THE SUPERNATURAL
AND NATURAL SELECTION

Studies in Comparative Social Science
A series edited by Stephen K. Sanderson

Titles Available

Revolutions: A Worldwide Introduction to Political and Social Change, Stephen K. Sanderson (2005)

Plunging to Leviathan? Exploring the World's Political Future, Robert Bates Graber (2005)

The Depth of Shallow Culture: The High Art of Shoes, Movies, Novels, Monsters, and Toys, Albert Bergesen (2006)

Studying Societies and Cultures: Marvin Harris's Cultural Materialism and Its Legacy, edited by Lawrence A. Kuznar and Stephen K. Sanderson (2007)

The Supernatural and Natural Selection: The Evolution of Religion, Lyle B. Steadman and Craig T. Palmer (2008)

Judaism in Biological Perspective: Biblical Lore and Judaic Practices, edited by Rick Goldberg (2008)

Forthcoming

Conflict Sociology: A Sociological Classic Updated, by Randall Collins, updated and abridged by Stephen K. Sanderson

THE SUPERNATURAL AND NATURAL SELECTION

THE EVOLUTION OF RELIGION

Lyle B. Steadman
Craig T. Palmer

Taylor & Francis Group

LONDON AND NEW YORK

First published 2008 by Paradigm Publishers

Published 2016 by Routledge
2 Park Square, Milton Park, Abingdon, Oxon OX14 4RN
711 Third Avenue, New York, NY 10017, USA

Routledge is an imprint of the Taylor & Francis Group, an informa business

Library of Congress Cataloging-in-Publication Data

Steadman, Lyle B.
    The supernatural and natural selection : The evolution of religion / Lyle B. Steadman, Craig T.
Palmer.
        p. cm.
    Includes bibliographical references.
    ISBN-13: 978-1-59451-565-1 (hardcover : alk. paper)
    ISBN-13: 978-1-59451-566-8 (paperback   )
    1. Religion. 2. Psychology, Religious. 3. Supernatural. I. Palmer,
Craig. II. Title.
    BL51.S628 2008
    200—dc22

                                                                        2008005983

Designed and Typeset in Adobe Garamond by Straight Creek Bookmakers.

ISBN 13 : 978-1-59451-565-1 (hbk)
ISBN 13 : 978-1-59451-566-8 (pbk)

For Marc, Caroline, Craig, and Dane
and
Fran and Amber

Contents

Preface and Acknowledgments

THE ORIGIN OF THE ARGUMENTS in this book can be found in a cold-blooded murder that was observed forty years ago by Lyle Steadman while doing fieldwork among the Hewa of Papua New Guinea. That occurrence, recounted at the start of Chapter One, made two facts painfully clear: (1) religion remains a puzzle to those attempting to explain it, and (2) understanding religion can be a matter of life and death. In this book, we propose an original and testable hypothesis to answer the questions of what defines religion and why religion has persisted for thousands of years. It will be argued, with evidence presented, that:

1. Religion is distinguished, and hence is definable, by the communicated acceptance by individuals of another individual's "supernatural" claim, a claim whose accuracy is not verifiable by the senses. The distinctive property of such acceptance is that it communicates a willingness to accept the influence of the speaker nonskeptically. While supernatural claims are not demonstrably true, they are asserted to be true. They can be shown to be metaphorical, but metaphors of a special type: Their status as metaphor is denied by the acceptors.

2. The most important immediate effect of religion (an effect identifiable both to the participants and outside observers) is that the explicit acceptance of a supernatural claim regularly creates cooperation like that between a parent and child and, consequently, siblinglike cooperation between coacceptors. Close kinship terms, such as father, mother, brother, sister, and child, are regularly used in religious behavior to foster these relationships.

3. Ultimately, the most important effect of religious behavior, the effect that continuously influences its frequency through time, is that it has increased the number of descendants of the religious participants.

The premise underlying this book is that an important effect of any behavior (and therefore religious behavior), the effect that continuously influences its frequency in succeeding generations, is its impact on the descendant-leaving success of those exhibiting it. Because behavior always involves some inheritable elements, it is continuously being influenced by natural selection. Behavior that promotes descendant-leaving success tends to increase in frequency in succeeding generations; when it does not promote such success, it tends to die out. This was Darwin's great insight. To emphasize the fact that Darwin realized the importance of inheritable elements without knowledge of genes, we will use the term "Darwinian selection" to emphasize that any inheritable and replicable element (including both genes and traditions) will be subject to the form of natural selection Darwin envisioned.

Religious behavior itself is a significant force. It is influential, and its most important and identifiable effect is in its creation of enduring family-like cooperation between nonfamily members. Religion tends to be traditional, meaning that it tends to be passed from ancestor to descendant. Because of this, it has influenced its own frequency through time in its descendant-leaving influence on participants. We shall argue that the fundamental and continuing source of both traditions and human nature is neither the hedonistic psyche of individuals nor any group to which they belong. Instead, it is individual ancestors (including parents) and their influence on their descendants, particularly through that which is inheritable, *including traditions,* and this influence responds to selection. Thus, our explanation differs markedly from both traditional social science explanations of religion and recent explanations of religion based on evolutionary psychology.

To make these arguments, we rely heavily on ethnographic descriptions of traditional kinship-based religious activities rather than on behavior from modern world religions. Most of the influential explanations of religion that have been produced over the last few centuries have focused on these traditional religions, and hence, our evaluation of them must also have this focus. More important, traditional kinship-based religions not only predate world religions but were the only form of religion for most of the time that religious behavior has existed. Thus, explanations must be able to account for this behavior, as well as the behavior observed in modern religions.

More people than we can possibly acknowledge have contributed to the creation of this book, but we would like to thank Reed Wadley, Scott Wright, Jennice Wright, Jesse McMinn, Robert Daly, Jon Lanman, and Joshua Crabtree.

We would like especially to thank those who have worked mightily on various drafts of this book: Kathryn Kyle, Patricia Kontak, Amber Palmer, Chris Cassidy, Donald Brown, and particularly Melissa Johnson, who contributed to many chapters but in particular to the chapter on divination.

We would also like to thank the following publishers:
Elsevier Limited for permission to publish parts of:

Steadman, L. B., and C. T. Palmer. 1995. "Religion as an Identifiable Traditional Behavior Subject to Natural Selection." *Journal of Social and Evolutionary Systems* 18(2): 149–64.

Palmer, C. T., and L. B. Steadman. 1997. "Human Kinship as a Descendant-Leaving Strategy: A Solution to an Evolutionary Puzzle." *Journal of Social and Evolutionary Systems* 20(1): 39–51.

Wiley-Blackwell Publishing, Ltd., for permission to publish parts of:

Steadman, L. B., and C. T. Palmer. 1994. "Visiting Dead Ancestors: Shamans as Interpreters of Religious Traditions." *Zygon: Journal of Religion and Science* 29(2): 173–89.

Steadman, L. B., and C. T. Palmer. 1997. "Myths as Instructions from Ancestors: The Example of Oedipus." *Zygon: Journal of Religion and Science* 32(3): 341–50.

Pamela J. Stewart and Andrew Strathern, coeditors of *Journal of Ritual Studies,* for permission to publish parts of:

Palmer, C. T., L. B. Steadman, and C. Cassidy. 2006. "Traditional Religious Ritual Sacrifice: Cultural Materialism, Costly Signaling, or Descendant-Leaving Strategy?" *Journal of Ritual Studies* 20(2): 33–42.

Oceania Publications for permission to publish parts of:

Steadman, L. B. 1985. "The Killing of Witches." *Oceania* 56: 106–23.

Katherine A. Lancaster, managing editor of *Ethnology,* for permission to publish parts of:

Steadman, L. B., C. T. Palmer, and C. F. Tilley. 1996. "The Universality of Ancestor Worship." *Ethnology* 35(1): 63–76.

The science of man proceeds, after all, by successive steps of demythologization; and that begins with the attitude of skepticism.

—George Park (1974: 11)

Chapter 1

Religion: What Needs to Be Explained?

> I find [the existing theories of religion], as they have been propounded, unacceptable in that they contain contradictions and other logical inadequacies, or in that they cannot, as stated, be proved either true or false, or finally, and most to the point, in that ethnographic evidence invalidates them.
> —*Evans-Pritchard (1965: 18, see also pp. 1–2)*

IN THE EARLY 1960S, an anthropologist lived among the remote highland Papua New Guinean tribe known as the Hewa. He was about to witness an example of religious behavior—in fact, an example typical of what constitutes "religion" in the anthropological literature (see, for example, Boyer 2001: 1–2; Lehmann and Meyers 1993). Early one morning, a cry from across the steep mountain valley woke him. This cry signaled the death of a friendly, elderly woman to whom, only the day before, the anthropologist had given a small but precious box of matches in exchange for a baby wild pig she had found hiding motionless in the forest.

Two days later, when the anthropologist asked the killers why they had slain this seemingly harmless old lady, they said it was because she was a cannibal and had eaten the viscera of an elderly man who was one of their kinsmen. They determined this not by any evidence of such an act (for example, a cut on the old man's body or an eyewitness account) but by asking the dying man to identify who had eaten his internal organs. They even suggested to him the names of the possible cannibal. The old man was too near death to respond, so instead they examined leaves they had placed on his chest, which they claimed

1

identified the cannibal as the woman who lived across the valley from them, about ten miles away.

As the anthropologist listened, he learned that this woman was alleged to be a *pisai,* a person said to cause death by secretly opening someone up, devouring his or her internal organs, and then closing the victim up without leaving a trace. Although the relatives and neighbors of the old woman scornfully dismissed the cannibal accusation as a lie, the killers showed no doubt, saying that if they had not killed her she would have continued eating the internal organs of others. They claimed that they were protecting all Hewa from a vicious cannibal.

Although the anthropologist had seen no evidence whatsoever that the elderly, dying man had been opened up, or that any of his internal organs were missing, to the men of his group there seemed to be no question that a *pisai* had caused his death. The only question debated was the identity of the *pisai,* who was finally "divined" (see Chapters Nine and Eleven) as the elderly woman living across the valley. The puzzled anthropologist had noticed nothing unusual about her behavior, and certainly nothing to indicate that she was a cannibal. Indeed, compared with adult Hewa men, who often engage in lethal violence, she seemed strikingly harmless.

Anthropologists are often delighted to hear talk about things such as cannibals and witches because it is sure to make their description of another culture more interesting, exotic, and entertaining. However, in this case, the talk was far more serious than just an engaging anecdote. Instead of being satisfied by "discovering" the cause of the elderly Hewa's death, the men used this discovery to justify killing a harmless old woman who, on the basis of all evidence available, was innocent of such a crime. As the bewildered anthropologist listened, the men told him that they had walked at night through the forest to the *pisai's* house and killed her at dawn with axes and arrows as she slept, each member of their party inflicting a wound. They then swiftly returned to their own group, stopping just long enough at a stream for a brief magical ritual (see Chapter Eight), to await the possible retaliation by the *pisai's* close relatives, who would use arrows and axes, not magic or unidentifiable cannibalism, to avenge her death.

Realizing that this apparently sociable and harmless woman had been brutally murdered, the anthropologist questioned the killers further. What evidence did they have that the man's viscera had been eaten? Did they not see that the old man's death had been due to age and other natural causes? What evidence did they have that the woman they killed had been guilty of any misbehavior, let alone secretly devouring the man's internal organs while he lived? Whatever doubts they may have had regarding these issues (discussed in detail in Chapter Eleven), they accomplished their mission, and they left the anthropologist, Lyle Steadman, and later his student and colleague, Craig Palmer, to ponder what

had happened. Why had adult humans asserted claims that could not be verified by their senses? Why had other adult humans agreed that those unverifiable
claims were true? And why had they used such claims to justify killing a woman
who, on the basis of their own senses, was innocent? Since this incident is a
typical example of the type of behavior anthropologists refer to as "religious,"
explaining the killing of an innocent woman in the highlands of Papua New
Guinea would require an explanation of religious behavior. This book attempts
to provide that explanation.

We provide a description of the events that started our inquiry into religion to
demonstrate that the lament by the anthropologist Evans-Pritchard at the start of
this chapter is more than just a dismal evaluation of the lack of progress in some
esoteric field of social science. As long as Evans-Pritchard's conclusion remains
true, humans will remain ignorant of the causes of one of the most powerful
influences on human behavior. Thus, Evans-Pritchard's description of the flaws
found in explanations of religion provides both a guide and a justification for our
attempt to find a more acceptable explanation. The quotation serves as a guide
because to produce a more scientifically acceptable explanation of religion it is
necessary to avoid the flaws found in previous explanations. Evans-Pritchard's
words serve as a justification because the ability, or inability, to explain religion
has practical consequences. As the story about the Hewa woman demonstrates,
those consequences can be a matter of life and death. One only need look to
history or current world events to see the frequency with which religion has such
life-and-death consequences.

The scientific study of religion, like the scientific study of anything, requires
rigorous objectivity, precise definitions, and skepticism. This book aims to satisfy
those requirements. However, the scientific study of religion is more complicated
than the scientific study of other human behaviors, because it verges on paradox.
The accuracy of religious statements is not empirically demonstrable. Yet, in
order to increase our knowledge of religion, it is essential that the accuracy of
our propositions be demonstrable. In the study of religion we are confronted
with the problem of making statements that must be subjected to skepticism
about statements whose acceptance depends on nonskepticism.

Evans-Pritchard asks the question that has guided the study of religion:
"How does it come about that people capable of logical behavior so often act in
a non-logical manner?" (1965: 94). Our book is unique among social science
explanations of religion because it does not attempt to answer that question. The
reason is that we do not assume religious behavior to be necessarily nonlogical. To
understand the reason for this fundamental departure from earlier approaches,
we must examine exactly what identifiable behavior the words "religion" and
"religious" refer to. To accomplish that, we must make explicit the reasons why

anthropologists, and their readers, classify the behavior just described among the Hewa as "religious." In short, we must define religion.

The Nature of Religion

It is essential to identify, as best we can, the necessary and sufficient elements that distinguish the phenomena of religion. That would specify not only what we need to account for but also what to test hypotheses against. In this endeavor, it is crucial to avoid the tendency of including in our definition things that are sometimes, *but not always,* associated with what we distinguish as religious. For example, while eating may accompany religious behavior, we do not label all acts of eating as religious. Eating does not distinguish religion. Similarly, people gathered together may or may not be considered religious. Gathering together is not distinctively religious and thus is not part of an acceptable definition. Sacrifice is also often associated with what we distinguish as religious (Bulbulia 2004; Sosis and Ruffle 2003), but once again, many instances of sacrifice are not considered religious, and many things that are considered religious do not involve sacrifice. The same is true of various emotions that are sometimes, but not always, associated with what is distinguished as religious (see Sosis and Alcorta 2003). Submissive body postures, such as kneeling or lying prostrate on the ground, are also frequently, but not always, associated with religious behavior (see Feierman 2006). Explaining why such behaviors are sometimes associated with religious behavior is a worthwhile endeavor, but none of these things are in themselves what humans distinguish as necessarily religious.

Even combinations of these behaviors are not necessarily religious. For example, in the Trobriand ceremony called *milamala* (described below), there is feasting, dancing, rejoicing, and gift-giving. All occur among the Trobriands in other contexts we would not consider religious. In modern societies similar activities occur at parties, social dances, and birthday celebrations. Clearly, although such combinations of behavior may occur in religious ceremonies, they are not necessarily religious. Many activities occur at a Christian church service, and yet gathering together in a building, singing, speaking, reading, dressing up, and consuming bread and wine may occur in contexts not considered religious. What then do people use to distinguish religious behavior from nonreligious behavior?

According to almost all scholars, it is the supernatural, meaning literally "beyond nature" (and hence, beyond identification by the senses), that distinguishes religion. For example, Levinson defines religion as "the relationship between human beings and the supernatural world" (1996: vii). Evans-Pritchard, although specifically rejecting the term "supernatural," associates religion with "mystical" ideas, those ideas that are not derived, or logically inferred, from observation (1937: 12; 1965: 108–10). He points out (1965: 108) that "religion concerns beings which cannot be directly apprehended by the senses." Tylor, often referred to as the "father" of cultural anthropology, based his definition of religion on "spiritual beings" (1958: 9). The French sociologist Levy-Bruhl equates religion with the "mystical" or "prelogical" (which, he argues, "wholly" characterizes primitive mentality) (1966: 96, 447), pointing out that such thought is not verifiable by the senses (ibid.: 61). Lowie, along with Marrett and Goldenweiser, specifies "supernaturalism" as "the differentia of religion" (1952: xvi). Horton (1960) defines religion by reference to entities "inaccessible to normal observation" and "unobservable beings"; Goodman (1988) on the basis of "alternative realities"; van Baal (1981) as the "non-verifiable world"; Yinger (1977) as the "superempirical"; James as "the belief that there is an unseen order" (1902: 53); and Spiro as "culturally patterned interaction with ... 'superhuman beings'" (1966: 96).

Recent evolutionary approaches have largely followed these earlier approaches in assuming that religion is defined by the supernatural. For example, Newberg, D'Aquili, and Ruse refer to "a realm of beings and forces beyond the material world" (2001: 66). Burkert calls religion a "tradition of serious communication with powers that cannot be seen" (1996: 177). Hinde defines religion as "systems of beliefs that have always been unverifiable" (1999: 2). Atran refers to "supernatural agents" (2002: 4), and Boyer states that religion "is about the existence and causal powers of nonobservable entities and agencies" (2001: 7)—or, in other words, "supernatural matters" (ibid.: 307). Finally, Sosis and Alcorta refer to the "ineffable and unknowable aspects of religion that separate it from ordinary perceptual experience" (2003: 265).

Even definitions not explicitly based on something supernatural imply the importance of something unidentifiable in distinguishing religion. For example, Garrett (1974: 168; see also Schneider 1970) noted that Berger's (1974) definition based on "transcendence" refers to the "non-empirical." Durkheim's definition (1961, first published 1912), based on the "sacred," which he defines as something "set apart" or "forbidden" and that "inspires respect," also requires a supernatural aspect, since to be set apart, forbidden, and respected is not necessarily to be sacred (and hence, not necessarily religious; on this point, see also Eliade 1987; Goody 1961; Swanson 1960).

Reference to something supernatural is also crucial to *functional* definitions of religion. Something supernatural is obviously implied in Luckmann's (1967: 49) reference to "the transcendence of biology." Functional definitions that replace "supernatural" with words such as "powerful," "pervasive" (Geertz 1966), and "ultimate" (Bellah 1964; Yinger 1970) have been repeatedly demonstrated to be too inclusive (see Berger 1974: 127; Machalek 1977: 398; Spiro 1966: 90; Weigert 1974: 484). Underlying this overinclusiveness of functional definitions is the fundamental problem that establishing the function of something still leaves open to debate the question of what that something is. This is why Spiro argues that "social solidarity, anxiety reduction, confidence in unpredictable situations, and the like, are functions which may be served by any or all cultural phenomena—Communism and Catholicism, monotheism and monogamy, images and imperialism—and *unless religion is defined substantively,* it would be impossible to delineate its boundaries" (1966: 90; emphasis in original).

The importance of the supernatural in delineating the boundaries of religion is evidenced in the examples used to support functional definitions. For example, Geertz states:

> For what else do we mean by saying that a particular mood of awe is religious and not secular, except that it springs from entertaining a conception of all-pervading vitality like mana and not from a visit to the Grand Canyon? Or that a particular case of asceticism is an example of a religious motivation, except that it is directed toward the achievement of an unconditioned end like nirvana and not a conditioned one like weight-reduction? (1973: 989; see also Asad 1983)

Whether or not mana and nirvana are "all-pervading" and "unconditioned," one obvious difference between these entities and the Grand Canyon and weight-reduction is that the former cannot be identified by the senses, whereas the latter two can.

Hulkrantz (1983: 231), after pointing out the crucial role of things unidentifiable in the definitions of theorists such as Muller, Frazer, and Robertson Smith, concludes that "religion cannot be defined without reference to the concept of the 'supernatural.'" Wells (1921: 275), after referring to the similar emphasis on the unidentifiable in the definitions by Plato, Kant, and James, concludes that "regard for correct usage of the term requires that religion be defined in such a way as to include supernatural belief."

Thus, although there may be considerable disagreement among social scientists about what else religion involves, there is general agreement that it involves alleged elements, entities, or forces not identifiable by the senses. In this book, we refer to such phenomena as supernatural.

Since the supernatural is "beyond nature," and hence, beyond identification by the senses, it cannot by itself be used to identify religion. Although social scientists sometimes write as though they were reporting their direct observations of supernaturals, they typically do not actually claim to observe them. In reading such reports, it is clear that what has actually been observed are *statements* people make about supernaturals. Geertz tells us that Javanese possessing spirits called "*lelembuts* ... can make one ill or drive one crazy. The *lelembuts* enter the individual's body, and if one is not treated by a native Javanese curer ... one will die." Geertz, however, supports this statement not by showing evidence that the *lelembuts* actually do such things, but by showing that the Javanese *say* they do (1960: 16).

Consider this description of a ceremony Malinowski observed in the Trobriand Islands of New Guinea:

> During the *milamala* [ceremony] the *baloma* [spirits of the dead] are present in the village. They return in a body ... where preparations are made to receive them, where special platforms are erected to accommodate them, and where customary gifts are offered to them, and whence, after the full moon is over, they are ceremonially but unceremoniously driven away. (Malinowski 1954: 172)

What is it about this activity that identifies it as religious? We suggest it is the *claim* made by the people engaged in the activity that it is the actual presence of supernaturals—spirits, gods, unseen forces—that makes the activity religious. Malinowski does not claim to have seen these spirits, even though he writes the passage as though the spirits of the dead actually come to the *milamala* ceremony. Malinowski, like Geertz, supports his claim about the presence of the spirits of the dead at the *milamala* ceremony by reporting *statements* made by the Trobriand Islanders, not by presenting evidence that such spirits exist.

What can be identified about supernaturals is what people *say* about them; if no one said anything about them, they would have no discernible existence. To identify religious behavior, therefore, it is neither necessary nor possible to identify supernatural phenomena; only *statements* about such phenomena need be distinguished. Because supernaturals cannot be identified, the accuracy of such statements has the distinctive quality of being unverifiable. Evans-Pritchard emphasizes this quality in his description of the alleged activity of Zande witches: "The whole act of vampirism is an incorporeal one: the soul of witchcraft removes the soul of the organ" (1937: 35). The fact that the alleged witch can be observed lying in bed at the time he or she is said to be devouring his or her victim does not challenge the truth of this statement, for it is his or her soul, a nonobservable part of his or her being, that is said to commit the atrocity. Nor does the fact that the alleged victim appears to be intact challenge the assertion that his or her soul has been devoured. Thus, one cannot determine whether or not this supernatural event has taken place; the accuracy of such a claim cannot be established. Evans-Pritchard did not witness it, nor does he attempt to convince us that he has. At the same time, no facts can be cited to disprove the claim.

Because supernaturals cannot be identified, correlations involving them cannot be demonstrated; a supernatural cannot be shown to be correlated with any observable event. Until supernaturals can be identified by natural means (at which point, by definition, they would cease to be supernatural), there is no way of determining which exist and which do not. On the basis of evidence, both the assertion of the existence of a supernatural and the assertion of its nonexistence must be seen as equally true or equally false, and neither statement can be logically accepted over the other.

During activities traditionally called religious, statements referring to something supernatural are regularly made (see Boyer 2001: 1–2). We propose that unlike all of the behaviors that are sometimes associated with religious behavior, *certain talk about supernaturals is the only activity that is distinctly religious.* Meeting other people in a building and singing is not necessarily religious. Yet going to a "House of God," singing *hymns,* listening to *sermons,* reading from the Bible, and taking communion are all commonly regarded as religious. The only activity distinctively religious is the *talk* about supernaturals. Some people consider Thanksgiving a religious holiday, while others do not. Whereas those celebrating it usually come together with their families and eat a large, traditional meal, some families, in addition, say prayers thanking God for what he has given them. It is not the eating or gathering together that is religious, therefore, but rather the prayers, the statements referring to something supernatural.

Yoga originally was (and to many people still is) considered religious. Its body postures and breathing exercises were justified by their contribution to an individual's spiritual improvement—a supernatural benefit. Yet many individuals practice these same exercises without any reference to the spiritual. In that case, the activity is not said to be religious. The exercises themselves are not necessarily religious, but the supernatural discussion that sometimes accompanies their performance is.

Although the term "religious" is often extended in ordinary usage to include the activities occurring with religious behavior, these activities are not themselves distinctively religious. The term "religious" is also often extended to refer to activities in which no talk about supernaturals is currently occurring, *but which people associate with talk about something supernatural.* Certain activities, such as taking communion or spinning a prayer-wheel, are almost always justified or explained by religious statements. It is the justification or explanation that is religious.

Thus, while statements referring to supernaturals are regularly used to distinguish religion, activities merely associated with such statements are not necessarily religious. Explaining why certain behaviors are sometimes associated with religious behavior is an important task in its own right, and great progress is being made toward such explanations (see Chapter Two). Explaining these things does not, however, explain religious behavior per se.

Belief

Although social scientists, as opposed to religious or theological writers (see Verkamp 1995), generally do not attempt to account for statements claiming the existence of supernaturals by the reality of the supernaturals, they almost invariably attempt to account for such statements by *belief* in supernaturals. Probably the most widely accepted definition of religion is something like "belief in the supernatural." The problem with this definition is that, unlike knowledge, which is identified in others by the correlation between identifiable phenomena and their behavior, *religious belief* cannot be identified by correlations with *supernatural* phenomena. Hence, such beliefs can only be *assumed* to exist in the minds of individuals, to motivate their behavior, and to be identifiable simply by observing the individual's *talk*. This point is crucial because it is this assumption of belief, and only this assumption of belief, that has made the explanation of religion an attempt to explain "nonlogical" behavior.

This assumption of belief may also be why the study of religion has made such little scientific progress. Although it *may* be true that religious rituals and statements are consequences of beliefs in supernaturals, the problem of identifying religious beliefs is rarely confronted. An author's claims about the beliefs of the people he or she studies, like those about supernaturals, are usually supported by citing people's statements. But there are obvious problems with such claims.

First, people can consciously lie about what they believe. Because of the potentially disagreeable consequences of a "no" answer, most Europeans in the Middle Ages would presumably have answered the question "Do you believe in God?" by saying "yes," no matter what they believed. On the other hand, in the Soviet Union of the 1950s a "no" answer would have been more acceptable than a "yes." How is one to determine who is the "true believer" and who is not? Second, individuals may exhibit different degrees of certainty about supernatural phenomena. It is often the experience of ethnographers that when people are questioned about supernaturals they exhibit some uncertainty, even to the point of asking the ethnographer for guidance. Although none of the Hewa paid any attention to Steadman's questions concerning the lack of evidence that the elderly man's viscera had been eaten during the initial public discussion to identify the *pisai,* several individuals did confide to the anthropologist in private that they, too, had wondered about such absence of evidence (see also Malinowski 1954: 167). Did these individuals believe in *pisai* or not?

Many authors have pointed out problems with the "simplistic approach to religious belief" (Hilty 1988: 243; see also Hahn 1973; Kirsch 2004; Saler 1973) that assumes a direct equation between people's statements and their beliefs. Evans-Pritchard warned that "statements about a people's religious beliefs must always be treated with the greatest caution, for we are then dealing with what neither European nor native can directly observe" (1965: 7). Authors making such criticism almost invariably assume that the problem of identifying beliefs can be solved "indirectly," merely by observing other behaviors. For example, some cognitive psychologists refer to the difference between "explicit belief" (what people say) and their actual or "implicit beliefs," which the psychologists assert are identifiable through nonverbal behaviors (see Barrett 2004; Boyer 2001: 305). This argument is illustrated by Evans-Pritchard's claim that the Azande's invariable consultation of the poison oracle before making important decisions demonstrates that they believe in its efficacy (Evans-Pritchard 1937: 261; see also Saler 1973). However, there are problems with this argument. For example, many scholars attempting to explain the ritual taboos of fishermen have assumed that the efficacy of a taboo is believed only when people state their belief *and* actually follow the taboo (see Mullen 1969; Poggie and Pollnac 1988; Poggie, Pollnac, and Gersuny 1976; Tunstall 1962; van Ginkel 1987; Zulaika 1981). A study of Maine lobster fishermen, however, found that some fishermen observed taboos that they denied "believing in," and other fishermen failed to observe taboos in which they professed belief (Palmer 1989). Such behavior appears to falsify the assumption that beliefs can be deduced from either talk or nonverbal behavior. Just as humans can say things they don't believe, they can also act like things they are not: humans can be actors. When faced with contradictions between statements and accompanying behavior, how can we decide whether it is the talk or the action, or neither, that reflects the person's belief? Any of these choices appear to be arbitrary—merely a guess—and hence, unacceptable in scientific analyses. Or as Radcliffe-Brown so aptly noted, "For as long as we admit guesswork of any kind social anthropology cannot be a science" (1979: 52).

The problem of our inability to identify belief cannot be solved by claiming to have a scientifically acceptable degree of certainty about the probability that an individual believes the supernatural claims he or she makes. Such probabilities could be calculated about the claim that the identifiable *behavior* of making a supernatural claim (for example, saying "I believe Jesus Christ is the son of God") will be followed by subsequent patterns of behaviors (such as attending a Christian church service within the following month), but determining the probability of correlations between two such observable behavior patterns tells us nothing about the probability that the individual does or does not actually believe Jesus Christ is the son of God.

Another clear example of inconsistency between certain claims and other behaviors is Boas's description of the case of a Kwakiutl Indian named Quesalid, who was skeptical about the alleged supernatural powers of shamans. Quesalid told Boas that in an attempt to expose shamans, he became an apprentice curer and learned all of the tricks designed to give the appearance of supernatural powers, including the one that involved appearing to suck out a "bloody worm" (the alleged cause of a disease) from the patient's body. By the time he had finished his training, however, Quesalid had gained quite a reputation as a curer. He continued to practice as a shaman, very successfully, in spite of claiming, in private, disbelief in their powers. Such an example suggests that the participation in activities asserted to involve supernaturals, even involving religious leaders, does not necessarily require belief. Except for his conversations with Boas, to all outward appearances, Quesalid behaved the same as other shamans who did not reveal (at least to Boas) their skepticism, and was even more successful than most (Boas 1930: 1–41; see also Levi-Strauss 1963a: 175–78; Radin 1957; Wadley, Pashia, and Palmer 2006).

There are many activities that, when examined, can be found to be inconsistent with religious statements made by the participants. Elkin (1964) reports that Australian Aboriginal peoples believe that a man can be killed through sorcery by pointing a sharpened stick or bone at him and singing a special chant. Yet when Aboriginal peoples, including other sorcerers, decide that an overly active sorcerer should be stopped, they try to kill him with a spear. Why would they risk their lives in a direct attack if they believed that sorcery is sufficient? We are not claiming that these behaviors prove the participants *don't* believe in their supernatural claims, rather we are simply arguing that from their behavior we cannot tell what supernatural beliefs they hold.

The difficulties caused by the possibility of false statements, uncertainty, and inconsistencies in statements and other behavior force one to question the validity of *any* claim of an individual's religious beliefs. The difficulty in identifying such religious beliefs, however, goes beyond these problems. The fundamental quandary is that religious beliefs, as they are assumed to exist inside the mind, are not themselves accessible to observation. There is no method known that can identify the internal entities called religious beliefs. Only statements and actions, not the religious beliefs that are so often assumed to motivate them, are distinguishable.

Those who attempt to study religious behavior scientifically, as opposed to theologically, do not generally use statements about supernaturals to conclude that those supernaturals exist. Rather, nearly all social scientists use statements about religious beliefs to conclude that those religious beliefs exist, and then go on to make claims whose accuracy cannot be demonstrated. People may make statements about what is inside their head. If a person says he or she believes in ghosts, he or she may believe in ghosts. Indeed, there may even be ghosts—there is no evidence that can disprove such a claim. However, when religious beliefs are claimed to be the cause of behavior, the cause is unidentifiable, and hence, the claim unverifiable. Claims about the existence of religious beliefs should be recognized for what they are: mere assertions of something supernatural, equivalent in truth value to assertions about the existence of spirits, ghosts, and gods.

Several authors have come close to recognizing this profound problem in the scientific study of religion, but, perhaps because of an inability to see an alternative, they have all failed to face up to it. Rappaport recognizes that what distinguishes religious ritual from nonreligious ritual is not beliefs but rather supernatural claims, or what he calls "unverifiable propositions" (1979: 262). For example, he states that "a religious ritual *always* includes an additional term, such as a statement about or to spirits" (ibid.: 260, emphasis in original). The realization that it is certain talk, not certain beliefs, that is identified as religious leads Rappaport to ask the question of whether or not participants in religious rituals actually believe the supernatural claims they make. Although he has just finished stressing the fact that humans can lie (ibid.: 261), he ignores this possibility and concludes: "It is thus plausible to assume a belief on the part of at least some of the participants in the existence of deceased ancestors; to assume otherwise would make nonsense of the proceedings" (ibid.: 262). In this statement Rappaport acknowledges that he cannot tell how many, or which, of the participants actually believe the supernatural claim, for he implies that the behavior of believers and nonbelievers is indistinguishable. Hence, the ritual will make just as much "sense" whether all, or some, or none of the participants believe in their claim. There simply is no logical basis for his conclusion that it is safe to assume that "some" must believe because all of the activities identified as religious could be performed by a nonbeliever, and no one would be able to tell.

Speculating about beliefs by introspection or otherwise is still speculation. Speculating about what could be a cause is not identifying or discovering causes. The analyst's claims about religious beliefs, like the supernatural claims of the individuals he or she is studying, are invulnerable to disproof by evidence. When such claims cannot be verified, counterclaims cannot be resisted, other than arbitrarily. Only identified correlations increase knowledge. When unidentifiable correlations are asserted, the procedure itself is more characteristic of religious activity (see below)—a religion of science perhaps—than a science of religion.

Perhaps the clearest statement of this problem has been made by Needham. In regard to the Penan of interior Borneo, Needham reports that, although he had been accustomed to saying that "they believed in a supreme god," he suddenly realized that he had no evidence at all to this effect. Not only that, but "I realized that I could not confidently describe their attitude to God, whether this was belief or anything else. ... In fact, as I had glumly to conclude, I just did not know what was their psychic attitude toward the personage in whom I had assumed they believed" (1972: 1).

Needham is also virtually alone in realizing the profound implications of this fact:

> The question then was whether the reports of other ethnographers were much better founded, and what evidence these really had that their subjects believed anything. Clearly, it was one thing to report the received ideas to which a people subscribed, but it was quite another matter to say what was their inner state (belief for instance) when they expressed or entertained such ideas. If, however, an ethnographer said that people believed something when he did not actually know what was going on inside them, then surely his account of them must, it occurred to me, be very defective in quite fundamental regards. (Ibid.: 1–2)

We agree. Indeed, the uncertainty, controversy, and lack of progress characterizing most studies of religion ("stagnation" is the term used by Geertz [1966: 1]) may be a direct result of the use of claims whose accuracy cannot be assessed. Because counterclaims cannot be logically resisted, analyses based on such assertions lead often to either cultlike devotees or acrimony and confusion.

However, this does not lead us to Needham's dismal conclusion that "[t]he solitary comprehensible fact about human experience is that it is incomprehensible" (1972: 246). Although beliefs are not identifiable, behavior is, and that aspect of humans can be studied. Indeed, the study of religion has made some progress because of the detailed accounts of what has actually been observed (see Murdock 1971). What is needed is a testable explanation of this observable religious behavior.

Defining Religion

What we are proposing here is nothing more than that the study of religious behavior be restricted explicitly to phenomena identifiable by the senses, and that hypotheses be limited to the proposal of correlations between such phenomena. We can examine only those things that are examinable, look only at the things that can be looked at, and listen only to those things that can be heard. To assert the existence of things not identifiable (including belief) does not increase knowledge.

We assume that behavior can be identified by the senses, that English speakers mean something by the term "religion," and that this category of things includes identifiable behavior. Therefore, given that religious behavior occurs and that it can be verifiably distinguished from other kinds of behavior, there would appear to be no reason why a careful examination of religious behavior should not increase our understanding of religion. Although religion may be more than that which can be identified by the senses, this fact does not threaten the assumption that our verifiable understanding of religious behavior can be increased significantly by focusing on what is identifiable. Spiro notes that "a theory of the 'existence' of religion must ultimately be capable of explaining religious 'behavior'" (1966: 99). Although religion may consist of more than identifiable elements, the impossibility of verifying the existence of such elements should threaten directly the accuracy of any statement alleging them.

For those who wish to argue that statements about things that are not verifiable by our senses are nevertheless true, the burden is on them to propose a standard to evaluate the accuracy of such statements. Neither the internal consistency of an argument nor a popular vote is sufficient to establish its truth. Theological arguments can be both entirely consistent and said to be true by whole populations, and yet contradict one another.

Our proposed approach overcomes several other obstacles previously seen as problematic in the study of religion. Scholars have claimed that the existence of societies with languages lacking a word translatable as "religion" prevents a universally applicable definition of religion (see Benson 1977; Cohn 1962; Hulkrantz 1983; Kohn 1967; Mandelbaum 1966). The realization that what needs to be defined is only the identifiable behavior referred to when the word "religion" is typically used literally by English speakers makes the presence or absence of a word translatable as "religion" irrelevant to the task of determining if religious behavior occurs in a given society. This is because the word "religion" clearly does not only (or even necessarily) refer to the act of uttering the word "religion" or its equivalent. Similarly, practitioners denying that their activity is religious do not necessarily challenge a definition of religion. For example, denials that Zen Buddhism, Alcoholics Anonymous, and Channeling are religious are likely to remain unconvincing for most English speakers as long as their activities continue to include talk of such supernatural matters as nirvana, a Higher Power, and reincarnation. Both of these types of objections are overcome because the presence or absence of talk about supernatural things, not the presence or absence of the word "religion," is what is crucial to determining if something is religious.

Furthermore, the requirement emphasized here, that hypotheses be verifiable, overcomes the problem of ethnocentricity or preconceived notions. It is this standard that permits one to ignore completely the origin of a hypothesis—whether it comes from a dream, a mistake, or a cultural inclination. Thus, one need not accept the assertion of a writer or analyst that he or she knows the true, but unidentifiable, meaning of certain cultural symbols. The claim that since "religion is essentially of the inner life, it follows that it can be truly grasped only from within" (Evans-Pritchard 1965: 121) is not good enough. Surely, if an argument were to be accepted only on the claim that it was made by someone who has truly grasped the religion from within, authors could simply profess to be true believers. Requiring verifiable hypotheses avoids the fruitless debates over whether one must be a true believer in order to make accurate statements about religion (see Nelson 1986; Segal 1985). The fundamental test of any hypothesis is whether it refers to identifiable elements and events, and whether it is consistent with them.

How then can attempts to scientifically explain religion proceed once the need to exclude unidentifiable beliefs from those explanations is accepted? We suggest the answer is simply by restricting hypotheses to what can be identified as religious, certain *talk,* and the identifiable effects of that talk. In other words, religious behavior can be studied in the same way as any other form of communication.

But exactly what is the talk that distinguishes behavior as religious? Or more broadly, what is the definition of religion? Although a claim of the existence of something unidentifiable by the senses appears necessary for behavior to be distinguished as religious, such a claim alone is not sufficient. A claim asserting the existence of something nonidentifiable may be considered evidence of being demented, perhaps even the basis for incarceration. An outright lie, a claim of seeing a unicorn, or flying saucer, the interpretation of a dream, a claim of being a teapot, a claim based on misperception, may all be "supernatural" assertions by definition, but are not normally considered religious (see Douglas 1975: 75). Certainly none is distinctively or necessarily religious.

To make further progress toward a definition of religion that specifies its necessary and sufficient elements, one that can withstand skepticism based on our senses, let us focus on the first element in the definition of religion being "belief in the supernatural." According to the *Shorter Oxford Dictionary,* cited by Hinde, "belief" means *"mental* assent to or acceptance of a proposition, statement, or fact, as true, on the ground of authority or evidence" (1999: 34, emphasis added). Religious beliefs, since they "are not subject to empirical verification" (ibid.: 34), can be defined as *mental* assent to or acceptance of a *supernatural* proposition or statement on the ground of authority. Although it may be that such a statement was made by a supernatural itself, such a source cannot be verified. More important, while it is possible that the person is experiencing "*mental* assent," the only thing that can be identified, by *both* social scientists and "believers," is the *explicitly communicated* assent or acceptance of another person's claim about something supernatural.

When a person makes a supernatural claim we do not necessarily conclude that he or she is religious. But when others regularly communicate their acceptance of that claim, it would be difficult to conclude that such behavior is not religious.

To understand the importance of communicated acceptance of a supernatural claim in distinguishing religious behavior, consider claims about Sasquatch, or "Bigfoot." Most current claims about the existence of this creature are considered silly. However, such claims in the context of Native American cultures are likely to be considered part of the peoples' religion. The only identifiable difference between the first and the second is the absence of communicated acceptance in the former. Communicated acceptance of another person's supernatural claim communicates commitment, but it does not imply belief. Communicating acceptance of another person's supernatural claim can be seen as a promise to accept the speaker's influence in certain respects. Hence, the sincerity of the communication will be judged by the receiver, and others, in the same way we judge any sincerity—by subsequent *behavior,* not by identifying beliefs. What behavior? In this case, behavior that shows continued acceptance of the speaker's influence.

Thus, we propose, as a testable hypothesis, that religious behavior is distinguished, and hence, can be defined as, the *communicated acceptance of a supernatural claim.* That is, *the communicated acceptance of another person's claim as true that cannot be shown to be true by the senses* constitutes the necessary and sufficient elements identifying behavior as religious.

This definition can be tested by examining what people identify as religious. For example, since a supernatural claim is a claim that, on the basis of the observer's senses (which is all one can depend on), is not demonstrably true, this definition implies that if such a claim did turn out to be demonstrably true, it would no longer be supernatural, and hence its acceptance no longer religious. If this definition can withstand skeptical evaluation of our literal uses of the word "religious" (for example, see the list of examples of religious behavior provided by Boyer 2001: 1–2), the essential task in the study of religion will be to account for the communicated acceptance of supernatural claims. Evans-Pritchard asserts that "religious conceptions can only be derived from experiences" (1965: 77). If this is true, the main task in the study of religion would be to identify the experiences leading to such a communication of acceptance.

In the following chapters we shall argue that our definition distinguishes the myriad of identifiable behaviors referred to as religious, from claims about *pisai* to assertions about the resurrection of Jesus. Further, we shall argue that different types of religious behavior discussed by anthropologists (for example, ancestor worship, totemism, myth, shamanism, magic, divination, witch accusations) are delineated by distinctive supernatural claims. Hence, the explanation of these specific behaviors that make up the general category of religion will require identifying the specific consequences of communicating acceptance of these distinct supernatural claims.

Before engaging in these arguments, however, we need to establish how the definition of religious behavior proposed in this first chapter directs explanations of religion in a fundamentally different direction from previous attempts. By excluding unidentifiable beliefs, the definition proposed in this chapter changes the question that explanations of religion attempt to answer.

Chapter 2

Previous Explanations of Religion

THE DEFINITION OF RELIGION proposed in Chapter One changes the question that needs to be answered, and thereby changes the entire direction taken by attempts to explain religion. To fully understand the significance of this change, we must first examine the question that has guided previous attempts to explain religion. Because of the assumption that religion is defined by *belief* in things supernatural, previous explanations of religion have focused on explaining these beliefs. Evans-Pritchard correctly noted that this has left these earlier explanations of religion attempting to answer the question "How does it come about that people capable of logical behavior so often act in a non-logical manner?" (1965: 94). More recently, this question has been rephrased to the simpler question of "Why do people believe weird things?" (Shermer 2002). In this chapter, we shall first examine the answers provided by the classic social science explanations, and then turn to those provided by recent explanations based on evolutionary cognitive psychology, which often focuses on the subset of "weird" things referred to as "counterintuitive."

Summaries of the types of explanations of religion (and many of their flaws) are available in numerous other books, most notably Evans-Pritchard (1965) and Boyer (2001). Instead of repeating all of those criticisms, we will focus on demonstrating how these explanations share the common fatal flaw of attempting to explain something (religious beliefs) that cannot be identified by the senses. This means that they are all subject to the second type of problem listed by Evans-Pritchard in 1965: they cannot be shown to be either true or false. In Chapter Three, we will present an alternative explanation of religion that avoids this flaw by attempting to answer a different question: Why do people communicate their acceptance of statements that are not demonstrably true by the senses?

Classic Explanations of Religious Beliefs

Classic explanations of religious beliefs are representative of the fundamental types of explanations of behavior in general. Hence, our examination will begin with these fundamental explanations. Virtually all social scientists assume that human behavior is not aimless. Even though it may not be successful, even though it may not achieve its goal, behavior, nevertheless, is assumed to have an aim. The use of the concept of efficiency, for example, implies a goal, an aim. The problem emerges when one tries to identify that aim, for the identification of even the immediate aim of behavior is not so obvious. First, any consciousness that may be involved is not itself identifiable, so it must remain irrelevant in identifying an aim. Further, we cannot identify an aim simply by a result, or the frequency of a particular result, for behavior does not have to achieve success—many aims or goals are not realized. For example, most people lose when buying a lottery ticket. Is that their aim?

A clue to identifying aim is the realization that inanimate objects can cause things to happen. Although the sun warms the earth and rocks crack when heated, we do not say that rocks and the sun are aimed at achieving such effects. Inanimate objects are not said to have an aim because they are not alive. Aim is implied, however, in almost every answer to a "why" question in regard to life: the roots of plants are said to seek water, leaves seek the sun, most animals seek living things (such as food, mates, offspring, and so forth) and seek to avoid predators. But the effects—even regular effects—of animal behavior are not necessarily their aim. The ground, for example, is regularly depressed, and insects killed, when trod upon, but such effects are not normally the aim of walking. This leads to the question of what constitutes the aim of the behavior of living things.

Two basic kinds of answers to this question have long been used to account for human behavior. They can be referred to as "psychological" and "sociological." The psychological assumes that human behavior is hedonistic, that it is determined by self-interest, and that the aim of behavior is to satisfy that interest. In contrast, sociological explanations assume that behavior (or "social behavior") is determined by the interests of a group, and hence, the aim of the behavior is to reflect, maintain, or otherwise satisfy that group. We will follow both Evans-Pritchard (1965) and Boyer (2001) in categorizing the classic explanations of religion into the sociological (those of Levy-Bruhl, Durkheim, and others) and the psychological (those of Marrett, Malinowski, Tylor, Freud, and most others).

Psychological (Hedonistic) Explanations

> Man is motivated by a single principle: to achieve pleasure and to avoid pain.
>
> —*Kenneth Gergen (1969: 10)*

Hedonism is based on the assumption that the aim of behavior is to maximize pleasure and avoid pain. Hedonism "is a cornerstone of social science," writes Gergen, a social psychologist. In his 1975 presidential address to the American Psychological Association, Campbell stated that "the dominant modern psychologies are individualistically hedonistic, explaining all human behavior in terms of individual pleasure and pain." That is true also of social psychologists, who explain virtually "all social interactions in self-serving terms" (1975: 115).

The first problem with hedonism as an explanation of human behavior is that, to actually qualify as a scientific explanation of behavior, it must be testable. To be testable, it must specify exactly what "pleasure" behavior is aimed at obtaining. As soon as one particular pleasure is specified—sex, food, confidence, and so on—such propositions are easily contradicted by evidence. Although people sometimes seek such things, they may also avoid them.

Perhaps the behavior that most clearly contradicts the idea that living things maximize *any* specific thing *for themselves* is parental behavior. Parental behavior everywhere includes gifts to offspring of resources important to their survival. In every human society mothers and fathers regularly give more material goods and food, time, and effort to their offspring than they receive in return, and thereby diminish their own survival and pleasure possibilities. When young, offspring are not in a position to reciprocate, and by the time they are old enough, they often begin putting their resources into their own offspring. Resources regularly flow from ancestors to their descendants, and this is a characteristic of all life. To argue, as do many (for example, Erasmus 1977: 18; Harris 1974: 284–85), that human parental behavior is an investment for "old age benefits" (a kind of old-age insurance) is likewise untenable, for parental behavior is exhibited in all mammalian species. Surely, a mother rat does not care for her offspring so that they will return the favor when she is old. Furthermore, while such a theory assumes self-interest to explain parental behavior, what accounts for the motivation of children when they choose to care for their elderly parents? This behavior cannot be explained as *their* old-age insurance policy. The argument that children can be socialized to help their aged parents does not protect this argument, for if the behavior of children can be so taught, so too can the behavior of parents by their own parents. Economic self-interest, therefore, does not account for parental behavior. The basic flaw of arguments based on hedonism as the fundamental motivation is that they are inconsistent with Darwinian selection (Darwin 1994, originally published 1859), the only continuous and directional influence on inheritable, replicable elements yet discovered.

The ease with which hedonism is falsified the moment it is put into a testable form is the reason that hedonistic explanations often refer to *unspecified* pleasures as the goal of human behavior. Although we may all agree that when individuals choose a course of action, they do so somehow because they want to, such an assumption can be simply synonymous with behavior: when behavior occurs, "wanting to" is assumed. There is no behavior, therefore, that can challenge this assumption. It is applied post hoc and hence does not increase our knowledge of humans; it does not facilitate successful prediction.

To say that a baby smiles because he or she wants to, because it gives him or her pleasure, is safe but specious. As social scientists we seek to understand why particular activities tend to occur and others do not. To say that everything humans do is aimed at increasing their pleasure and avoiding pain—whether they exploit others or sacrifice for them, whether they invest their wealth in stocks or spend it on concerts, whether they become alcoholics or teetotalers, whether they are frugal or spendthrifts, whether they struggle to live or commit suicide—is to say nothing.

Psychological (Hedonistic) Explanations of Religion

Both Evans-Pritchard (1965) and Boyer (2001) find it useful to divide psychological (that is, hedonistic) explanations into the categories of intellectual and emotional. Intellectual explanations of religion argue that the aim of religious behavior is to explain, or make sense of, phenomena. This attainment of an explanation increases pleasure by alleviating uncertainty. Emotional explanations propose a more direct connection between religious behavior and the attainment of pleasant feelings and/or the avoidance of unpleasant ones.

Intellectual Explanations

The intellectual explanation of religion is based on the following assumptions. First, humans find their inability to explain any and all aspects of the world unpleasant. Second, this discomfort is so intense that it leads them to *believe* explanations even when those explanations are contradicted by the evidence of their senses. This *belief* in the unverifiable propositions put forth to explain some phenomena thus reduces the discomfort caused by a lack of explanation. This is a common explanation of origin myths, but it is perhaps best exemplified by Tylor's (1958) explanation of religion based on the concept of souls as a means of explaining such things as shadows, reflections, and, most important, dreams.

The first problem with intellectual explanations is the fact that the alleged *belief* in the asserted explanation cannot be identified. All we can identify are what people *say* is the explanation for some phenomena, not whether or not they actually *believe* in that explanation. This flaw alone makes intellectual explanations untestable. The second problem with intellectual explanations is the lack of evidence that a failure to explain something necessarily produces discomfort. Even the most educated humans are unable to explain much of what they experience, and they seem perfectly content with that situation, directing their explanatory efforts toward only a small subset of unexplained things. The next obvious problem with intellectual explanations of religion is the "nonlogical" nature of supernatural claims as "explanations." Given that supernatural claims, by definition, are not supported by the evidence of the senses, why should they be taken as explaining anything? Once awake, a brief discussion with those individuals "seen" in dreams would reveal inconsistencies in the dreams that would falsify the hypothesis that dreams necessarily involve the souls of individuals (Durkheim 1961; Evans-Pritchard 1965). For early theorists such as Tylor and Frazer (see Chapter Eight), their explanation of why "primitives" had this nonlogical belief was simple—they were not only ignorant but also deficient in their reasoning. Criticism of that explanation led to more explanations of religion using emotions.

Emotional Explanations of Religion

The explanation that supernatural claims were believed simply because primitive people were intellectually deficient was destroyed by Malinowski's fieldwork (see Chapter Eight). This led Malinowski, following the work of Marrett, to seek a new explanation of the nonlogical religious behavior of humans. Since all humans are capable of logical behavior, something must temporarily remove this ability to allow for religious beliefs. Malinowski hypothesized that it was intense emotion that interrupted the normally rational functioning of the human mind and made religion possible. Malinowski argued that religion and magic (discussed in Chapter Eight) occur when a gap in practical or scientific knowledge leads to uncertainty or danger beyond man's ability to influence events, hence causing unpleasant and intense anxiety. Nowhere is this anxiety greater than in regard to death. Religion, with a belief in the afterlife, gives the pleasure of confidence and reduces the pain of anxiety.

This argument, that the aim of religion is to give confidence, is inconsistent with the facts. Because the correlations alleged by religious statements cannot be identified, there is no objective basis for confidence in them. Rather than a rain dance giving confidence that rain will fall, it should do the opposite, for, identifiably, it has no effect on the frequency of rain. Nor does religion necessarily reduce anxiety, for it may create it: by talk of hell, the devil, original sin, evil spirits, and so on. Indeed, some religious rituals appear designed to instill fear (Whitehouse 1996). If religion were to promise everyone heaven regardless of their behavior, it would be more consistent with the anxiety reduction argument, but religious leaders everywhere emphasize consequences, which encourages certain behavior and discourages other behavior.

The argument that people are religious because it makes them feel less anxious or euphoric is equally assailable. Both sex and alcohol can promote such feelings, but few would call them religious. Nor must religious leaders "express" such feelings when doing their job; Catholic priests need neither exhibit nor induce euphoria when performing Mass. Such emotions (which would include the so-called religious thrill and awe), therefore, are neither necessary nor sufficient elements of religion (see Evans-Pritchard 1965: 43–47). However, the fundamental problem with emotional explanations is that they assert unverifiable beliefs as the cause of the desired emotion.

Sociological (Group) Explanations

Social phenomena are born, not in individuals, but in the group.
—Emile Durkheim (1961: 263)

The second major kind of explanation used by social scientists is that human behavior is determined by a group. The aim of human behavior is thus sought in its effect on the group. The first problem with group explanations is the typical absence of an objective definition of what is meant by "group" (Palmer, Fredrickson, and Tilley 1997). *Webster's Dictionary* defines the term as "an assemblage of objects having some relationship, resemblance or common characteristic." But all objects can be said to share some characteristic (being an object, for example), and hence, any two objects can be declared to be a group. If we are interested in identifying influences on human behavior, however, the mere sharing of a physical feature, such as size, shape, or appearance, common territory, name, or even descent, may be irrelevant. Because some individuals are more than six feet tall or share common descent does not mean that they necessarily influence one another. Further, it is mutual influence or, more specifically, cooperation that is fundamental to what we usually mean by a *social group*. Human behavior is obviously influenced by the behavior of other individuals—indeed, all traditional behavior (i.e., behavior copied from parents and other ancestors) presumes this. If we seek the causes of human behavior, we must identify the influence of other individuals (Murdock 1971; Palmer, Fredrickson, and Tilley 1997).

Durkheim and his followers (and many others), however, often argue (or imply) that social behavior results not from particular individuals but from a group, because the group is more enduring than the individuals constituting it. Such an argument precludes defining a group by its actual membership, for the loss or addition of one member would necessarily change it. If a group's actual membership is irrelevant to its identification as a group, the meaning of a group would then be something like that of the *Webster's* definition: objects sharing a common characteristic. Indeed, a shared name is often cited as the evidence that is used to identify a social group (see, for example, Durkheim 1961: 122–23). The fact remains, however, that humans, as well as stones, can be called by the same name without implying mutual influence. Thus, we suggest, by not defining this crucial term explicitly, social theorists have tried to have it both ways: a group as a set of regularly cooperating individuals that somehow endures beyond the existence of those individuals—literally a contradiction.

Identifiably, the source of cultural behavior, including religion, is other individuals whose behavior is copied, whether or not they form a group (Murdock 1971). The lack of a definition of a group compounds the second problem of explicitly identifying the relevant group. Is it the household or family? Or is it the village, clan, tribe, or society, however they are defined? Could it be the human race, or mammals, or vertebrates, or even life itself? When behavior is explained by a group, that group must be identified. The larger, more enduring categories, such as tribes or societies, influence the individual far less than smaller groups, such as the family or household. But the smaller, more influential groups have less endurance—individuals often live in more than two or three households during their lifetime. Categories such as clans, while longer enduring, are usually not social groups (see below). In the still larger and less influential categories, such as tribes or societies, the boundaries are often difficult to identify. Intermarriage often occurs between such categories, and when that happens offspring will have close relatives in each, thus continually confusing the distinctiveness of the categories. Furthermore, the gain or loss of members through death or departure regularly changes the composition of all groups.

A third shortcoming of group explanations is that they do not account for the discrimination found, indeed implied, in all social relationships. Parents regularly favor their own children over others and influence them to favor each other over more distant kin. Hence, even in a Hutterite colony, "Biological brothers function as a closely cooperating subgroup within the larger cooperative" (Hostetler and Huntington 1996: 93). Within families individuals cooperate differently with their father and their mother, and in still other ways with individual siblings and children. Individuals treat each other differently not only according to impersonal criteria such as age, sex, and appearance but also according to their remembered uniqueness and behavior toward one another. Further, such discrimination among individuals takes place both internally and externally to the designated group.

The fourth problem with group explanations is that they are often circular. Commonly, they assert that the group causes the phenomena in question while at the same time implying that such phenomena cause the existence of the group. This is perhaps best seen in the most influential group explanation of religion, put forth by Durkheim.

Sociological (Group) Explanations of Religion

Although Durkheim's basic argument is that religion is a consequence of a group—or at least that a group is a necessary condition for the existence of religion (and indeed anything social)—he also writes that religious beliefs create a group's unity. This circularity can be seen in the following: "The really religious beliefs are always common to a determined group. ... [T]hey are something belonging to the group, and they make its unity. ... Wherever we observe the religious life, we find that it has a definite group as its foundation" (Durkheim 1961: 59).

Another clear fact opposing Durkheim's argument that the function of religion is either to reflect or maintain a group is that religious behavior (by following a prophet, for example) can create groups. In addition, because new religious groups are often created out of existing groups—out of existing social relationships—they are often seen as threatening those relationships. Thus, new religious groups are often created at the expense of existing groups and may even destroy them.

Our final contribution to the list of flaws found in group explanations of religion is that group explanations are based on unidentifiable beliefs. Although Durkheim claims that beliefs "consist in representations," he writes that between "beliefs and rites ... there is all the difference which separates thought from action." Further, "it is possible to define ["distinguish"] a rite only after we have defined the belief" (ibid.). Therefore, according to Durkheim, religious practices are identified only by beliefs. But religious beliefs, as alleged internal phenomena, cannot be identified, and hence responded to, by others. Consequently, beliefs cannot be shown to "unite ... all those who adhere to them," for they can be distinguished neither by religious participants nor outside observers. To the extent that religion is acquired from others, it must be based on perceptible behavior. Although members of many religions invariably speak of the importance of faith, it is not faith but actions (including talk of faith) that can influence other individuals.

All of these flaws intertwine in Durkheim's explanation of the religious behavior of Australian Aboriginal peoples in *The Elementary Forms of the Religious Life* (1961). According to Durkheim, the fundamental group of Australian Aboriginal peoples was the clan, which he at times labeled "society" (ibid.: 245, 265). This group was the basis of their religion: "The clan was able to awaken within its members the idea that outside of them there exist forces which dominate them and at the same time sustain them, that is to say in fine, religious forces" (ibid.: 245). In other words, their social group, their clan, caused them to believe in religious forces.

However, in perhaps every Australian tribe there is a word that is usually translated as "the Dreaming" or "the Dreamtime," meaning for most writers the "religion" of the Aboriginal peoples. Durkheim focused on the Aranda (or Arunta) whose word for this phenomenon was *alcheringa.* As will be discussed in Chapter Five (on totemism), the Aranda word *alcheringa,* and perhaps an equivalent word in all other Australian tribes, literally means "ancestors"—not religion, the dreaming, the group, society, or even the clan. A clan is a set of codescendants who personally bear the name of their common ancestor. Because of clan exogamy ("marrying out"), as well as other reasons, individuals bearing the same clan name typically are scattered throughout at least the tribal area; they do not live together as a group. Australian Aboriginal peoples identify sets of codescendants, but these are not exclusive: individuals are members of every set of codescendants from whose common ancestor they can trace descent through either parent. This usually means five or six such categories, sometimes more. Furthermore, they discriminate individuals within the various categories on the basis of genealogical distance (Palmer and Steadman 1997). In addition, the set of individuals with whom a person lives often changes because individuals often change their residence (see, for example, Evans-Pritchard 1940; Hart, Pilling, and Goodale 1988; Palmer, Fredrickson, and Tilley 1997).

It is the worship of their variously identified ancestors, not groups, that constitutes Aboriginal religion. A term equivalent to *alcheringa* is extended, metaphorically, in every tribe perhaps, to refer to virtually all important behavior encouraged by ancestors: rituals, law, respect for the dead and the old, women who have just given birth, and newly initiated kinsmen—virtually every social tradition (see, for example, Elkin 1964: 188–85; Hart, Pilling, and Goodale 1988: 96; Stanner 1956: 51; Tonkinson 1991: 20–23, 95). Australian Aboriginal peoples do not worship their group; they worship their ancestors, the source of their traditions and their kinsmen (Steadman, Palmer, and Tilley 1996).

Evolutionary Psychology

Explanations of human behavior based on Darwin's theory of evolution by natural selection are part of an approach to explaining human behavior that was called sociobiology but now is usually referred to as evolutionary psychology (see Wright 1994). These kinds of explanations have reinvigorated the study of religion. Yet, despite their differences, from our perspective, many of these approaches share a number of strengths and weaknesses. Their foremost strength is that they are based on the only comprehensive explanation of living things that is currently scientifically acceptable. Some of these evolutionary explanations also focus on the communicative aspects of religion and how they can promote cooperative social relationships, the effect of religious behavior we propose here. Unfortunately, recent evolutionary explanations of religion also tend to have several common flaws. First, many of them suffer from the lack of an accurate, explicit definition of religious behavior. This leads them to attempt to explain behaviors only sometimes associated with religious behavior, instead of religious behavior per se. Second, evolutionary explanations of religious behaviors that focus on the promotion of cooperative social relationships rely on explanations of altruism that are not sufficient to account for the patterns of human altruism found associated with religious behavior. Finally, and most important, recent evolutionary explanations have followed the earlier social science explanations in assuming that religious behavior is produced by unidentifiable beliefs in supernaturals.

The assumption that people believe the supernatural claims they make has been made in the work of essentially everyone who has responded to Wilson's observation that "[r]eligion constitutes the greatest challenge to human sociobiology" (Wilson 1978: 175; see also Alexander 1979, 1987; Blackmore 1999; Boyer 2001; Burkert 1996; Campbell 1975, 1991; Dawkins 1998, 2006; Dennett 2006; Giovannoli 1999; Hinde 1999; Irons 2001; McClenon 1994, 2002; Moore 2000; Newberg, D'Aquili, and Ruse 2001; Richerson and Boyd 1989; Sosis and Alcorta 2003; Wilson 2002). This is true also of the closely related, but broader, field of cognitive psychology. Thus, evolutionary psychological explanations of religion parallel the older classic explanations in trying to answer the question, Why do people believe weird things? Whether they see religion as an adaptation created by either individual level or group level selection (see Wilson 2002: 44–45), or just an evolutionary by-product (Boyer 2001), they all attempt to explain religious *belief* (although sometimes the term "belief" is replaced with the terms "memes" or "psychogenes").

Perhaps the most popular evolutionary explanation of religion is that the "erroneous" reasoning that leads to religious beliefs (which in turn cause religious behaviors) is just a side effect of a variety of evolved psychological mechanisms. The proposed mechanisms include intuitive ontologies, the memorability of counterintuitive representations, theory of mind, and hypersensitive agency detection. In the words of Boyer, religious beliefs are the result of the "successful activation of a whole variety of [evolved] mental systems" (Boyer 2001: 298; see also Ashbrook and Albright 1997; Barrett 2000, 2004; Kirkpatrick 1999; Neese and Lloyd 1992; Pinker 1997; Pyysiainen 2004). Other researchers propose that the religious beliefs assumed to cause religious behavior are adaptations instead of merely by-products. One influential version of this view sees religious behavior as a form of "costly signaling": a hard-to-fake, and therefore honest, signal of commitment (see Atran 2002; Irons 2001; Sosis 2000). Individuals sending this signal by participating in forms of sacrifice encouraged by religion (allegedly because of their belief in the supernatural claims they make) can be trusted to be reliable reciprocators. Some versions see this behavior as an adaptation that was favored by selection at the level of the individual, while others see it as an adaptation produced through the process of group (or multilevel) selection discussed below (Wilson 2002).

Despite the variety and complexity of evolutionary explanations, they all have been built upon the assumption that people believe in the supernatural. This is a major flaw because evolutionary theorists have not solved the problem of identifying belief. For example, Sosis and Alcorta suggest that participants in emotional religious rituals can be assumed to believe because "[t]he ability of religious ritual to elicit emotions makes it difficult for nonbelievers to imitate, and renders it a powerful tool for social appraisal. As a result, ritual practices promote trust and commitment among adherents, thereby providing a foundation for cooperative group enterprises" (Sosis and Alcorta 2003: 270). This method of identifying belief fails in three ways. First, as noted by Evans-Pritchard (1965: 20–47), in regard to previous attempts to explain religion by emotion, this method of identifying religious belief suffers from the fact that emotion is not a necessary, nor even a common, aspect of religious behavior. In regard to magic, Lessa and Vogt go so far as to state that "the performance of magic is routine, and while the ritual may appear to be dramatic, it is almost always nonemotional" (1979: 332). This lack of emotion in no way makes the ritual any less religious, nor is it taken by the participants as evidence of disbelief. Second, when "emotion" is part of a ritual, participants rarely seem interested in noticing whether the "facial expressions and body language generated by emotion differ from those under voluntary control" (Sosis and Alcorta 2003: 270). In fact, as Evans-Pritchard again points out, the proper emotion involved in rituals is often obviously voluntary: "The expression of emotion may be obligatory, an essential part of the rite itself, as in wailing and other signs of grief at death and funerals, whether the actors feel grief or not. In some societies professional mourners are employed" (1965: 45). Once again, this voluntary emotion does not make the ritual any less religious, nor is it claimed to reveal the identity of nonbelievers. Finally, and most fundamentally, Sosis and Alcorta *assume* that the participant activating the nonvoluntary muscles are doing so as a result of belief in whatever supernatural claims are being made during the ritual, instead of its being in response to any of a countless number of other possible causes of emotion including the potentially, and identifiably intense, social interaction during the ritual.

Another means of supposedly distinguishing believers from nonbelievers employed by some evolutionary authors is the use of recent technological advances to identify changes in certain areas of the brain during experiences such as meditation (Newberg, D'Aquili, and Ruse 2001). These changes are then claimed to be the cause of beliefs in the supernatural and hence the root of religion. The first problem with this approach is that identifying these brain activities is not the same as identifying religious beliefs: identifying such brain activities would not answer the question of whether the individual believes in God, gods, the claims of shamans, or any other supernatural claim. The second problem with this approach is that any distinctive brain activities associated with religious behavior that may exist have been only recently detectable, and are thus clearly not what humans normally call religious. It is only when supernatural *claims* are made, whether about these states or anything else, that people can identify religious behavior. Newberg and colleagues admit that "extrapolating meditative practices and their results to all religious experience is not a simple step" (ibid.: 40). The real problem, however, is that the words "religion" and "religious" are used to refer to many behaviors that do not involve any kind of distinctive experience. Surely many religious behaviors— instances of communicated acceptance of supernatural claims—are made in the absence of any unusual brain activities. Attempting to determine the evolutionary basis of unusual brain activities is an important endeavor, but these attempts will not constitute an evolutionary explanation of religion.

The assumption that religious *belief* must be explained in order to explain religious behavior has led evolutionary psychologists to explanations that are very similar to past social science explanations. Like numerous evolutionists, Giovannoli replaces "beliefs" with "memes" in his explanation. He then attempts to explain religion by "psychogenes," a class of memes (Giovannoli 1999: xvii) that he defines as "*beliefs with perceived inheritance value* that are replicated between or within generations" (ibid.: xvi, emphasis in original), or simply "beliefs that people find acceptable" (ibid.: xvii). Because he still assumes the reality of religious beliefs, now called memes, he essentially replicates earlier explanations of religious behavior. He starts by asking a version of the question that, as Evans-Pritchard noted, has always guided theorists: "My initial motivation for writing this book was to determine why rational minds are capable of believing in myth" (ibid.: xviii). He then makes the same assumptions that are found in the century-old explanations of religion, such as the supposition that the first people to practice religion and magic had a striking lack of intellectual ability: "A key factor in these beliefs is that our ancestors lacked the capacity to distinguish between real and spirit worlds" (ibid.: xxvi). Like Malinowski, however, he realizes that even early humans must have been able to produce accurate explanations: "The evolutionary advantage of seeking explanations for why events occur may be that our ancestors were better able to respond to recurring events and not merely treat them as if they were happening for the first time" (ibid.: 50). Thus, he is forced to account for how this rational thought gets interrupted and results in religious belief. His answer simply adds some recent knowledge about the human brain to the basic assumption that people temporarily lose their rational thought: "It appears that an unfortunate aspect of this survival trait is that the left hemisphere, in attempting to ascribe meaning to events, often *incorrectly links* cause and effect, thereby creating a false memory of events and their meanings" (ibid., emphasis added). This is simply a repetition of Malinowski's explanation, with a few new hypothesized details about the proximate mechanisms involved in the temporary "erroneous reasoning" of people who are claimed to believe in religion.

We fully agree with the proposition that evolved psychological mechanisms are operating during all behavior, including behavior labeled religious (Palmer and Steadman 2004). Identifying the proximate and ultimate explanations for these mechanisms is an important contribution to the study of evolution and human behavior. For example, advances in brain imaging and other aspects of neurophysiology can potentially complement our approach by increasing knowledge of the proximate physiological mechanisms producing religious behavior, as long as they are correlated with identifiable behavior instead of assumed beliefs in the supernatural. However, the specific explanations of the involvement of these mechanisms in religious behavior per se, as stated, are unacceptable because they assume that religious behavior is necessarily a consequence of "supernatural" beliefs. If recast in a form that is not dependent on the untestable assumption of religious belief, many of these approaches have potential for explaining both human behavior sometimes associated with religious behavior and, in some cases, religious behavior per se.

Particularly promising are explanations of both sacrifices and strong emotions as behaviors that act as costly signals of commitment to social relationships (Irons 2001; Sosis 2000; Sosis and Alcorta 2003). Although sacrifices and emotions are not necessarily religious, they are often associated with religious behavior. Thus, when these explanations are restricted to identifiable behavior (that is, the behavior of the person sending the signal and the subsequent changes in the behavior of the person being influenced by the signal), they are consistent with, and complement, our explanation of religious behavior by explaining why sacrifices and emotions are sometimes associated with religious behavior per se.

We suggest, however, that even if recast in a form that does not require the assumption of belief in supernaturals, evolutionary explanations of religious behavior still suffer from an inadequate understanding of the evolutionary causes of human altruism. Perhaps the clearest way to demonstrate this point is to follow Boyer (2001: 181–87) in categorizing evolutionary explanations of religion by the evolutionary explanations of altruism upon which they draw (ibid.). Our own explanation of the sacrifices and other altruistic acts encouraged in religions is found throughout the book, but especially in Chapter Ten on taboo, pain, and sacrifice (see also Palmer, Steadman, and Cassidy 2006a).

Kin Selection

In the 1960s, Hamilton (1964) proposed *kin selection* (or as he preferred to call it, *inclusive fitness*) to account for altruism between kin. Given the frequent occurrence not only of altruism but also of the use of kin terms (for example, father, mother, brother, sister) to encourage such altruism, it is not surprising that kin selection is often mentioned in explanations of religion. For example, certain aspects of religious behavior are seen as by-products of evolved mechanisms produced by kin selection to promote altruism among close kin.

As has been suggested elsewhere (for example, Palmer and Steadman 1997; van den Berghe 1979: 91), the key problem with Hamilton's argument is that it can account only for altruism that occurs between very close kin. Even with first cousins, for example, the chances of two individuals sharing the same gene by common descent are small. And yet humans everywhere exhibit altruism toward quite distant kin and, in modern societies, toward nonkin. Such altruism, or social behavior, found in every religion, must be accounted for by any explanation of religion offered. We suggest that this can only be accomplished by focusing on the ability of ancestors to pass on traditions that promote cooperative behaviors among many future generations of descendants.

Reciprocal Altruism

To account for social behavior between distant kin or nonkin, and the emphasis religions typically place on moral behavior in general, some have proposed what is usually called *reciprocal altruism* (compare Wright 1994). Darwin himself used this concept to explain the origin of morality: "[As] the reasoning powers and foresight of the members became improved, each man would soon learn from experience that if he aided his fellow-men, he would commonly receive aid in return" (1871: 163).

Explanations of religious behavior based on costly signaling theory often focus on the relationship between religion and reciprocal altruism. Costly signaling theory, however, ignores the influence of ancestral traditions that encourage sacrifice. This is crucial because reciprocal altruism, emphasized in costly signaling theory, really isn't altruism at all. Instead, it is aimed at enhancing one's own survival or reproduction. Although at times we obviously do exhibit behavior that is consistent with "tit for tat" (for example, I'll help you if you help me), the forms of sacrifice typically encouraged by religion are certainly not limited to that type of behavior.

Group Selection

The third evolutionary concept influencing explanations of religion is group, or "multilevel," selection. Group selection is the idea that selection can take place between groups as well as between individuals or genes. Group selection has been seen as an explanation of forms of altruistic behaviors not explainable by kin selection or reciprocal altruism. This concept comes up in explanations of religion because religions often encourage forms of altruism that may reduce survival and reproduction. Hence, religion is hypothesized to have evolved because it helped certain groups outsurvive other groups by influencing their individual members to be altruistic for the good of the group. For example, Wilson's answer to the question of why people believe in magical rituals that don't work as claimed is that the *beliefs* work in other ways to benefit the group: "Even massively fictitious beliefs can be adaptive, as long as they motivate behaviors that are adaptive in the real world" (2002: 41), adaptive meaning beneficial to a group.

Evolutionary criticisms of group selection (see Williams 1966) have undergone a significant reappraisal during the past two decades and are currently the subject of much debate. Regardless of how these debates are resolved, group selection explanations of human behavior are faced with the problem of identifying the particular religious groups that have been around long enough to be a result of selection by outsurviving other groups. Thus, the same lack of enduring social groups distinguished by common religious behavior that caused such a problem for Durkheim's group explanation of religion is also a problem for evolutionary multilevel selection explanations of religion (Palmer, Fredrickson, and Tilley 1997). Further, groups do not reproduce and leave descendants; individuals are the genetic product only of individual ancestors. Because of their genetic and environmental uniqueness, each individual is a unique descendant-leaving strategy. Although an individual may contribute to the welfare of a group at his or her own descendant-leaving expense, his or her inheritable elements will tend to be less frequent in subsequent generations.

Religion does indeed encourage altruistic behavior, including forms of altruism not explainable by current evolutionary concepts. Hence, an acceptable explanation of religion requires a new evolutionary explanation of altruism, one that focuses on descendant-leaving strategies (Palmer and Steadman 1997). We agree that religious behavior can have powerful adaptive results, although for the descendant-leaving success of individuals, not groups. In addition, there is no need to assert the existence of unidentifiable beliefs, since these beliefs cannot be demonstrated to have any effects at all. What "works" (what has identifiable effects) is the behavior, not the alleged "beliefs." Hence, it is the identifiable effects of religious behavior as a form of communication that can increase significantly our understanding of religion.

Explaining Hewa Witch-Killing

All of the explanations just discussed would assume that the behavior by the Hewa that resulted in the murder of the elderly woman was caused by *belief* in *pisai*. These explanations would attempt to make sense of the behavior of killing an innocent old woman by explaining why the Hewa *believe* some humans can devour the insides of other people without leaving a trace.

Hedonistic explanations would argue that believing in the claim that individuals can consume the viscera of others nonidentifiably somehow made the Hewa feel better. An emotional hedonistic explanation might assert that such a belief made people feel less anxious, although the opposite would seem more likely. Such an explanation might also assert that this emotion was so pleasant that it prevented the Hewa from exercising their normal powers of observation. The so-called intellectual hedonistic explanation might focus on how the Hewa needed to explain the elderly man's death, and that the pain caused by a lack of an explanation was so great that it led them to believe an explanation that contradicted what their senses told them about the world. In either case, the increased pleasure provided by the *belief* that a *pisai* had caused the death somehow outweighed any discomfort that might be caused by believing the world was inhabited by individuals who could commit unobservable cannibalism, going on a dangerous raid to kill an innocent woman, and risking being killed in retaliation by her kin.

A group explanation of the Hewa's behavior would focus on how the alleged belief in *pisai* was both caused, and maintained, by some group. The small set of people living within an hour's walk of one another would probably be selected as the significant group, since the behavior obviously destroys social relationships among individuals in larger categories of Hewa. The problem of the constantly changing membership in these small groups, the discrimination among individuals that makes every relationship within that group unique, and the crucial social relationships with individuals in different such groups would need to be overlooked. The fact that the "group" as an enduring, unchangeable entity is simply a reified abstraction that identifiably consists only of individuals who have various relationships with one another would be similarly ignored.

Evolutionary psychology would merely add hypotheses about which evolved psychological mechanisms might be involved in producing this unidentifiable belief, whose asserted existence is untestable. They might hypothesize that the belief in *pisai* is simply a by-product of mechanisms evolved to interact altruistically with kin, or reciprocally with nonkin. Or they might propose that the belief in *pisai* is a product of multilevel selection and exists today because it has helped groups with this belief outsurvive groups without it. Or they might propose that the belief is an adaptation produced by individual-level selection because it produced costly signals of commitment such as the risk of being killed during the attack on the alleged *pisai* or the retaliation that might follow. Although going on the raid may indeed be a costly signal of commitment, this explanation does not require the assumption of belief.

Taken individually or in combination, these explanations fail to produce a testable explanation of the behavior of the Hewa. In all cases, the key problem is the lack of evidence that such a belief in *pisai* is actually held by *any* Hewa. To develop a testable explanation requires rephrasing the question about what needs to be explained.

Conclusion

In order to be scientific, hypotheses proposed to account for religion, indeed anything, must refer to things identifiable by the senses. Only so far as a hypothesis refers to identifiable elements is the hypothesis verifiable, or falsifiable;

only to the extent that its referent is identifiable can it be shown to be wrong. The aspect of religion that can be studied, the part that is observable to both participants and outside observers, is religious behavior. Religious behavior is identified by the communicated acceptance of a claim asserting the existence of something not identifiable by the senses. No other behavior is necessarily religious. Therefore, religious behavior implies communication, and, hence, cooperation. It involves the communication of the willingness to put aside one's own senses—one's skepticism—and to accept the influence of another person nonskeptically.

Although the study of religion usually focuses on what are called the "belief systems" of a society, such "systems," to the extent they exist, apparently are learned from, and hence depend on, behavior that can be observed or heard. Despite this fact, there has been a curious inattention not only to religious behavior itself but also to the question of how religious activities have come to be widespread. The identifiable consequences of religious behavior must inevitably influence individuals in their choice of whether to repeat the behavior and encourage it in others (including their descendants). These consequences can be identified by social scientists.

It is confounding to argue that the function of religion is to relieve anxiety, when it sometimes increases it; or to maintain a group, when it sometimes breaks it; or to increase knowledge, when the truth of religious statements is distinguished by their nondemonstrability. Because the hypotheses proposed in the rest of this book specify observable phenomena, they are vulnerable to disproof and hence may be shown to be wrong. Either the correlations alleged may be shown not to occur, or other, more general facts may be discovered. Should that turn out to be the case, the approach taken here would be vindicated. When a hypothesis is shown to be wrong, it can be discarded; others can be proposed, and we can advance beyond the practice of resurrecting those century-old chestnuts whose validity is either contradicted by evidence or cannot be assessed.

In the study of religion, the primary question is "What is religious behavior?" Is it the expression of unidentifiable beliefs? If so, the task should be to identify how individuals come to believe in things for which there is no evidence. *Or,* is religious behavior a form of communication? If it is, the task is to identify the effect of such communication on others. This book attempts to identify this effect.

Chapter 3

Changing the Question

THE DEFINITION OF RELIGIOUS BEHAVIOR as the communicated acceptance of another person's supernatural claim changes the question that needs to be answered when explaining religion. Instead of asking why people have illogical *beliefs* that cause them to behave in a nonlogical manner, the question becomes why do people make, and communicate acceptance of, supernatural claims. In this chapter we outline our explanation of religion. The first step in this explanation is to see religious behavior as a particular form of communication.

Religious Behavior as Communication

The claim that religious behavior is a form of *communication* is in contrast to the common assumption that the most significant effect of religion lies in its *expression*; religion is said to express people's beliefs, values, emotions, needs, confidence, even their social structure. Indeed, communication itself is often said to be self-expression. Although much has been written on communication and communication theory (and this is not the place to discuss it adequately), it must be emphasized that communication is not simply expression. Expression (from the verb *ex-press,* meaning literally "to press or squeeze out," such as juice from grapes) is often used as a synonym for communication. For example, we are taught in school how "to express ourselves." Communication, however, occurs only when a message sent by one organism is received by another. Religion is communication; it is not simply the expression of internal states: needs, anxieties, aggression, awe, desire, greed, or anything else that may be expressed or squeezed out. The most significant effect of communicative behavior—the only effect that can account for its persistence through generations—is its influence on the behavior of others through their senses. This is as true of religious behavior as it is of any other form of communication.

This is not to say that the communicator consciously intends to influence others in that way; intentions and motives are unobservable. For example, we know that a baby's smile tends to communicate because we notice it and it often influences our behavior. But babies smile before they have experienced the effects of their smiling; even blind babies will smile without ever having observed other smiles or the reaction to their own smile (Wilson 1978: 62). Although we cannot say whether the baby intends to produce a particular effect with its smile, we can say that smiling is a form of communication that elicits certain identifiable responses in other individuals. It is only by identifying such responses that one assumes one has communicated. In the same way, the social scientist must identify certain responses to determine the particular message communicated. Because the intentions of the communicator are unobservable, they must not be assumed. Such assumptions are not only unverifiable, they are unnecessary. The important and identifiable consequence of communication is on the behavior of those who receive the message. Having distinguished communication from expression, we are left with the problem of identifying the important effects of religious behavior.

Religious Behavior as Denied Metaphor

Religious behavior appears to be distinguished by the communicated acceptance of another person's supernatural claim. Most of these claims refer to one of three categories:

1. *Techniques,* such as those distinguishing magic and divination.
2. *Living human beings,* such as shamans, prophets, witches, people who are possessed, and speakers of "tongues."
3. *Humanlike beings,* such as souls, spirits, ghosts, dead ancestors, devils, monsters, zombies, and more recently, space aliens.

What distinguishes all of these supernatural claims is that they appear to be responded to as metaphor, but metaphor of a special kind: their metaphorical status is *denied* and they are asserted to be literally true. Thus, we suggest that religious behavior is a specific kind of communication, *a metaphor whose metaphorical status is denied.*

A metaphor is an analogy that is distinguished as a statement that cannot be shown to be true. "The feature of metaphor that has most troubled philosophers is that it is 'wrong': it asserts of one thing that it is something else" (Percy, cited in Geertz 1973: 210). But it is not a lie, for it is not aimed at deception. People understand a metaphor by converting it into a simile: "That man is a rat" is understood as "that man is like a rat (in some respect)." However, a metaphor is not the same as a simile because it is, based on the senses, an untrue statement, and therefore its acceptance communicates a tacit agreement to act as if, or to pretend that, the untrue statement is true. Consequently, acceptance of a metaphor, because it is untrue, implies a kind of collusion, a conspiracy, which is a form of cooperation.

A supernatural claim is likewise distinguished by being untrue according to the senses. The wafer and wine taken at communion by Roman Catholics is said to be literally the blood and body of Christ, despite remaining, on the basis of the participants' own senses, wine and a wafer. What distinguishes them as Christ's flesh and blood is the "supernatural" claim. Communicating explicit acceptance of such a claim communicates a willingness to accept the speaker's influence nonskeptically, and thus a willingness to cooperate, to collude, with the speaker. *What distinguishes a religious claim from an ordinary metaphor is the denial that it is a metaphor, that it is claimed to be literally true.* The effect of that denial is to promote much greater collusion between the speaker and the follower, and among the cofollowers, than is achieved by ordinary metaphor. This is because the acceptance now includes the claim that the statement, untrue according to the senses, is, in fact, true. Ordinary metaphors, in contrast to religious metaphors, are acknowledged to be false.

For example, totemism (as discussed in Chapter Five) is distinguished as religious by the claim that a certain set of humans are truly members of a non-human species, such as rats. They deny they are only *like* rats. To communicate acceptance of a metaphor, then, in contrast to accepting an explicit simile, communicates a willingness to suspend skepticism. To communicate acceptance of a religious metaphor is to communicate one's willingness to suspend skepticism even when challenged about the truth of the metaphor. For instance, some Australian Aboriginal peoples claim to be actual kangaroos (or witchety grubs, owls, and so forth) because, they say, their father was one, and his father was, and so on. One anthropologist reported that an old man, when asked if he were *really* a kangaroo, was so emphatic in his answer that tears came to his eyes when he asserted that he was indeed a kangaroo—and he might have passed a lie detector test on that subject. And yet, no human kangaroo has ever been reported trying to mate with an actual kangaroo, none has ever been reported resisting the killing and eating of actual kangaroos, as they certainly would if their human kangaroo clan brother were killed and eaten. Indeed, while they may refrain from eating kangaroos themselves, human kangaroos perform rituals that are said to increase the reproduction of actual kangaroos *so that other, nonkangaroo humans may hunt and eat them.* Furthermore, human kangaroos are *exogamous:* they are not allowed to marry human kangaroos; they may marry only a human owl, crow, or the like. All human kangaroos, therefore, have one parent who cannot be a kangaroo but instead will "be" a member of another species, unlike anything seen in nature. Nevertheless, they communicate their acceptance of their ancestor's claim that they truly are kangaroos, and thereby encourage a form of cooperation among distant kin, their fellow clan members.

The communicated acceptance of a religious metaphor because it includes the claim that it is literally true (that it is not metaphor) communicates and creates significantly deeper collusion than the acceptance of a normal metaphor. Indeed, the collusion, and hence cooperation, engendered by the acceptance of religious claims may be the fundamental function of religious behavior.

It is possible that the meaning of every religious claim, like metaphors generally, lies in their implied similes. For example, talk of souls implies the continued existence of an individual after he or she dies, literally a contradiction. The simile? We should *act* (to some extent) *as if* the dead individual were still alive. For Roman Catholics, taking bread and wine at communion *is like* taking Christ into their body, it is *like* incorporating Him. Fellow human kangaroos should act toward one another, in certain respects, *as if* they were members of a separate species. In the course of this book we shall suggest the similes underlying common religious claims.

The explicit, communicated acceptance of a claim that cannot be verified by the senses communicates *a willingness to suspend skepticism,* to suspend the critical use of the senses to examine the accuracy of an assertion. To communicate acceptance of a claim whose truth cannot be demonstrated communicates *a willingness to accept another person's influence nonskeptically,* without regard to one's own senses. But then what causes a person to communicate his or her willingness to accept another person's influence nonskeptically? When a person *says* he or she believes that X is true, he or she implies a memory of certain experiences that led him or her to that statement. Indeed, when asked, he or she will often specify some of those experiences. Let us suggest at this point some possibly crucial experiences that are identifiable both to the social scientist and the participants in religious activities.

The Kinshiplike Nature of Religious Behavior

What are the identifiable experiences that lead people to communicate acceptance of another person's supernatural claim? Nonsupernatural experiences can be cited that lead to communicating acceptance of the claim that 2+2 = 4, or of how to make an ax or a house. But, by definition, *actual* experiences of supernatural phenomena are identifiably irrelevant to people's supernatural claims. What then are the identifiable experiences that lead people to communicate such acceptance? Merely hearing the claims, obviously, is not sufficient, for such claims can be easily ignored, even ridiculed. We suggest that the answer to why we communicate acceptance of some supernatural claims, but not others, lies in the most fundamental of all cooperative relationships in our species—the relationship between parent and child.

Although a child regularly accepts the influence of his or her parent nonskeptically—indeed, he or she is rarely in a position to judge it—a parent, on the other hand, is often skeptical of claims made by his or her child. As a hypothesis to be supported in later chapters, we propose that the prior behavior of the speaker whose supernatural claim is accepted will be similar to that of a parent. There is considerable evidence that the speaker shows parental-like interest in his or her followers, and the submissive postures of people communicating acceptance of a religious leader's supernatural claims, such as during many forms of prayer (see Feierman 2006), communicates the followers' childlike acceptance of, and obedience to (Bouchard 2007), parental influence. Indeed, religious leaders are often called "father" or "mother" explicitly. A common expectation, therefore, should be to receive parental-*like* behavior from him or her, and kinshiplike cooperation from cofollowers, themselves often called "siblings."

There is another important experience, that of the identified and remembered consequences of the religious behavior itself. When individuals witness the consequences, including social consequences, of any behavior, their decision to repeat, modify, or abandon that activity inevitably will be influenced. When individuals do choose to modify or even abandon traditions, their decision to do so is often influenced by their remembered experiences of that traditional behavior, including its effect on others.

In the following chapters we shall argue that the most significant proximate effect of religious behavior, the effect that has led to its persistence, is in its encouragement of enduring family-like cooperation between distant kin, kinsmen in different families, or, more recently (during the past few thousand years), between nonkin. We shall argue also that religious behavior is an adaptation; the ultimate (or evolutionary) cause of religion is that such cooperation has promoted, not just the reproductive success of individuals over one generation (Blume 2007) but also the leaving of descendants of those involved over many generations. It is in the effect of kinshiplike behavior that the success of both primitive and modern religions—from the simplest form of ancestor worship found in tribal societies to modern "world" religions such as Judaism, Islam,

Hinduism, Buddhism, and Christianity—can be understood. It is this same general effect that can account for the persistence and frequency of magic (including sorcery), divination, taboos, the telling of myths, and even the killing of witches. To the extent that such religious activities are traditional, their persistence depends on cooperation between ancestors and descendants—they depend on kinship cooperation.

Specifically, we shall propose and support the following definitions and hypotheses:

Ancestor worship (Chapter Four), as religious behavior, is distinguished by the claim that dead ancestors influence, and are influenced by, their living descendants. The rituals associated with such claims have the dual effect of promoting cooperative relationships between the kinsmen involved, descendants of those ancestors, and encouraging respect for the influence of those ancestors—the source of both their kinsmen and traditions. We propose that it is the encouragement of kinship relationships and the transmission of traditions that can account for the persistence and spread of the claims and rituals involved in the apparently universal worship of ancestors in all societies without a modern, prophet-created religion (Steadman, Palmer, and Tilley 1996).

Totemism (Chapter Five) is identified by the claim that *an ancestor, and hence his or her descendants, has a supernatural relationship with a natural category, such as a plant or animal.* The most important effect of this metaphor, the effect that can explain its persistence, is the metaphorical embellishment of social relationships among a set of living codescendants.

Through *myths,* or traditional stories (Chapter Six), ancestors vicariously transmit experiences to their descendants to encourage them to cooperate in various ways with one another. The various supernatural claims involved in myths not only suggest that such claims are significant but also depend upon nonskeptical acceptance by the listeners.

Magic (Chapter Eight) is distinguished by the communicated acceptance of a claim that certain *techniques* have a supernatural effect, one that cannot be demonstrated. The identifiable effect of such claims and techniques lies in their communication of sexual desire, anger, support, concern for someone's well-being, and so on. The general effect of such messages is to promote particular kinds of cooperation. Black magic, or sorcery, which communicates anger, is a substitute for violence.

Divination (Chapter Nine) is identified by the supernatural claim that certain techniques are supernaturally influenced by events, including events in the future. Such claims cannot be shown to be true. The most important effect of divination is that it reduces responsibility in decision-making, and thereby reduces the acrimony that can result from bad decisions.

An individual's acceptance of supernaturally justified *taboo, pain, and sacrifice* (Chapter Ten) communicates a willingness to suffer for those, including ancestors, who encourage such acceptance and thereby promotes the willingness of everyone involved to suffer for one another. This is a defining feature of social relationships.

A *witch* (Chapter Eleven) is an individual accused of being supernaturally evil. The killing or injuring of a witch includes the communicated acceptance of the supernatural accusation. Because actual evidence is irrelevant, by such acceptance individuals uniquely communicate their willingness to support, and cooperate with, the accusers in harming or killing the accused. We propose that people accept such accusations and support such actions in order to intimidate a category of people who pose an identifiable threat to their social hierarchy. The witch is a symbol used to communicate a readiness to use violence to protect the hierarchy on which their social relationships are based.

The acceptance of a claim that a *shaman* (Chapter Seven) or *prophet* (Chapter Twelve) has supernatural powers communicates uniquely a commitment by the acceptors to the shaman's or prophet's influence. Although the task of a shaman is to lead traditional religions of (mainly) identified kin (see Steadman and Palmer 1994), the activity distinguishing a prophet is the creation of a modern cult, maintained by his or her representatives or priests. Although ancestral cults are distinguished by the creation of family-like relationships between distant kin, modern religions (including the world religions) are distinguished by such relationships between nonkin, individuals who (usually) by virtue of *alleged* descent from a creator God are only *said* to be kin of a supernatural kind. The acceptance of the claim of supernatural descent communicates a willingness to act like a kinsman toward actual (and potential) cofollowers.

The common thread running through all of these activities is the encouragement of individuals to sacrifice themselves in various ways for others: the encouragement of selflessness. The willingness to sacrifice lies at the heart of social relationships; it is the sine qua non of human societies. By encouraging voluntary sacrifice, religious behavior creates and strengthens social relationships between individuals. As a result of the force of Darwinian selection, traditional religious behavior that has become widespread has favored the descendant-leaving success of the participants and has thereby increased the frequency of the religious activities themselves.

Determining the truth of the above hypotheses depends on empirical identification of the facts asserted. Although statements whose facts cannot be so identified may be true, simply asserting them does not make them so. In an enterprise such as science, which is concerned with the demonstrable accuracy of statements, the statements proposed and considered must be restricted to those whose accuracy is subject to skepticism based on our senses. The above hypotheses must be so judged.

The transmission of traditional behavior depends on social relationships. Not only is religion usually traditional, it also helps to create and maintain the social relationships through which many of the traditions themselves are transmitted. In the following chapters we attempt to demonstrate that the most significant effect of religion, the effect that can account for its persistence through time, is that it encourages "close" kinship behavior between either distant kinsmen or, more recently, people said to be like kinsmen. We propose that it is this effect that has promoted the leaving of descendants. To the extent that religion is traditional, it depends for its perpetuation on cooperation between ancestors and descendants. It depends literally on kinship cooperation.

The next question is how to incorporate traditions, including religious traditions, into the framework of evolutionary theory. To provide an ultimate (or evolutionary) explanation of religious behavior we must answer the question of how religious traditions have been successful descendant-leaving strategies of our ancestors.

Darwinian Selection and Traditions

The most powerful, identifiable influence on all organisms, including humans, is their ancestors, living and dead; all living organisms are influenced profoundly by their ancestors' genes. In addition, many animals acquire and hence are influenced by, behavior of their ancestors that becomes traditional (Avital and Jablonka 2001). The influence of traditions has become uniquely and overwhelmingly powerful among humans. Living ancestors, such as parents and grandparents, influence their living descendants directly, and, through the transmission of some of their behavior to their descendants, they can influence distant descendants yet to be born. In this way, humans are influenced by the traditions deriving from very distant ancestors. That is why we use the term "descendant-leaving success" (DLS) rather than "reproductive success," because the latter focuses attention on the number of surviving offspring rather than more distant descendants (Palmer and Steadman 1997). The evolutionary success of parental (and grandparental) behavior is judged not by the number of offspring, or even living grandchildren, but by distant descendants.

Recognizing the relationship between ancestral influence through traditions and success in leaving descendants has enormous consequences for the understanding of human behavior. Ancestral influence comes from individuals distinguished necessarily by success in one activity: they each left descendants.

Not a single one of our ancestors, perhaps back to the beginning of life on earth, failed in this regard. That is no mean achievement, for in every population many individuals fail. Indeed, every living individual has a substantial chance of failing to leave descendants. Thus, all organisms are descendants of ancestors who successfully left descendants, yet only some become ancestors themselves. While our existence implies ancestral success, it does not imply our own future success. Hence, the failure of organisms to leave descendants in no sense challenges the fact that all are products of such success.

Acquisitions from ancestors are invariably associated with descendant-leaving success. But still more important is the fact that anything replicable and acquired from ancestors is subject to Darwinian selection. Although such selection has come to refer only to genes, our use of the term "Darwinian selection" is consistent with how Darwin used the term to describe the process he discovered more than a century ago, whereby anything inheritable and replicable can influence its own frequency in later generations. Such a process obviously includes traditions, for they are both inheritable and replicable. Anything inheritable *and* replicable (while land or gold, for example, may be inheritable, they are not replicable) that promotes the leaving of descendants (offspring, grandchildren, great-grandchildren, and so on) tends to increase in frequency in subsequent generations, along with the descendants; anything that reduces such success tends to disappear.

Humans, therefore, like all living organisms, are continuously being fashioned out of the *descendant-leaving success* of their particular ancestors. Both genes and traditions are inheritable elements by which human ancestors influence the behavior of their descendants. The frequency of those genes and traditions responds to their own descendant-leaving influence. Traditions are distinctive not because they are learned behavior, or even learned behavior acquired from others (that is, culture); they are distinctive because they are learned behavior acquired from ancestors and, hence, subject to selection.

Because of the process of Darwinian selection, defined here specifically as *the influence of inheritable, replicable elements on their own frequency in succeeding generations,* it is human ancestors who have been selected to be most interested in what their descendants learn, for descendants represent directly the ancestors' descendant-leaving stake. It is for this reason that parents and grandparents are the ones who most encourage offspring to acquire and support the traditions constituting their religious, governmental, and economic behavior. Indeed, it is primarily parents who maintain such behavior (Castro and Toro 2004). Humans leave descendants not by mere reproduction but also by carefully influencing their living descendants for many years. Because of the importance of traditions, humans who do not transmit, or support the transmission of, traditions to their descendants have tended to leave fewer descendants than those who do. In all human societies, traditions regularly include the encouragement of cooperation among codescendants, including *distant* codescendants. Religion regularly includes such encouragement. By being traditional, the frequency of religious behavior, therefore, should respond to its own descendant-leaving influence.

Returning to our observation that essentially all researchers of human behavior assume that human behavior has an aim (Chapter Two), we propose a new answer to the question of what that aim might be. To identify the cause of anything requires identifying certain prior conditions or events correlated with that thing. Thus, the cause of the *aim* of behavior, like the cause of any behavior, is discoverable only from the past. Identifiably, the most powerful, continuous, directional event influencing the frequency of any behavior is the influence of that behavior on the descendant-leaving success of the organisms in the past that exhibited it. The *effect* of inheritable elements that increases their own frequency in later generations is the most important *cause* of their increase.

Effect, as cause, occurs also with learning behavior. It is the memory of past correlations—in particular, the remembered effect, or consequence, of past behavior—that influences the decision whether to repeat that behavior. When individuals are influenced to act because of their memory of past consequences of that act, we speak of that behavior as having an aim—namely, the achievement of those past consequences. Thus, because of his or her remembered experiences, a hunter can be said to be aiming his or her arrow at a deer, trying to shoot it, even though he or she may not be successful. Nevertheless, by identifying certain past experiences he or she has had with that behavior, including *vicarious* experiences, we can conclude that his or her behavior is indeed aimed at shooting the deer.

The influence of memory, of course, is itself influenced by Darwinian selection. Not only are the kinds of things remembered influenced by genes (which are continuously subject to selection), but if we ask why the hunter seeks a deer, and then why he or she eats and shares it with his or her family, for example, we are led quickly to the conclusion that such behavior is indeed a descendant-leaving strategy. This is true even considering the possibility that this behavior may fail, for it is only success in leaving descendants that has fundamentally increased the frequency of this behavior in the first place.

More precisely, replication is the key to aim. The replication of genes and remembered experiences (including cultural behavior) distinguishes both life and learning, respectively. Aim is nothing more than the attempt to replicate a past result. The aim of tree roots is to interact with the environment in ways that were favored by selection in the past. The same is true of a human hunting a deer. In order to replicate the killing of a deer, the hunter tries to replicate the hunting and shooting techniques that he or she experienced as "successful" in the past. These techniques, in contrast to others he or she has experienced, were chosen because of the results he or she remembers them achieving. In his or her attempt to replicate certain past experiences, the hunter takes the deer home and shares it with his or her family, all of which are part of his or her ultimate replication—the reproduction of those genes involved in his or her behavior. Aim is created by "successful" past effects, the success ultimately determined by the replication of the genes involved. Thus, aim implies Darwinian selection, and that is why it is restricted to biological organisms. Furthermore, the replication involved in selection and memory is not only the basic cause of aim, it is what constitutes aim. To the extent that behavior has an aim, it is to replicate certain past effects—either remembered correlations or the genes involved in the behavior.

It is within this context that the concept of "culture" can be best understood. Culture has been the focus of anthropology since its beginnings. An explicit definition of culture, however, has never been widely accepted. Clearly, while the term refers to something learned, it does not refer to just anything learned, for many organisms exhibit some learning and are not said to exhibit culture. The essence of culture is not that it is learned, but that it is something learned and copied from one individual by another, occurring in the first individual and then *replicated* by the second. Therefore, what distinguishes culture, identifiably, is copied behavior. Only to the extent that it is copied do we speak of culture; it is only the repeated, learned part of behavior that is *identified* as culture. Cultural behavior, then, exhibited by one individual implies another individual from which it was copied. Culture, *identifiably,* is behavior that is experienced, remembered, and then copied, as Darwin implied by his use of the word "imitation."

Despite the unparalleled dominance of the use of "culture" in the field of anthropology, the behavior that has played such a crucial role in human evolutionary history is more accurately labeled by the word "tradition." A tradition is cultural behavior copied from, and sometimes encouraged by, ancestors. Traditions have been favored by selection when they promote the descendant-leaving success of ancestors. This approach provides an answer to the debate over the relationship between culture and biology that has dominated much of the history of social science (Brown 1991; Freeman 1983).

Claims of cultural inheritance as being independent of biological inheritance, whether made by nonevolutionary social scientists or evolutionary biologists (Boyd and Richerson 1985; Dawkins 1976; Pulliam and Dunford 1980), are erroneous. Culture is not the "superorganic" force that some social scientists have claimed it to be. Nor, as Dennett (1995) has pointed out, does culture consist of "memes" that parasitize minds independent of psychological (that is, biological) adaptation as claimed by certain biologists (for example, Blackmore 1999; Dawkins 1976). When inheritance is properly considered as a phenotypic phenomenon influenced by both genetic and environmental factors, traditional cultural behavior is inherited the same way as any other aspect of the phenotype—by inheriting the genetic and environmental factors that interact to produce the phenotype (see Thornhill and Palmer 2000: 24–29).

Although nontraditional culture is important in many parts of the world, that is a recent development. Close, enduring contact between nonkin is rare in tribal societies. It is the force of traditions that causes humans to favor closer kin over more distant kin. Such traditions have been selected for because children *not* favored by their own parents are less likely to leave descendants than children so favored. Parents encourage cooperation among their offspring, who are siblings of one another. For the same reason, grandparents encourage cooperation among their grandchildren, who include cousins of one another. And more distant ancestors, through traditions, encourage cooperation among more distant codescendants (see Palmer and Steadman 1997). All learning organisms that exhibit parental care can benefit their offspring by what they have learned in their own lifetime. But learned behavior that can be copied by descendants, like genes, can influence very distant descendants. This surely is the fundamental significance of traditions.

It is neither the hedonism of the individual nor the survival of the group that has fundamental consequences. The basic reason why particular behaviors are widespread is that, in the past, they have helped the ancestors of the living organisms to leave descendants, and thereby have increased in frequency along with their descendants. The essential flaw in psychological and sociological theories is that they are inconsistent with the fact that all living organisms are the result of success in leaving descendants influenced profoundly by inheritable elements that respond continuously to selection. Although evolutionary psychology has incorporated the significance of genes that have been favored by natural selection, it has largely ignored the role of traditions.

The Aim of Religious Traditions: Social (Moral) Behavior

Religious behavior is a form of social behavior. Much human social behavior tends to be traditional in that it comes from, and is encouraged by, ancestors. Such ancestral influence cannot be explained by common conceptions of either natural or sexual selection that ignore traditions, *for it is at their expense.* Darwin recognized this crucial feature of morality.

In *The Descent of Man,* Darwin confronted the problem of morality—the "moral faculties which distinguish [man] from the lower animals" (1871: 158). Darwin attempted to explain the selection for moral behavior by its contribution to a group—the community or, especially, the tribe—arguing that such behavior would make a group stronger in competition with other groups:

An advancement in the standard of morality ... will certainly give an immense advantage to one tribe over another. There can be no doubt that a tribe including many members who, from possessing in a high degree the spirit of patriotism, fidelity, obedience, courage and sympathy, were always ready to give aid to each other and to sacrifice themselves for the common good, would be victorious over most other tribes; and this would be natural selection. (Ibid.: 166)

And again: "[A]lthough a high standard of morality gives but a slight or no advantage to each individual man and his children ... , an advancement in the standard of morality ... will certainly give an immense advantage to one tribe over another" (ibid.).
And finally:

Let it be borne in mind how all-important, in the never-ceasing wars of savages, fidelity and courage must be. ... Obedience ... is of the highest value, for any form of government is better than none. Selfish and contentious people will not cohere, and without coherence nothing can be effected. A tribe possessing the above qualities in a high degree would spread and be victorious over other tribes. ... Thus the social and moral qualities would tend slowly to advance and be diffused throughout the world. (Ibid.: 161–62)

But Darwin, himself, saw the flaw in his own argument:

It is extremely doubtful whether the offspring of the more sympathetic and benevolent parents, or of those which were the most faithful to their comrades, would be reared in greater number than the children of selfish and treacherous parents of the same tribe. He who was ready to sacrifice his life ... rather than betray his comrades, would often leave no offspring to inherit his noble nature. The bravest men ... would on an average perish in larger numbers than other men. Therefore, it seems scarcely possible ... [that] such virtues ... could be increased through natural selection, that is, by the survival of the fittest. (Ibid.: 163)

As Darwin recognized, the key problem with moral behavior is that it involves sacrifice, which is at the expense of either one's survival, reproduction, or both. For many writers, including Darwin (ibid.: 229), being "social" means acting as a member of a (social) group. But a mammalian mother is "social" to her young, regardless of any group. The term "social" (for most writers) also implies *interaction*. However, while social behavior *does* imply two or more individuals, it does not imply interaction, for one individual (such as a mother) can help another (such as her offspring) who does not realize it. Thus social behavior is not necessarily interactive. Nor does interaction imply social behavior, for there is much interaction between individuals—enemies, for example, trying to kill one another—that is not social. A sociopath may interact with others without being social. Social behavior requires only that one individual help another at his or her own expense. From a Darwinian perspective, that expense is either reduced survival or reproduction, or both.

Thus, social behavior implies sacrifice. Parental care is the epitome of social behavior, and it reduces the parent's own chances of reproduction and survival. As Darwin noted, "Everyone knows how strong the maternal instinct is, [even] in opposition to the instinct of self-preservation" (ibid.: 83–84). *Cooperation* is an example of social behavior, for each of the individuals involved has made himself or herself responsive to, and hence vulnerable to, the other. Moral behavior is obviously similar to social behavior, as here defined.

As Darwin noted, "moral" behavior is doing "good" *for others*. That is because much, if not most, of the behavior that is usually called "good" or "moral" involves altruism (for example, sacrifice) toward other people. It is important to note that we use these terms in accordance with this standard usage, but we do not claim that what is typically called "good" or "moral" is actually good or moral, or necessarily desirable, in any absolute sense. We are not making a moral judgment about how people ought or ought not to behave. We are only describing the kind of behavior often encouraged by religious behavior with the terms typically used to label that kind of behavior. To leap from such a description of how the world is to how the world ought to be is to commit the naturalistic fallacy. Readers interested in our opinions about the absolute moral goodness or badness of religious behavior, or even whether this is a meaningful question, can turn to the last few pages of this book, where we address the issue.

For now, the important point is that in evolutionary terms, doing "good" to others often means promoting their survival and mating potential at the expense of one's own survival and mating potential. Thus, both moral behavior and social behavior imply sacrifice. If moral behavior is not synonymous with social behavior, then perhaps it must be a type of social behavior: *social behavior encouraged by others,* particularly ancestors. This encouragement by others is the source of what we "ought" to do, which, according to some (for example, Wright 1994), is the definitive feature of moral behavior.

Let us present an alternative hypothesis to account for what is typically labeled social, or "moral," behavior. Consistent with Darwin's natural and sexual selection, it focuses on individual success in leaving descendants, not group selection. The hypothesis is this: social, or moral, behavior has been selected for as a strategy of ancestors. To the extent that an individual, by his or her behavior, can influence the behavior of his or her offspring, *and through the offspring, more distant descendants,* the behavior of the descendants is part of that ancestor's strategy to leave descendants and must be so evaluated.

What distinguishes humans from other animals is not their appetites, but the suppression of those appetites, which everywhere is encouraged by ancestors through the transmission of the behavior we call traditions. A tradition is a phenotype copied from ancestors, whose expression, like all phenotypes, depends both on particular genes and a particular environment. When such inheritable behavior increases the likelihood of leaving descendants, it tends to increase in frequency along with the descendants. Furthermore, any genetic mutation that facilitates the expression of a successful tradition will also tend to increase in frequency along with the descendants.

Traditions imply *restraint on carnal appetite.* Such appetite is the main cause of competition, conflict, and violence. In all tribal societies, religious leaders, representing ancestors, encourage self-restraint through taboos and promote cooperation through rituals. The time-consuming activity of transmitting traditions involves parental (and hence, ancestral) sacrifice (Steadman and Palmer 1997). In modern societies, this transmission includes formal education, which invariably is supported by parents with school-aged children. Accepting the influence of ancestors, rather than following one's own desires, is a sacrifice of one's own personal desires. Traditions also imply kinship cooperation, for their expression and transmission depend on cooperation between living ancestors and their descendants. In all traditional societies—the societies of all our distant ancestors—kinship identification and cooperation are *traditionally* encouraged well beyond second cousins, often involving hundreds, sometimes thousands, of codescendants (Palmer and Steadman 1997).

The main restraint on the appetites of *nonhuman* animals is the threat posed by other individuals. This is a threat that restrains humans as well. But, in addition, humans actively encourage restraint, sacrifice, and cooperation among their descendants, through traditions, especially religious traditions. Morality involves both restraint and sacrifice for others at the expense of satisfying one's own appetite.

The following claims will be supported in detail in the following chapters. The function of religion is not to satisfy our appetites, our desire for confidence, reduction of fear, and so forth, as so many have argued, but instead to encourage sacrifice, which has the effect of promoting cooperation and restraint among cofollowers. Indeed, all religions encourage moral behavior among the followers. Buddhism, for example, argues that all suffering comes from desire (that is, appetite), and Buddhists are encouraged to restrain, even extinguish, their desires, which has the obvious effect of reducing competition, violence, and the like, which stem from desire. Islam, meaning literally *submission* (to Allah via Muhammad and his Koran), requires Muslims to pray five times a day, give alms to the poor, fast each year during the month of Ramadan, and make at least one pilgrimage to Mecca.

The fundamental religion of all traditional small-scale societies (and hence, the religion on which *all* others must be based), to be described in Chapter Four, appears to be ancestor worship. Its aim—the cause of its persistence through time—is that it promotes cooperation among codescendants of the same ancestor and respect for his or her traditions. Kinship cooperation and traditions are the basis of all human societies. Most lateral cooperation is the result of accepting a common hierarchy, and in simpler societies everywhere, the hierarchy consists of ancestors, or kinsmen, who speak for dead ancestors (Steadman and Palmer 1994, 1995). Prophet-created "modern religions" influence their followers to behave *as if* they were kin, often calling the alleged creator, and the prophet, "father" or "mother," and each other, "brother" and "sister."

Darwin noted:

> As no man can practise the virtues necessary for the welfare of his tribe without self-sacrifice, self-command, and the power of endurance, these qualities have been at all times highly and most justly valued. ... The American savage voluntarily submits without groan to the most horrid tortures to prove and strengthen his fortitude and courage; and we cannot help admiring him, or even an Indian Fakir, who, from a foolish religious motive, swings suspended by a hook buried in his flesh. (1871: 95–96)

What distinguishes humans from the other animals is not his or her "needs," "wants," or "appetites," but the extent to which he or she suppresses them. This does not make us any better or worse than any other species, just different. Human appetites are not very different from other mammalian appetites, and even that of reptiles and birds: for sex, food, and the power to gain them. Darwin saw that our appetites are not distinctive. With the "lower animals," man shares the instincts of "self-preservation [and] sexual love" [read "lust"] (ibid.: 36). He goes on to write: "The lower animals, like man, manifestly feel pleasure and pain, happiness and misery. ... [They] are excited by the same emotions as ourselves" (ibid.: 39). He continues: "[M]an and the higher animals, especially the Primates ... have the same senses, intuitions and sensations—similar passions, affections, and emotions, even the more complex ones" (ibid.: 48). The question before us is: how has morality, which is at the expense of one's own carnal appetites for survival and reproduction, been selected for?

The virtual obsession with a lateral, or group, explanation has prevented social scientists from appreciating the vertical influence of ancestors on their descendants—not just genetically but also through the influence of traditions, especially on their descendants' social behavior toward one another. If we lived in a highly traditional society it is much less likely that this fundamental feature would have been overlooked, for in such societies everything good is explained by ancestors; indeed, the explicitly stated aim of life is to live according to the ancestors! The transmission of traditions, as well as the genes on which such behavior depends, has long been a crucial part of the way individual humans have increased the frequency of their genes in distant generations.

Any genetic mutation that facilitates the expression of a successful tradition will tend to increase in frequency along with the descendants. It is likely, therefore, that most of the genes distinguishing us from chimpanzees, our closest animal relatives, were selected because they facilitated behavior involved in traditions, such as ax-making, speaking, religious and hierarchical behavior, and so on.

One thing Darwin and others failed to appreciate is that when offspring imitate a parent's behavior, it is a form of inheritance, but unlike wealth, it is replicable, and therefore transmittable to further descendants. Thus, such imitation can significantly increase the parent's, as well as the offspring's, chances of leaving descendants, for the offspring thereby acquire behavior that has been successful. Darwin, however, did see the inheritance of copied behavior in birds. He writes that "the actual song, and even the call notes, are learnt from their parents, or foster parents. ... Nestlings, which have learnt the song of a distinct species ... teach and transmit their new song to their offspring" (ibid.: 55). But for men and monkeys, Darwin speaks only of imitating their "fellow-man" (or -monkey) in their community or tribe, not their parents (ibid.: 57). His failure to recognize that traditions are inheritable may be related to his acceptance of Lamarck's (and Wallace's) idea of the inheritance of acquired characteristics, as, for example, when he writes that "handwriting is certainly inherited" (ibid.: 58), or when he states that "an inherited habit" is "an instinct" (ibid.: 47). In short, if we learn something in our lifetime that can be somehow genetically transmitted to descendants, why speak of the inheritance of behaviors through imitation? But Darwin's contemporaries in the social sciences did no better, for they, too, tried to explain culture, or imitation, by the group. However, imitation is important among mammals in general, and it doesn't require a group. When a mother coyote discovers a water hole, a new hunting technique, or a safe place to sleep, such important information can be acquired by her offspring simply by following her (imitating her by going along the same path) (see Avital and Jabloka 2001).

Although Darwin used "social" and "imitation" to refer to communal behavior, his own personal life shows his keen awareness of the influence of *individual* ancestors on their descendants. Wright, in his analysis of Darwin's life, perspicaciously notes first that "the transmission of moral instruction from old to young parallels the transmission of genetic instruction and is sometimes indistinguishable in its effects" (1994: 218). Wright then writes: "[T]his fidelity of moral transmission is plain in Darwin. When, in his autobiography, he extols his father—his generosity, his sympathy—he might just as well have been talking about himself. And Darwin would in turn work to endow his own children with solid [moral] skills" (ibid.: 218). In Wright's words, Darwin "felt compelled to teach [his children] the virtues of kindness" (ibid.: 156).

Conclusion

The vertical influence of ancestors on their descendants has not been fully appreciated as the basic cause of morality and social behavior. Such behavior involves reduced competition and greater cooperation among codescendants. Reduced competition and increased cooperation increase the ability of individual codescendants to compete successfully with nonkinsmen, or distant kinsmen, when competition occurs for any scarce resource: land, space, animals, mates, and so on. An individual with a greater number of supporters who are willing to sacrifice for him or her is more likely to win against an individual with fewer supporters. As anthropologists have long recognized, in primitive societies one's influence is closely related to the number of kin one can identify.

Religious behavior, such as the Hewa's talk about *pisai,* is highly traditional. Traditional behavior is subject to selection. The universality of religious behavior indicates that it has been favored by selection. That is, the religious behavior of individuals has had the effect of increasing their descendant-leaving success. This brings us to the question of how the tradition of religious behavior has been so favored. For example, instead of asking why the Hewa believe in *pisai,* the question should be what the identifiable effects of communicating acceptance of such supernatural claims have been, and how they account for the manner in which this traditional behavior has helped the ancestors of the current Hewa successfully leave descendants. Our answer to this specific question about the Hewa will be provided in Chapter Eleven, but to fully understand that answer, we must first examine the close connection between religion and kinship, a connection seen most saliently in ancestor worship.

Chapter 4

In the Beginning: Ancestor Worship

> Why, if we are believers, is the one and only true god the God of our parents and grandparents?
>
> —*Thompson (2001: 130)*

> Ancestor cults ... can only be understood when they are viewed as part of a whole set of family and kin relationships.
>
> —*Evans-Pritchard (1965: 111)*

THUS FAR, we have put forth an explanation of religion in general. However, the word "religion" is simply the label of a category of behavior that includes numerous specific behaviors that all have some identifiable part in common: the communicated acceptance of a supernatural claim. Rarely does the religious behavior of humans consist of the communicated acceptance of simply the general claim that supernaturals exist. Instead, humans communicate acceptance of many different specific supernatural claims, such as "*pisai* can consume someone's viscera." The rest of this book uses our general explanation of religion to generate testable explanations of the different types of supernatural claims that make up the category called religion. We start with what appears to be the most common supernatural claim found in traditional societies.

The Universality of Ancestor Worship

Anthropologists have long made the point that religious behavior takes place in all known human societies. Wherever people have managed to survive and reproduce, they have communicated acceptance of supernatural claims. A key to explaining how and why this situation has come about lies in another, previously unappreciated, universal aspect of human behavior. Not only do humans everywhere communicate acceptance of *some* supernatural claim, but it is possible that in every human group studied by anthropologists, individuals have communicated acceptance of the *same* one: the claim that *dead ancestors are still alive and can influence the living and be influenced by the living*. Why, out of all the myriad supernatural claims possible, would individuals in all known human groups make, and communicate acceptance of, this particular claim? Answering that question would clearly be a major step in explaining religion.

The ubiquity and antiquity of ancestor cults was assumed in the nineteenth century by Spencer (1972) and Tylor (1958). However, claims of ancestor interaction with the living are not recognized today as universal because the focus of anthropology has usually been on differences rather than similarities. This has led to overly narrow definitions of both "ancestor" and "worship." Often the term "ancestor worship" is restricted to those societies in which the dead are explicitly called by a term that is translated as "ancestor," thereby excluding societies whose religious practices concern claims about ghosts, shades, spirits, souls, totemic plants and animals (see below), or merely the dead.

The role of ancestors is also obscured in many descriptions of societies whose religions are based on more general, and hence, supposedly nonancestral, spirits or gods. An example of this is the hunters and gatherers living in the Kalahari, once referred to as the !Kung of Namibia (Africa). Although Lee (1984: 103) states that the !Kung's "religious universe is inhabited by a high god, a lesser god, and a host of minor animal spirits," he also states that "the main actors in [the !Kung's religious] world are the *//gangwasi,* the ghosts of recently deceased !Kung" (ibid.).

The failure to see the connection between ancestors and spirits or gods often causes societies to be excluded from the ancestor worship category. Lehmann and Myers state that "when the living dead are forgotten in the memory of their group and dropped from the genealogy as a result of the passing of time (four or five generations), they are believed to be transformed into 'nameless spirits,' non-ancestors" (1993: 284). Similarly, Tonkinson claims that the Mardu lack ancestor worship because they cannot remember the names of specific distant ancestors, despite the fact that their religious rituals focus on "ancestral beings" (1978: 21–22, 195). The Yąnomamö provide a similar example because their religion is said to be shamanic (see Chapter Seven) and concerned with spirits instead of ancestors. Although it is true that Yąnomamö religion involves shamans ingesting hallucinogenic drugs and controlling spirits known as *hekura,*

Chagnon reports that "when the original people [the *no badabö*] died, they turned into spirits: *hekura*" (1983: 92). Since the *no badabö* were clearly the ancestors of living Yąnomamö, ancestors are central to Yąnomamö religion. Indeed, it is crucial to realize that whenever there is reference to ghosts, spirits, or the dead in a religion, ancestors will be present, if not predominant, in this category.

An overly narrow definition of the term "worship" is also often used to claim that certain societies lack ancestor worship. Many societies do indeed lack ancestor worship if the meaning of worship is restricted to elaborate ceremonies involving ritualized sacrifices. If, however, the term "worship" is used in the broader sense of reverence or respect shown ancestors, accompanied by the communicated acceptance of supernatural claims about communication between dead ancestors and their living codescendants, the universality of ancestor worship is a definite possibility. At the very least, claims of communication between dead ancestors and their living codescendants appear to be a human universal. For example, such behavior is reported in not only all of the ethnographic descriptions of societies coded by Swanson (1960) as having "ancestor worship" but also in *every* society coded by Swanson as *lacking* ancestor worship (see Steadman, Palmer, and Tilley 1996).

Lehmann and Myers observe that "a belief in the immortality of the dead occurs in all cultures" (1993: 283). We suggest this is because ancestor worship implies the idea of souls. A soul becomes significant only after the person dies, for it refers to the continued existence of an individual after death. It is the *soul* of the ancestor that is said to continue to exist, and to influence and be influenced by the descendants, which distinguishes ancestor worship as religious behavior. Why is it that everyone is said to have a soul, even though some may have no offspring? At birth, all individuals are potential ancestors, and therefore are said to have a soul, even though it is not very significant until they become actual ancestors. Thus, it is ancestor worship (whose importance we shall soon see) that may account for the universal talk of souls.

Ancestors not only provide us with our genetic material; they are also the source of traditions and kinsmen, resources essential to humans everywhere. By encouraging respect for ancestors, ancestor cults promote both respect for living kinsmen and the transmission of traditions between them. We shall argue that it is this effect that can account for the ubiquity and apparent antiquity of ancestor worship. By requiring cooperation, ancestor worship rituals thereby encourage cooperation among the participants, who are codescendants of one another.

Cooperative behavior, like all aspects of living things, is a product of both genes and countless environmental factors, which can include living ancestors. When the influence of ancestors, living and dead, is not accepted, their descendants (kinsmen of one another) are unlikely either to identify one another as kin or to cooperate with each other. Traditions—implying acceptance of ancestral influence—will be lost. Therefore, disregarding one's ancestors (and hence, traditions and kinsmen) has two important consequences: (1) it disrupts the acquisition of "successful" behavior (behavior that has allowed the ancestors to survive and leave descendants), and (2) it eviscerates the influence of those individuals themselves on their own descendants. It is difficult to guide one's descendants when one has defied one's own ancestors. Ancestor worship, by encouraging filial piety, encourages respect for both kinsmen and traditions. That is the basis not only of human society but, more important, of human descendant-leaving success.

There are many situations and rituals in which both living and dead ancestors are honored, but what distinguishes ancestor worship as religious is *the communicated acceptance of the claim that dead ancestors can influence, and be influenced by, their living descendants.* Such influence is not identifiable, and hence, the referent of the claim is supernatural; it is a religious claim. It is on the living that the influence of such talk can be identified by both the participants and outside observers.

Religious rituals that focus on ancestors thus strengthen kinship ties and the traditions on which they depend: "Evidently the family-cult in primitive times, must have greatly tended to maintain the family bond: alike by causing periodic assemblings for sacrifice, by repressing dissensions, and by producing conformity to the same injunctions" (Spencer 1972: 218). The claim that ancestors can influence the living and be influenced by them would be a part of such rituals because it strengthened kin ties and the transmission of traditions in two ways. First, the reference to long-dead ancestors provided a means of involving many more codescendants than the few who could trace their common ancestry through only a few generations. Second, as Rappaport points out, supernatural claims—which would include references that dead ancestors influence the living and are influenced by them—establish "the quality of unquestionable truthfulness" (1979: 262). Such claims about ancestors promote the acceptance of traditions because "although one can argue to a point with an elder, no one questions the wisdom and authority of an ancestor" (Lehmann and Myers 1993: 285; see also Fortes 1976: 2). The cost of questioning what dead ancestors are claimed to say is usually prohibitively high because of the rejection of traditions and kin such skepticism implies.

Ancestor worship is not restricted to simpler societies. Japanese Shintoism involves ancestor worship, including the worship of the ultimate ancestress, Amaterasu, from whom all Japanese are said to descend (see, for example, Molloy 1999: 238). In addition, a creator God, a more distant ancestor, is found in most modern religions. To show the particular effect of ancestor worship on kinship cooperation and the transmission of traditions, we turn now to the religious behavior of the Lugbara of Africa. In Chapter Five, we shall examine the ancestor worship of the Australian Aboriginal peoples, whose "totemism" has been seen by some social scientists as the most primitive form of religion known.

The Lugbara

The Lugbara are one of the populations of the Bantu speaking peoples of Africa. The Bantu of today (who speak more than four hundred related languages and cover much of sub-Saharan Africa) may be descendants of a small population living some two thousand years ago in what is now Nigeria. The Bantu, therefore, seem to represent "one of the greatest movements of people in history" (Schneider 1981: 34), and the extraordinary descendant-leaving success of what were probably only a few individuals in that ancient population.

The Lugbara, as is true of all the Bantu-speaking peoples, are said to have "no cults of God or his subdieties, only cults of the ancestors" (ibid.: 189). Therefore, it is possible that the amazing success of the Bantu in leaving descendants had something to do with their ancestral cults. Let us examine such cults.

The Lugbara number almost a quarter of a million people and occupy a plateau on the border between the Democratic Republic of Congo and Uganda. They live mainly in small settlements and support themselves by keeping livestock and growing crops for cash and consumption. In *Lugbara Religion,* Middleton writes: "God made the world. ... [T]he hero-ancestors and their descendants, the ancestors, formed Lugbara society. The rules of social behaviour are 'the words of our ancestors'" (1960: 27). Middleton also writes: "The relationship between God and the ancestors is difficult to discover. It is never made explicit. Every lineage has its own ancestors, but God is everywhere, in a relationship of equal intensity with all lineages" (ibid.: 28). Note here that God, by making the world and creating humans, is the first ancestor, making all the Lugbara codescendants of one another.

Middleton writes that the Lugbara erect small stone shrines to a dead ancestor one year or so after his or her death. Usually a man builds a shrine to his dead father, but he also builds shrines to his mother's mother and mother's sister, his mother's brother, and in some places, his father's mother's brother. He can also inherit shrines from his father. There are also shrines dedicated to the ancestors in general and shrines that are said to be occupied at different times by the ghosts of various more distant patrilineal ancestors. Offerings of food and beer, and the sacrifice of cattle, goats, sheep, and fowl, are made at these shrines (ibid.: 46–71).

The Lugbara say that the ghosts of their dead ancestors can punish living descendants who offend them. The ghosts are said to be concerned with, and can be offended by, behavior that threatens the kin ties of their descendants. They are said to punish "sins" by causing the offender or his wife, child, or younger sibling to become sick. According to the Lugbara, "a man who persistently offends and insults his close kin is a 'man with sin'" (ibid.: 22). These sins include striking or fighting a kinsman older than oneself, swearing or shouting at a kinsman, deceiving a close kinsman by stealing or cheating or lying, quarreling with a kinsman, a woman quarreling with her husband, or striking him or denying him the exercise of the rights he holds in her, and a man failing to carry out the duties of a guardian or heir. These social offenses bring a man "shame" (ibid.: 38–39). An elder who is particularly offended at the bad behavior of one of his close kinsmen is said to be able, by his anger or feeling of "outrage," to invoke the ghosts against this man or woman.

When someone becomes sick, oracles are consulted to decide what ancestors have been offended and by whom, or who may have invoked the ghost. The type of sacrifice to be made (beer, a cow, a goat, for example) is then determined. If the family head is not an elder, he calls on the ritual leader to conduct the sacrifice, which may be attended by a large variety of kin. Members of the "family cluster" (the local group of several related families) attend, along with those of closely related families and "representatives" from many related lineages (ibid.: 118–19).

During the ceremony, ritual addresses made by each of the attending elders are directed toward both the living and the dead. The first address usually gives a summary of the problems—quarrels, hard feelings, failure to pay proper respect to either living kin or dead ancestors—which are then discussed in detail at a second address. Such statements are said to reassure the ghosts that "the living are now in harmony and that the breach caused by the offender is mended" (ibid.: 93). These addresses give a traditional history of the lineage leading up to the present events, including a listing of disputes and how they were resolved, and conclude by stressing "that there should be no discord within the kin-group, that the girls should bring in good bridewealth and not behave promiscuously and so destroy the lineage, and that their wives should bear good and obedient sons" (ibid.: 94).

Here the emphasis is not on punishing the offender; rather, it is on forgiveness. Everyone recognizes that a sacrifice "is an occasion on which they must clear their hearts of animosity towards one another and unsettled and festering quarrels must later be aired and made up" (ibid.: 97). The Lugbara say that the ritual addresses of current problems are heard by the ancestral ghosts, who "will rejoice that they and the living are now in harmony" (ibid.: 93). The elders then spit on special leaves to "show their hearts are good" (ibid.: 95), demonstrating that all is forgiven and that they are at peace with one another.

These rituals, like rituals everywhere, are distinguished by stereotyped co-operation, the significant effect of which—their aim—is to encourage future nonstereotyped cooperation among the participants. By participating, the individuals communicate their promise to put aside their animosities. Such a public pledge makes it difficult for people to justify continuing their disputes, for they have publicly indicated that it is best to make up and get along with one another. In short, these rituals are used by elders to influence younger codescendants to settle their differences. Those who are quarreling have an opportunity to end their animosities without accepting blame for the problem. In addition, by their participation, individuals communicate that they forgive each other, which thereby limits their future criticism of the offenders.

The sacrificial animal is killed and cut up, and a small portion of the meat is placed in the shrine. The "feeding" of the ancestors at a sacrifice is said to appease their anger, and the Lugbara say they have an obligation to feed them, just as they must feed their living kin (ibid.: 55). Some of the meat is cooked and eaten in a communal meal "with the ancestors" by the patrilineal descendants of the ancestor (ibid.: 118–20). The uncooked meat remaining is distributed among these same people and, in addition, the rest of the kin attending the sacrifice (ibid.: 120). We shall return later to this emphasis on patrilineality.

Middleton claims that the ancestor worship of the Lugbara is aimed at influencing the relationship between the living and the dead. According to Middleton, the Lugbara *believe* that the dead are as much a part of their social life as the living, and ghosts are said to enter into direct, personal, and responsible contact with the living (ibid.: 54). "The dead are kin, but in most cases they are senior kin, and the living should behave towards them as towards senior living kin" (ibid.: 21). Further, he writes:

> The lineage includes both living and dead members: "Are our ancestors not people of our lineage? They are our fathers and we are their children whom they have begotten. Those that have died stay near us in our homes and we feed and respect them. Does not a man help his father when he is old?" For the Lugbara, living and dead of the same lineage are in a permanent relationship with each other. (Middleton 1960: 25–26)

It is obvious, however, that this statement cannot be shown to be true; the Lugbara do not have an identifiable social relationship with their dead ancestors. The dead do not discernibly respond to or influence the living. These statements are metaphorical, with the basic simile being that they agree to act, in certain regards, *as if* they continue to have social relationships with their dead ancestors.

Indeed, some of the statements made by Lugbara themselves indicate their own recognition of this fact: "It is said, 'People say our ancestors live as we do, but we cannot see them and we do not know'" (ibid.: 28). And this illuminating statement: "I was told on one occasion that 'the ancestors died long ago. Who knows whether they hear or not?' My informant was immediately checked not as being cynical and impious, but because he had spoken improperly rather than untruly" (ibid.: 93).

Although no one can objectively identify whether or not the ancestors hear the ritual addresses spoken at sacrifices, it is clear to everyone that the attending kinsmen do. Although ancestors are never actually seen eating the sacrificed meat or drinking the beer, the living relatives are. Identifiable, both to the Lugbara and the anthropologist, is the effect of the religious behavior on living kinsmen. This identified effect inevitably must influence the future decisions of the Lugbara in regard to repeating, modifying, or even abandoning such behavior.

According to Middleton, "Most of the social interaction of any Lugbara individual or family is with kinsmen" (ibid.: 20). The "family cluster," averaging about forty people, consists generally of several men related patrilineally (perhaps a pair of brothers and their grown sons) with their wives and young children, plus other relatives and their families, including perhaps a sister of one of these men or a sister's son. Occasionally, someone labeled by Middleton as a "non-relative" lives with this group, who attaches himself as a "client" to a wealthy individual (ibid.: 8–10). But important social relationships for the Lugbara are by no means limited to kin living together, the family cluster. Middleton reports that "individuals have personal ties with individual cognates [kin] and affines [in-laws] over a wide area" (ibid.: 20). In fact, the Lugbara identify far more relatives than this statement suggests, and this identification, along with the cooperation encouraged among them, has important consequences.

Of what he calls the "inner lineage," Middleton writes: "The most important [obligations] are that personal kinship terms are used between its members; homicide is regarded as fratricide" (ibid.: 149). In addition to identifying relatives by a set of kin terms, the Lugbara identify a great number of kin by patrilineally transmitted ancestral, or "descent," names. The Lugbara have about sixty clan names, each of which identifies, on average, about four thousand patrilineally related kinsmen (codescendants). One characteristic of Lugbara clans, like clans generally, is that they are exogamous (ibid.: 8, 19): members of the same clan must not marry each other. This marriage prohibition, by requiring that one's mother and father be of different clans, has the effect of ensuring each individual two sets of patrilineally identified relatives—the set of one's father and another of one's mother, a total averaging about eight thousand relatives. In addition, because the *offspring* of all females of both one's own patrilineal clan and one's mother's patrilineal clan are also identifiable kinsmen by virtue of *their* mother's patrilineal identification, perhaps eight thousand additional relatives for each individual will be identified. Hence, by such patrilineal clan identification, the average individual should be able to identify some sixteen thousand relatives (living codescendants). Clan names thus permit one to identify far more relatives than merely those bearing the name of one's own clan. And obviously all of these kin do not live together as a group, but instead are scattered throughout the land of the Lugbara.

Spouses frequently attend these rituals, even though they usually are not descendants themselves of the ancestor being worshipped. Why? The fundamental significance of affines (in-laws) is that they are actual or potential kin of your kin. For example, your wife and your mother-in-law (both in-laws) are the actual or potential parent and grandparent, respectively, of your children, forever. And your wife and your mother-in-law will have a lifelong interest in the welfare of those children.

Social relationships between relatives are regularly influenced by other relatives. Lugbara parents, like parents everywhere, encourage social behavior among their offspring: to avoid fighting one another, and to favor one another in various ways. In addition, each family cluster is under the authority of an elder, who controls the land and livestock. Part of his job is to keep the families together and to avoid the quarrels, fights, and hard feelings that can break them apart. The importance of the elder in encouraging social behavior among his dependents is evidenced by the fact that the breakup of a family cluster tends to occur only after the death of the elder "whose authority has hitherto kept the segments together" (ibid.: 15). Elders also influence the behavior among more distant relatives: "If there is a feud within the tribe, it is sooner or later stopped by the elders of the groups concerned" (ibid.: 113). Elders threaten to invoke the ghosts against any of their dependents who do not display proper kinship behavior. The dead ancestors themselves are held up as examples of how kinsmen ought to behave:

> "Our ancestors" are seen as good people who set an example that men should follow and who maintain the ideal of . . . social behavior merely by their having lived as they are said to have lived. A man who squanders lineage property or who by his actions weakens this system of authority is blamed as much for having failed to keep faith with the dead as for offending his living kin. (Ibid.: 26)

The statement that the ghosts, or more precisely, the elders by representing the ghosts, can punish behavior that threatens kinship relationships communicates to the offender the seriousness of his or her destructive behavior—that it is serious enough to deserve punishment. Also, if, in a ritual address, an illness is attributed to the offensive behavior of a particular individual, such attribution indirectly, but publicly, criticizes the offender.

Sometimes a sickness is said to be due to the fact that the ancestors are angry because they have not been "fed" enough, that their descendants are being stingy and failing to meet their social obligations. A man who fails to make sacrifices may be criticized for his stinginess, or his name may be put to the oracles as a possible cause of illness (he may even put forward his name himself). The obligation to feed the ancestors is said to be part of the general obligation to feed kinsmen; therefore, when a man is criticized for being stingy toward his ancestors, he is also being criticized for being stingy toward his living kin. He has himself probably eaten meat at the sacrifices given by his kin, for only a portion of the meat is left at the shrine; the rest is given to the living kin.

That religious behavior is not merely automatic, but rather that it involves individual choices and sacrifice, is seen in the criticism made by a Lugbara of a family that did not keep ancestral shrines: "These people are not real Lugbara. Have they no ancestors? Do they not respect them? Do they not even respect their fathers while they are alive?" (ibid.: 35). This statement also makes clear the connection between ancestor worship and social behavior among living kin. Failure to keep ancestral shrines is recognized as a rejection of the ties of kinship.

Therefore, when the Lugbara claim that antisocial behavior offends the dead and results in supernatural punishment of the offenders, its identifiable effect can be seen on the living codescendants. To the extent that those making the claim are influential, such a message should tend to have the effect of diminishing antisocial behavior between the living kinsmen.

But Why Make It Religious?

Even if it makes evolutionary sense to influence your descendants to cooperate with each other, why not simply tell them to do so? A crucial issue we shall be addressing throughout this book is why a *supernatural* claim is part of the communication. Why, for example, do the Lugbara not simply say that one's living kin are offended by such behavior?

Presumably the offenders, or their families, do not become sick any more often than do those who act like good kinsmen. Middleton presents no evidence that they do. Therefore, one might think that actual punishment of the offenders might be a more effective way of influencing their behavior than would the threat of supernatural wrath, whose effect cannot be identified. However, in this situation, by speaking for the ancestors and of their supernatural threats, instead of taking direct action against the offenders, an elder avoids displaying just the kind of behavior that he is trying to discourage. If he were to strike or injure his dependents when they quarreled or fought, he would be displaying behavior similar to that of the offenders. As one Lugbara sagaciously put it, "The work of an elder is to keep the territory without trouble. ... It is bad for a man to strike with his hand, or with his spear; now the ghosts strike on his behalf" (ibid.: 39). Similarly, when there has been feuding within the tribe, the elders mark a line on the ground and threaten to curse anyone who crosses it bearing arms. By threatening hostile individuals with a curse rather than physical punishment, the elders set an example, and thus discourage physical violence between kinsmen.

In addition, elders can criticize offenders indirectly, without themselves acting as the offended. If two kinsmen are fighting, their behavior can be discouraged without taking sides, without saying that one has wronged the other. It is simply asserted that the ancestors are angry with both for fighting.

Another problem presents itself. How can a threat of supernatural punishment be an effective means of influencing behavior, when such punishment cannot be shown to take place? A distinctive feature of supernatural claims about what dead ancestors want is that such claims cannot be disproved by evidence. The rejection of such an assertion, therefore, has the effect of rejecting the authority— the influence—of the individual who makes it and, perhaps, to some extent all those who make the same sort of statement. An individual faced with an assertion about something identifiable can cite evidence disputing it. An individual faced with a supernatural assertion about the desires of dead ancestors does not have that option. Fortes writes: "As my Tallensi friends used to say, one can argue with living elders but not with ancestors" (Fortes 1976: 2).

Consider, for example, the individual who is told, "If you don't behave like a good kinsman, the ghosts will send sickness to you or your family." He or she cannot disprove this statement. Since the only identifiable support for the assertion is found in the statements made by living people, he or she must reject them in order to reject the assertion. Such a rejection may disrupt his or her social relationships, something he or she may not be willing to risk. If he or she accepts the statement but continues the destructive behavior, that constitutes a demonstration that he or she still rejects the authority of those critics.

There is a more important consequence. To reject, deny, or ignore a traditional claim is not only to reject the person making it but also to reject one's ancestors, the source of both one's existence and one's traditions and kinsmen. The Lugbara say that the behavior of the ancestors is perfectly moral and social, and provides the example for all living kin to follow. Because the ancestors' behavior cannot be observed, this statement is unchallengeable. On the other hand, if individuals were told that the living elders were perfectly moral and well behaved, whose examples one should follow, one could challenge the statement by identifying any antisocial or selfish behavior they may exhibit. As one Lugbara pointed out, "Elders often quarrel among themselves like young men. They are men and all men have bad hearts. But the ancestors do not quarrel among themselves" (Middleton 1960: 17). Thus, supernaturals are a most appropriate model for ideal behavior—they are the only ones who can never fail to exhibit it.

The most fundamental advantage of distant ancestors over living ancestors is that distant ancestors are the source of many more kinsmen. For example, a parent can give an offspring only siblings, while a grandparent gives his or her grandchild first cousins. A great-grandparent can provide second cousins. Furthermore, one will generally have about twice as many first cousins as siblings, and about twice as many second cousins as first cousins, and so on. Thus, the more remote the ancestor, the greater the number of codescendants: with each further generation of ancestors identified, one roughly doubles one's codescendants.

The activities and statements that take place at Lugbara sacrificial rituals can be understood as communication that regularly encourages social behavior among identified kin. In Chapter Ten we discuss the identifiable effects of sacrifice; here, we want to mention only a few points regarding this matter. The offense cited as the reason for the sacrifice usually affects only people within the same family cluster. Yet many of the sacrifices are attended by a large number of distant kin, people who are not actually involved in the problem for which the sacrifice occurs. Middleton asks, "Why [should] a sacrifice that is concerned with the effects of sin upon the internal unity of a family cluster ... call for a congregation consisting largely of outside lineages?" (ibid.: 124). He offers no clear answer. We suggest the answer is that the man giving the sacrifice is concerned with more than the social relationships within his family cluster; he and his kinsmen share ancestors with individuals in these "outside lineages," with whom they are codescendants. When these "outsiders" attend the sacrifice, he has the opportunity to enhance his relationship with them through the sharing of his meat and his emphasis on maintaining good relationships with his kin. Those who attend do so because they recognize their relationship with the person making the sacrifice, or patient, and by attending, demonstrate their willingness to sacrifice for that relationship. And the rituals, like rituals everywhere, promote social behavior among the participants.

At Lugbara sacrifices there is an emphasis on patrilineal kinship. Although the kin who attend may be related to the "host" lineage through their mother, or their mother's mother or father's mother, for example, only the patrilineal descendants of the ancestors may sit near the shrine and actually eat and drink the food shared with the ancestors. The meat is only then distributed to representatives of the other codescendants that are linked to the ancestor through at least one female. Since relatives traced through both sexes are encouraged, and choose to attend, why is there this emphasis on those identified patrilineally?

We argued above that the significance of ancestral names is not that they identify an enduring group but that they allow the identification of many codescendants, considerably more than those in one's own patrilineage or clan. Patrilineal ancestral names allow individuals to identify their mother's *patrilineally* identified category of codescendants and, reciprocally, the offspring of one's own patrilineally identified females, who will be personally identified by the clan and lineage name of their own father. Therefore, rituals that emphasize those bearing the same patrilineal name are emphasizing only the *means* by which a much larger number of codescendants are identified—those who share the same ancestor—whether or not they themselves personally bear the name of that ancestor. It is only through such a name that most of these individuals can identify themselves as codescendants (Palmer and Steadman 2004).

We can draw certain conclusions from our examination of Lugbara religious behavior. It is distinguished by the claim that dead ancestors are still alive and continue to have a strong parental-like interest in the behavior of their descendants, particularly their social behavior toward one another. They, in fact, do this effectively through traditions they have transmitted when alive that include taboos, restraint on carnal appetites, and rituals. The rituals are distinguished, like rituals everywhere, by stereotyped cooperation that increases the likelihood among the participants of future cooperation. The overall effect of this encouraged cooperation is that competition and violence are reduced among the identified codescendants, making life safer, and also increasing cooperation, including trade, which increases the standard of living, and hence, the potential for leaving descendants.

We suggest that the combination of the traditional use of ancestral names to identify distant individual ancestors, and hence, large numbers of kin, and the rituals involved in the cults of ancestors, which promote enduring cooperation among these kin, may be the key to the tremendous descendant-leaving success of that small population of Bantu speakers living in Nigeria two thousand years ago. Such enduring cooperation among great numbers of identified kin may be the basis of their success in gradually replacing other peoples over much of sub-Saharan Africa.

One last point. We are arguing here that the significance of ancestral, or "clan" names is not that they identify a social group, a clan, or lineage, as so many have assumed (see Palmer, Fredrickson, and Tilley 1997). Rather, we are making the point that the significance of such names—the effect that favored their frequency through Darwinian selection—is that they allow the identification of many code-scendants, many (or even most) of whom do not live together in the same social group or bear the same ancestral ("clan") name. Therefore, because everywhere kinship distance is important, we predict that nowhere will second cousins sharing the same clan or ancestral name be systematically favored over first cousins who do not share the same clan name.

So-called "clan" rituals, involving individuals identified through an ancestral name, involve codescendants, regardless of their group affiliations and regardless of their residence. Thus, clan rituals are not aimed at, or reflect, a group as Durkheim (along with many anthropologists) mistakenly assumed in his analysis of Australian religion (1961). If clan rituals were aimed at maintaining the clan as an exclusive social group, as many have argued, why would codescendants identified by *other* clan names be regularly encouraged to attend and participate, and why would they do so? So far as we are aware in all "lineage systems" ever described, nonlineage members are encouraged to, and do, attend rituals. (For example, see Fortes's [1945, 1949] account of the Tallensi and Keesing's 1970 criticism of it. See also van Wing's 1938 account of the Bakongo [in Howells 1962: 166–77], which attempts, but fails, to explain the village as a clan.) This widespread phenomenon has never been satisfactorily explained. Further, if the maintenance of the clan as a social group were so important, why would they usually be exogamous, leading inevitably to the regular dispersal of clan members, with the residential groups consisting always of individuals identified by a number of clan or ancestral names? Clearly, to the extent that names are transmitted from ancestors to descendants, no group relationship is implied; descent identification and social groups of individuals are independent phenomena.

Ancestors in Modern Cultures

The significance of ancestors and traditions has become obscured in modern societies, influenced so strongly by both the breakdown of many traditions and the skepticism of science. But even the Roman skeptic Cicero noted that "we must never cease to hold fast to the gods" (1950: 413), or put another way, the ancestors. Although Cicero criticized divination as fraudulent, he recognized that skepticism endangered religion, and hence, traditions: "The annihilation of superstition does not involve the overthrow of religion. For it is judicious and wise that we should hold fast to the institutions of our ancestors by continuing to practice their solemnities and ceremonies" (ibid.: 460–61).

Human traditions everywhere are the result of cooperation between ancestors and their descendants. When individuals follow their traditions they are responding to the influence of their ancestors, who provide thereby the most appropriate symbol for rituals that encourage respect for both living kinsmen and traditions.

Arensberg reveals the connection between traditions and kinsmen when he writes of the Irish countrymen: "The past is a favorite topic; the 'old days' something of an obsession in the countryside. . . . For, where descent [read "kinship"] is a critical nexus of habitual relationship and old age the most honoured state, the past cannot fail to be the focus of interest" (1968: 108–9).

Because social rituals are distinguished by stereotyped cooperation between the participants, rituals have the effect of increasing the likelihood that the participants will cooperate in the future. When a common ancestor is the object of worship, the cooperation encouraged is between kin. In the Irish countryside today, cottages are often built with a West Room. This room of the "old people" is considered sacred (ibid.: 38–42, 107); children are prohibited from entering it, and it contains photographs of "departed" kin. In fact, it is an ancestral shrine, for near it are the paths of fairies, which old people become when they die. Or, as Arensberg writes, they "join 'them'"(ibid.: 184). Although *pisherogues* (or "superstitions") are strongly criticized by the Church and school, they have persisted throughout the fifteen hundred years since St. Patrick brought Christianity to Ireland. We suggest that the ancestral shrines, and related talk, persist because they promote kinship cooperation and respect for traditions among Irish countrymen.

In modern-day Mexico, a major annual ritual throughout the land is El Dia de los Muertos, a form of ancestor worship, in which living kinsmen visit the graveyard (sometimes called "panteon," from the Greek, meaning all gods or spirits) of their kinsmen and please them further by giving them their favorite food and drink. In the United States, at almost the same time of year, Halloween (the eve preceding All Saints' Day) occurs. Although today its function seems to be to promote good relations between disguised neighborhood children and homeowners, who give the anonymous children treats, in the past, as in Mexico today, it was a form of ancestor worship, and hence the symbolic elements emphasizing graveyards and skeletons.

Conclusion

The most significant and identifiable effect of ancestor worship, the effect that, through Darwinian selection, can account for its ubiquity and apparent antiquity, lies in its encouragement of cooperation among living kinsmen. More precisely, ancestor worship encourages family-like cooperation between nonfamily kin. By promoting such cooperation between kin, ancestor worship includes the promotion of the transmission of traditions from ancestors to descendants. Therefore, if it can be shown that participation in ancestor worship does not regularly increase kinship or family-like cooperation among the participants, the hypothesis presented in this chapter would be disproven.

Although others have attempted to account for the universal occurrence of religion through an examination of the "epidemiology of representations" (Sperber 1996), we suggest that what is actually needed is an examination of the evolutionary "epidemiology of supernatural claims." For example, *pisai* are not claimed to be the Hewa's ancestors. However, as is so often the case in traditional religious behavior, even when the behavior in question is not itself ancestor worship, the influence of ancestors is still necessary to explain the behavior. The Hewa talk about *pisai* because they heard their parents talk about *pisai,* and they observed the consequences of that talk. Each generation has replicated both that talk and those consequences. The talk of *pisai* and the killing of the woman accused of being a witch are traditional behaviors and hence part of the Hewa ancestors' descendant-leaving strategy. To understand exactly what part it played in this strategy we will need to examine the consequences of communicating acceptance of other types of traditional supernatural claims.

Chapter 5

Totemism

Perhaps the reason why the universality of ancestral cults as described in the last chapter has not been appreciated is the failure to recognize totemism as a form of ancestor worship. Lehmann and Myers state that a "major problem with Spencer's argument [that ancestor worship was the first religion] is that many societies at the hunting-and-gathering level do not practice ancestor worship. The Arunta of Australia, for example, worshipped their totemic plants and animals, but not their human ancestors" (1993: 284). However, totems are clearly ancestral in that they identify a person with a line of ancestors. Indeed, Harris points out that the Australian form of totemism "is a form of diffuse ancestor worship ... [because by] taking the name of an animal such as kangaroo ... people express a communal obligation to the founders of their kinship group" (Harris 1989: 405).

Once this fact is recognized, totemism ceases to be a distinct type of religion, much less the most primitive form of religion, as was proposed by both Durkheim and Freud (see below). Instead, totemism is an embellishment of ancestor worship. To explain this embellishment requires seeing totemism as metaphor.

Totemic-like identification is probably used metaphorically in every human society. Individuals are called by plant and animal names—he is a rat, pig, mule, good old bean; she is a fox, tiger, chick, peach—and social relationships among members of certain groups—sporting teams, for example—are identified often by names such as Tigers, Rams, Hawks, Bears, and so on. Furthermore, ancestral names, even in modern societies, are often "totemic": Fox, Tiger, Lion, Hawk, Gold, Stone, Moon, Wood, Steed, Brown, Clay, with sometimes only the spelling obscuring their "totemic" status—Browne, Greene, Foxe, Tyger, Pigg.

What exactly is the difference between the nonreligious totemic-like phenomena in modern societies and totems "proper," which are considered religious? In both cases, the most striking feature of any totem is that it is a metaphor, its claim not literally true. As discussed in Chapter One, "the feature of metaphor that has most troubled philosophers is that it is 'wrong': 'It asserts of one thing that it is something else'" (Percy, cited in Geertz 1973: 210). A human who is called a pig is not an actual pig. A team called the Rams does not consist of rams, but rather humans, and the same is true of an Australian kangaroo clan, despite its members' claim to the contrary. Totemic claims are metaphorical. Totems are religious when, and only when, their status as metaphor is denied. It is this denial, obviously untrue according to human senses, that requires, and thereby encourages, greater cooperation than that involved in the acceptance of acknowledged metaphor.

The religious behavior referred to as totemism is distinguished by the communicated acceptance of the claim that *an ancestor, and hence his or her descendants, has a supernatural relationship with a natural category, such as a plant or animal.* For example, among the Hewa, members of the Puali clan claim that their first ancestor emerged from a *Pu* plant. There are two important questions here: what does talk of a totem add to the humans so identified, and, second, what does the religious or supernatural claim add to this phenomenon?

In the strict anthropological sense, a totem is a metaphor that claims an association between its primary referent—kangaroos, for example—and the set of codescendants so identified—a lineage, clan, phratry, moiety, and so on. Because an ancestral name identifies a genealogical relationship, so too does the totem. The totemic rituals and taboos, by emphasizing the primary referent of the totem—the animal or plant—help to maintain its metaphorical status. Without such an emphasis, metaphors easily become unrecognized; the totem then becomes merely an ancestral name, such as the English family names cited above.

A totem embellishes an ancestral name, promoting cooperation among those so identified. Such embellishment is not trivial, for the care taken to select "totems" for sporting, fraternal, or religious groups or categories belies such a label. The passionate controversy surrounding the acceptance of the artichoke as the "totem" of the sporting teams of one community college in Arizona, as well as the Banana Slug as the "totem" of the University of California at Santa Cruz, indicates that such labels must be significant. Indeed, their widespread use proclaims this fact.

What does a "supernatural" claim add to the metaphor? Above all, the supernatural claim implies that the totem is not a metaphor—that it is, in fact, literally true. Hence, the acceptance of such a claim implies a denial of one's senses, one's own observations, and hence, communicates the acceptance of the influence of the persons making the (usually) traditional claim. Other behavior related to totemism (such as performing the totem's behavior in rituals and accepting prohibitions and taboos in regard to the totem) has the effect of elaborating and emphasizing the (denied) metaphor.

Individuals are often prohibited from eating their totem because by accepting a prohibition placed on the totem, one communicates respect, a willingness to suffer, for the symbol, and hence, for the kinship relationships it represents. Clearly, one is not communicating to the animal or plant. What is the identifiable impact of demonstrating such concern? Respect for a totem, much like the cross for Christians and crescent moon for Muslims, shows respect for those it symbolizes. Disrespect for a totem communicates the opposite. Showing a willingness to restrain oneself at the encouragement of others shows a willingness to cooperate with those others (see Chapter Ten). Thus, the acceptance of a taboo of one's clan totem communicates the importance of both those who encourage the restraint—the ancestors—and the descendants represented by it. The overall impact of such acceptance should be to promote kinship cooperation among fellow codescendants.

A totem is a metaphor and, as such, must be understood as a disguised simile. It identifies one thing by pointing out an association with something else. Second, it identifies and hence encourages social behavior and relationships between individuals, and therefore is often used to identify the relationships between members of a sporting team or religious group. Third, in the strict anthropological sense, the relationships identified, embellished, and thereby encouraged are between codescendants. Communicating acceptance of the claim that the metaphor is not a metaphor, but is instead literally true, increases the commitment communicated. Participation in the rituals involved in totemism, as in any social ritual, encourages future cooperation among the participants.

Australian Totemism

The most complex development of totemism known in the world is found among Australian Aboriginal peoples. Both Durkheim and Freud, publishing near the turn of the nineteenth century, argued that Australian Totemism focused on the clan and was the most primitive form of religion. Freud, in *Totem and Taboo* (1950), focused his argument of the origin of religion on the "most backward and miserable of savages, the Aborigines of Australia, the youngest continent, in whose fauna, too, we can still observe much that is archaic and that has perished elsewhere" (1).

Of these people, whom he had never seen, Freud writes: "It is highly doubtful whether any religion, in the shape of a worship of higher beings, can be attributed to them. . . . Among the Australians the place of all the religious and social institutions which they lack is taken by the system of 'Totemism'" (ibid.: 2).

Durkheim concurred that Australian totemism was "the most primitive and simple religion . . . actually known" (Durkheim 1961: 13). The argument presented in his formidable work *The Elementary Forms of the Religious Life* is based on this assumption. Evans-Pritchard summarizes Durkheim's thesis: "[P]rimitive religion is a clan cult and the cult is totemic. . . . Totemism is the most elementary or primitive . . . form of religion known to us" (Evans-Pritchard 1965: 56).

Anthropologists often continue to imply that when Australian Aboriginal peoples claim they are kangaroos, witchety grubs, blackbirds, and so on, they really mean it, and that they *believe* they are the same as their totem animal. Therefore, according to those anthropologists, to Australian Aboriginal peoples such claims are not metaphorical, but the expression of actual beliefs. Hippler claims that "the Yolngu (of Australia) appear to be a people strongly characterized by magical thinking. . . . Words are the thing. . . . Ceremonial words are themselves . . . loaded with the power to kill (1978: 226, 241). This assertion is consistent with Levy-Bruhl's position, that primitive thought was oriented toward the supernatural, that "the attitude of the primitive is very different. . . . Objects and beings are all involved in a network of mystical participations" including the relationship between a man and his totem (cited in Evans-Pritchard 1965: 80, 86). Levi-Strauss argues that "savage" thought (reflected by magical talk and ritual) is distinctive. He suggests the source of such thought by pointing out that magical practices "may sometimes succeed" (1966: 11), but later retreats from this position by noting that magic "lacks efficiency" (ibid.: 220). More recently, evolutionary psychologists have also assumed that practitioners of totemism believe their supernatural claims about being a member of their totem species, and Shore asserts that this belief "can easily be shown to be rational in both the *empirical* and *contextual* senses of the term" (1996: 170, emphasis in original; see also Boyer 1996, 2001; Guthrie 2001; Winkelman 2004).

In regard to Australian totemism, Durkheim states:

> Every member of the clan . . . believes that while he is a man in the usual sense of the word, he is also an animal or plant of the totemic species. In fact, he bears its name; this identity of name is therefore supposed to imply an identity of nature. . . . [T]he name, for a primitive, is not merely a word or a combination of sounds; it is part of the being, and even something essential to it. A member of the Kangaroo clan calls himself a kangaroo; he is therefore, in one sense,

an animal of this species. "The totem of any man," say Spencer and Gillen, "is regarded as the same thing as himself; a native once said to us when we were discussing the matter with him, 'That one,' pointing to his photograph which we had taken, 'is the same thing as me; so is a kangaroo (his totem).'" So each individual has a double nature, two beings coexist within him, a man and an animal. (1961: 156–57)

In this last sentence Durkheim contradicts himself. He should have written "each individual has a triple nature; three beings coexist within him, a man, an animal, and a photograph." But clearly that is absurd; the native not only distinguishes all humans (including "kangaroo" humans) from kangaroos, but also the two from photographs. Such discrimination is crucial for his or her existence. Obviously, the native recognizes that both the kangaroo and the photograph merely represent him or her, that they are symbols of him or her, and that they remind people of him or her.

Leach writes: "Australian Totemism ... has fascinated but baffled several generations of anthropologists. ... Australian aborigines classify the categories of human society by means of the same words which they use to classify the categories of Nature. It is only because we use words in a different way that we find this strange" (1966: 406–7).

That is not true. We do use words in this way, as the "mascots" of sporting teams demonstrate. The members of a team called the "Rams" often claim to be rams; they may associate themselves with an actual ram at a sporting event and may even characterize themselves in words and drawings as possessing ramlike characteristics such as power, aggressiveness, and bravery. No one can identify what the team members actually believe, but their behavior can be determined to be either consistent with such statements or not. One can identify the extent to which they behave like rams, noting, for example, that female sheep are not sexually pursued by the human "Rams." Indeed, the humans (and perhaps, even the actual rams) would consider such action outrageous. Nor do the human Rams care much about the condition of rams in general—whether they are well fed, protected, slaughtered, or eaten, as they well might care about human Rams. The same is true of Australian Aboriginal peoples.

The behavior of the Aboriginals demonstrates a systematic discrimination between real humans (of any type) and real kangaroos. Statements of the identity between the two categories, therefore, are only metaphorical; the kangaroos and humans are only alleged to be codescendants. The humans (no less than the actual kangaroos) demonstrably recognize great differences between the two categories. Humans never marry actual kangaroos. Indeed, as human kangaroos, they must not marry human kangaroos, but instead marry only human owls, or human witchety grubs, or human crows, and so on. Hence, because the category is exogamous, offspring always have one parent identified by a totemic species other than their own. Such a fact is quite contrary to anything Australians find in nature, as actual kangaroos, owls, crows, or witchety grubs mate only with individuals of their own species and give birth to the same. As noted in Chapter Three, kangaroo humans never complain when their "relatives" (the actual kangaroos) are eaten by other humans. On the contrary, they perform "increase" ceremonies said to be aimed at increasing the reproduction of actual kangaroos so that members of other clans—their kinsmen—may eat them!

As argued earlier, ancestors, because they are the source, are a particularly appropriate symbol to represent and encourage respect for kinsmen and traditions. The appropriateness of symbols is always relevant to their use in communication. The more abstract the symbol, the greater is the likelihood of misinterpretation. Thus, a drawing of a dog is, in most cases, a more appropriate representation of a dog than a drawing of a worm, bird, or tree. The use of English sounds in the formation of a new word is more appropriate for English speakers than that of foreign sounds. Scientific terms are appropriately coined from Greek or Latin. The key symbol selected to represent both the unity of Mexicans, and their separation from Spaniards and other Europeans, is the Lady of Guadalupe. She is claimed to be Mary, mother of Jesus, and thus associated with the Christian basis of Mexican unity, but she is recognized also as Indian—she stands without child in a half-moon, as did an Aztec goddess—and thus serves to distinguish the Mexicans from Spaniards and other Europeans. It is this appropriateness that led to her selection by Mexicans to represent them in their revolt against Spain (Wolf 1958) and her continued use to symbolize Mexicans today.

Why, then, are animal symbols so often chosen to represent humans? A full answer should cover all uses of such metaphor—the Ram football players, those called *cabron* ("ram") in Spanish, Australian Aboriginal "kangaroos," and a schoolboy coming to the United States from Australia called "kangaroo." We should also account for why animal names such as "ram" are used to distinguish inanimate objects, like the battering device. Such inquiry should seek to discover what it is that the metaphor evokes, its appropriateness, and should resist any claim of shared essences or spirits—claims that are no more than metaphors themselves.

What, then, can be said of Australian Aboriginals' use of names of nature to identify kinsmen (a set of codescendants)? The objects and animals chosen as totems are well known to the Aboriginals, and not just as food. One particular attraction toward a name of a species of animal or plant is that such a name already represents a category of related organisms (a species) and, hence, is particularly appropriate to represent a category of related humans. In other words, the totem communicates that the set of codescendants called a clan is *like* a separate species, distinct from other people. Similarly, but without the religious claim, a "ram" football team emphasizes its distinction; the difference between it and another football team is emphasized also by being a little like a separate species.

Australian Kinship

Elkin writes that "totemism is so much a part of a man's very being in Australia that it enters into all his social and ritual groupings" (1964: 207). Furthermore, "The obligations of kinship govern a person's behaviour from his earliest years to his death, and affects life in all its aspects; in conversation, visiting and camping; at the crises of life, namely, childbirth, initiation, marriage, sickness and death; and in quarrels and fights" (ibid.: 118). He also notes: "The Aborigines … reckon their relationships throughout the whole community and even beyond the borders of any one tribe. … In other words, [kinship] relationship is the basis of behaviour; indeed, it is the anatomy and physiology of Aboriginal society" (ibid.: 56).

Radcliffe-Brown strengthens this observation:

> In Australia we have an example of a society in which the very widest possible recognition is given to genealogical relationships. In a tribe that has not been affected by white intrusion, it is easy to collect full pedigrees for the whole tribe. Further, these genealogical relationships are made, in Australia, the basis of an extensive and highly organized system of reciprocal obligations. … [In] native Australian society [genealogical relationship] regulates more or less definitely the behaviour of an individual to every person with whom he has any social dealings whatever. (43)

Kinship relationships, because they are based on genealogy and, hence, birth, are always relationships between individuals, whether or not such individuals form groups. Radcliffe-Brown makes a very clear statement in that regard:

> The relationships between one person and another in the kinship system are individual relationships. In deciding what they are, appeal is always made to actual genealogical connection. … [As] to the suitability of a proposed marriage it is the genealogical connection between the two persons that is considered. … [W]hen the genealogical connection is too remote to be traced the natives fall back on a consideration of the section or subsection or the clan to which an individual belongs, but … in the minds of the natives themselves they are dealing,

throughout all the ramifications of the kinship system, with real genealogical relations of parent and child or sibling and sibling. (ibid.: 436)

The most significant identifiable effect of Australian totemism (or more accurately, ancestor worship) is that the rituals, by promoting social behavior among the participants, help to convert identified genealogical relations into social relationships. To the extent that the defining relationship between the members of the various categories is ancestral (and both Elkin and Radcliffe-Brown imply that it is), the relationship between the members is genealogical, not residential. Totems and totemic rituals, by embellishing genealogical relationships, encourage social behavior and relationships between those so identified. Indeed, when individuals living together identify themselves as kin, it is a result of their genealogical relationship, not their common residence.

The totemism rituals of Australian Aboriginal peoples are similar to those of the Lugbara. Both are said to be directed toward a common ancestor and, hence, are rituals of individuals identified as codescendants. In both, the alleged common ancestor is identified patrilineally, and in some cases, identified occasionally through the mother's (and sometimes even mother's mother's) patrilineal identification. Hence, the rituals of both peoples include the offspring, and grand-offspring, of females identified patrilineally. The identifiable effect of the Australian rituals is, like those of ancestral cults everywhere, to encourage respect for both living kinsmen and traditions.

The Australian rituals may be distinguished from those of the Lugbara in several ways. The most obvious may be that the common ancestor worshipped is said to be not human, but only humanlike—a "totemic" ancestral hero—a mythological being who is said to have not only created the patrilineal ancestors of the participants but also exhibited by word and deed the characteristics of their totem (Elkin 1964: 159). The crucial difference may be that the Australian ancestors, in contrast to most of those of the Lugbara, are not personally identified. All the relevant ancestors are distant.

The "clan" rituals performed by the Australians are mainly of three kinds: (1) those involving the initiation of new cult members, (2) rituals that re-enact the doings of the ancestral hero (which Elkin calls "historical"), and (3) magical rituals said to promote, or "increase," the fertility of the totem animal or plant—the alleged "codescendants" of the cult members—and perhaps even the fertility of the cult members themselves (ibid.: 200–203). Like all rituals, these have the effect of promoting cooperation among codescendants.

Additional rituals are performed that are said to be aimed at more remote ancestral gods or spirits, creators of larger categories of codescendants—tribes, for example, and sometimes even several tribes. It is not always clear in Elkin's writings, but apparently such rituals are conducted by the cult group, although individuals of many cult groups may participate, as in the corroborees. As one might expect, the ancestral term "father" or "mother" is often used to refer to these distant ancestral creators (ibid.: 225–32), making the codescendants "siblings" of one another. Again, the significant effect of such rituals lies in their encouragement of cooperation between identified codescendants, identified by a moiety, section, or subsection name, which refers to more distant ancestors and, hence, larger categories of codescendants than clans. By explicitly accepting such myths of ancestral gods, and participating in rituals directed toward those gods, cooperation is encouraged not only between individuals within the same totemic category but also between individuals in different categories and even tribes.

Radcliffe-Brown recognized the cooperative effects of certain rituals on distant kin:

> When a youth [of the Kariera or similar tribe] is to be initiated into manhood he is sent on a journey which lasts frequently for several months. ... During his journey he is treated as sacred wherever he goes and may therefore visit in complete safety hordes ["local clans"] that are at enmity with his own. He is normally taken first to a neighboring horde of the other moiety from his own, and is passed on from one horde to another until he passes out of his own tribe and may eventually reach a tribe at some distance from his own. Here he remains for a period and acquires some knowledge of the language. ... For the rest of his life the country through which he has travelled becomes his "road" along which he can travel to carry messages or for other purposes. Thus in a given horde there will be men having different roads. ... Now it seems that a man tries to obtain a wife from a distant horde on his own road, and sometimes succeeds in doing so. ... He establishes by this marriage a connection between his own children and this distant horde which is of course that of their mother. (1931: 446–47)

This would suggest that the most significant and identifiable effect of Australian totemic rituals—an effect recognized also by Elkin—is that they encourage cooperation among the individuals involved, invariably identified kinsmen. But Elkin does not attempt to account for these rituals and stories by such cooperation. He argues instead that the totemic rituals of the Australian Aboriginal exist because they are believed to prevent or shorten the period of such disasters as drought, floods, and disease, or at least provide confidence that these natural disasters are being controlled. Thus, by the performance of rites and circumspect behavior, "they assure themselves that their efforts [to control nature will] be rewarded" (Elkin 1964: 140). Elkin argues that totemism is a result of people's experiences with the disasters of nature. Faced with the "vicissitudes of life," the Aboriginal person turns to totemism for the confidence needed to cope; it is totemism that "rouses" him or her to action. For example, the totemic "increase" ritual "is a method of expressing man's needs. ... It is a system of cooperation with nature which is both economic and psychological in function; it expresses economic facts and needs and also provides confidence in the processes of nature (spiritually conceived and determined) and hope for the future" (ibid.: 205–6).

But from whence comes this alleged confidence? The rituals either influence natural calamities or they do not. As religion is distinguished by claims whose truth cannot be demonstrated, if such rituals did in fact influence nature in the way they are claimed to, it is difficult to justify their being called religious. Elkin implies that the rituals do not affect nature when he notes that the processes of nature are only "spiritually determined" by totemism. Nowhere does he suggest that the rituals work as alleged.

It is the concern for actual disasters that Elkin focuses on as the cause of totemism, not merely alleged or supernatural disasters. If we assume that the actual disasters are not perceptibly diminished by the rituals, we then have a problem in accounting for how individuals would come to be, and continue to be, convinced that disasters are controlled by such rituals. Elkin cannot have it both ways. If the concern for disasters is sufficient to lead to attempts to control them by ritual, the lack of any demonstrable efficacy of the rituals in influencing the disasters should lead to their abandonment. Certainly there should be no development of confidence in controlling or influencing the disasters, which is the basis of Elkin's argument.

In addition, if individuals did by some strange coincidence develop "confidence" and did perform the rituals on the basis of it, they might actually reduce their ability to deal with nature. By spending time on demonstrably ineffective techniques, the Australian Aboriginal person would not spend that time on hunting, building shelters, traveling to more bountiful areas, or accomplishing other things that might actually avoid the consequences of disasters. Totemism as a response to nature's disasters is not a convincing argument.

Levi-Strauss also rejects Elkin's argument, but he does so on the basis that it does not distinguish totemism from religion in general—that Elkin's explanation is true for all religion. Thus, according to Levi-Strauss, it is not only totemism but also all philosophy and religion, of whatever kind, that present the features by which Elkin attempts to define the first: "a philosophy which ... provides that faith, hope, and courage in the face of his daily needs, which man must have if he is to persevere and persist, both as an individual and as a social being" (Levi-Strauss, 1963b: 54, citing Elkin).

The problem exposed above in Elkin's attempt to account for totemism by the need for confidence applies also to Levi-Strauss's assertion about religion in general. If we assume that religious activities do not perceptibly diminish natural adversity, what would be the basis for any confidence that they do? And if the frequency and intensity of the actual adversity is, in fact, irrelevant, how can one reasonably argue that it is the adversity that is the cause of religion, and its persistence, in the first place?

Neither Elkin nor the Aboriginal peoples can identify the supernatural beings said to be influenced by the rituals, the supernatural relationships between the humans and their totem category, or the alleged beliefs in such phenomena. Therefore, their behavior cannot be explained objectively as a response to supernatural beings and relationships, or their beliefs in them. Because individuals cannot be shown to be influenced by such phenomena, their behavior cannot be accounted for by them. But individuals *can* respond to *claims* made about such phenomena, and they demonstrably do so, for such claims are usually traditional.

Conclusion

Instead of attempting to explain why their "theory of mind" and "cognitive fluidity" have somehow led Australian Aboriginal peoples to believe that they are members of a nonhuman species (Shore 1996; see also Winkelman 2002; 2004), we have attempted to explain totemism through examining its identifiable effects. Australian Aboriginal peoples of today are descendants of ancestors who came to Australia more than forty thousand years ago (see, for example, Hart, Pilling, and Goodale 1988). Living largely in great isolation from the rest of humanity, their traditions today represent a tremendous elaboration—a fine-tuning—of genealogical identification and kinship social relationships.

We have not attempted here to account for how or why Australian Aboriginal peoples have come to identify themselves with so many different ancestors, both patrilineal and matrilineal. But the significance, the function, of all such names is that they identify different sets of codescendants. The complicated cooperation required by the rituals creates and encourages social behavior among the participants.

Totems intellectually embellish and, hence, emphasize these social relationships. By implying an association between the kinsmen, on the one hand, and a species of plant or animal, on the other, totems decorate kinship relationships. Totemic rituals, taboos, and artwork (Coe 2003) embellish further such relationships. To show respect for a totem is to show respect for those individuals whose relationships it symbolizes. Therefore, a totem literally is a metaphor that represents a common ancestor and thereby encourages social behavior among the descendants of that ancestor.

A major enigma in regard to Australian Aboriginal peoples is the meaning and significance of the word *alcheringa,* or one of its variants in other Australian languages. Stanner puzzles over this most profound word of the Aranda tribe, which he translates as "Dream Time," although noting that it means "literally something like 'men of old.'" He writes that the Aboriginal person uses it for "his totem, or the place from which his spirit came, his Dreaming. He may also explain the existence of a custom, or a law of life, as causally due to The Dreaming" (1956: 51).

Similarly, Elkin states that such a word (*altjira,* in the tribe he studied) refers to physical "symbols of the great heroes of the eternal dream time" (Elkin 1964: 187), and merely by handling such a symbol, it "makes the individual sacred and a sharer of the sacred life of the tribal heroes. . . . [T]his term . . . also denotes the . . . myths and rites through which the initiated enter into this sacred condition, and indeed, the initiated themselves" (ibid.: 188, cf. 185).

If the *literal* meaning of *alcheringa* is indeed "men of old," as Stanner claims, then its other uses (including "the dreaming") must be metaphorical. Surely, the phrase "men of old" refers to ancestors, those who created the present descendants and their traditions. Thus *alcheringa*—literally "ancestors"—is extended metaphorically to identify the time of the ancestors, their descendants, all traditions, and the various symbols used to represent them, including their totem and their sacred sites. This word, or its equivalent, found perhaps in all other tribes (such as *pukimanii* for the Tiwi [Hart, Pilling, and Goodale 1988: 96] and *manguny/jugurr* of the Mardu [Tonkinson 1991: 20–23, 195]) metaphorically evokes the ancestral connection. That the Australian Aboriginal peoples themselves recognize the failure of "whites" (including anthropologists) to appreciate the crucial relationship between these ancestral elements can be seen in one Aboriginal person's statement to Stanner:

> *White man got no dreaming,*
> *Him go 'nother way.*
> *White man, him go different,*
> *Him got road belong himself. (Stanner 1956: 51)*

A man without respect for his ancestors will have neither kin nor tradition. He, indeed, has only himself.

Chapter 6

Myth

MESSENGER (from Corinth): Polybus was not your father.

SWOLLEN FOOT: Not my father? ...

MESSENGER: Long ago he had you from my hands, as a gift.

SWOLLEN FOOT: Then how could he love me so, if I was not his?

MESSENGER: He had no children, and his heart turned to you. ... [I was] your saviour, son, that day.

SWOLLEN FOOT: From what did you save me?

MESSENGER: The infirmity in your ankles tells the tale.

SWOLLEN FOOT: Ah, stranger, why do you speak of that childhood pain?

MESSENGER: Your ankles were riveted, and I set you free.

SWOLLEN FOOT: It is true; I have carried the stigma from my cradle.

MESSENGER: That was why you were given the name you bear.

SWOLLEN FOOT: God! Was it my father or my mother who did it? Tell me!

—*Sophocles c. 425 B.C.*

ALTRUISM, OR SACRIFICE, the basis of social relationships, does not occur automatically. It must be encouraged. To a considerable extent cooperation between close kinsmen is a product of parental encouragement. Similarly, cooperation between more distant kin is a product of the influence of more distant ancestors, through their living descendants. One fundamental way ancestors encourage such behavior in their descendants is through talk, including stories. When ancestors succeed in influencing their descendants to repeat that talk to their own descendants—in other words, to transmit traditional stories—they are able to influence the behavior of very distant descendants. When such stories contain supernatural claims, they are known as myths, and the communicated

83

acceptance of myths increases the influence of ancestors and their ability to promote cooperation among distant codescendants.

It is proposed here that a significant and identifiable consequence of traditional stories—a consequence that may account for their persistence—lies in their encouragement of altruism between kinsmen (see also Coe, Aiken, and Palmer 2006; Coe and Palmer 2007; Palmer et al. 2006b). To consider that possibility, this chapter analyzes one of the most famous myths ever written: Sophocles' tragedy *Oedipus Rex,* a play that has challenged interpretation for more than two thousand years.

Plato, the first known user of the term "myth," declared that it referred to no more than the telling of stories, usually containing legendary figures (Cotterell 1980: 9). According to *Webster's Dictionary,* a story is a communication of a succession of events involving plot, setting, and characterization. Stories thus include myths (as well as fables, parables, folktales, fairy tales, legends, operas, plays, novels, and movies). Myths are traditional stories that, like history, use the past to influence human behavior. Through myths, the audience experiences vicariously (and safely) the consequences of the characters' actions (Scalise Sugiyama 2001; Steadman and Palmer 1997). Myths are a form of religious behavior because they include supernatural claims (for example, legendary figures) of which people communicate their acceptance.

Oedipus Rex, "the masterpiece of Attic Tragedy" (Jebb 1966: 4), was attended, along with other plays, by the whole population of Athens at certain annual festivals. At the principal festival, held in the spring, perhaps seventeen thousand spectators came to experience "a cycle of dramatic performances presented amid high civic splendour and religious ritual" (Watling 1947: 8–9). *Oedipus Rex* was a part of Athenian religion.

The play's author, Sophocles, was a native of Colonus, on the outskirts of Athens, where a local cult honored the hero Oedipus, who was said to have been buried there. With "a firm reputation for great piety" (Gould 1970: 92), Sophocles devoted himself to the service of the state in art and public affairs, and in old age was regarded with affectionate respect and honored for his charm and his good temper (O'Brien 1968: 1; Watling 1947: 7). He lived for ninety years, through most of the fifth century, and "saw in succession the Persian invasions of Greece and their defeat, the growth of Athens as an imperial power and center of culture under the regime of Pericles, and the long, cruel, ruinous war with Sparta and her allies which began in 431" (O'Brien 1968: 1). Watling, writing of Sophocles, notes:

> At [his] birth, Athens was still in the infancy of her life as a free democracy, making her first experiments with the new machinery of popular government. During his

boyhood she was defending that life and liberty ... against the aggression of the powerful state of Persia. ... Through most of the fifty comparatively peaceful years during which Athens created and enjoyed the richness and breadth of a free social life and culture, Sophocles contributed to the expression of that culture in the theatre which was its prime temple, performing also in his course the public duties which were as much the province of the artist as of the man of action. (1947: 7–8)

From his sixty-fifth year on, the war with Sparta and her allies engaged and drained the forces of Athens and her miniature empire until all of Greece was divided by contrary ideals of statecraft and opposing ambitions for power. It was during this struggle, at about the age of seventy, that Sophocles wrote *Oedipus Rex*, "the masterpiece of his life's work ... , [according to] Aristotle, who has this play constantly at his elbow as the perfect type of tragic composition" (ibid.: 14).

The Oedipus myth, the basis of Sophocles' play, will be familiar to many readers, but, because of its importance here, we summarize its relevant features in Note 1. The two most influential analyses of this myth are both examples of the psychological (hedonistic) explanation of human behavior, as we discussed in Chapter Two. We critique these two famous analyses, along with others, before presenting our own.

The Psychological (Emotional) Explanation: *Sigmund Freud*

For Freud, *Oedipus Rex* symbolized his psychoanalytic theory; indeed, he argued that the play was the purest "expression" of the most basic human impulse (Freud 1950: 156–57). According to Freud, myths are "nothing but psychology projected to the outer world" (in Dundes 1962: 1033); myths, like dreams, express unconscious psychological conflicts. Thus, the followers of Freud analyze myths the way they analyze dreams, seeing them as symbolizing repressed desire. According to Freud, the Oedipus myth expresses two desires held by men that are fundamental and universal: to have sexual relations with their mother and to kill their father. His "Oedipus complex" refers to these two desires and their psychological effects, and constitutes the "nucleus of all neuroses." Indeed, "the beginnings of religion, morals, society, and art converge in the Oedipus complex" (Freud 1950: 156–57).

The chief difficulty with Freud's interpretation of *Oedipus Rex* is that it contradicts the play: there is no hint anywhere that Oedipus sexually desires his mother or wants to kill his father. On the contrary, he banishes himself from Corinth to avoid violating his presumed parents, and much later pierces his eyes the moment he discovers that he unwittingly had violated his *actual* parents.

Freud himself recognized this innocence when he writes that Oedipus "did all in his power to avoid the fate prophesied by the oracle, and who in self-punishment blinded himself when he discovered that in ignorance he had committed both these crimes" (Freud 1935: 290). Nevertheless Freud continues:

> [T]he hearer ... react[s] ... to the secret meaning and content of the myth it-self. He reacts as though by self analysis he had detected the Oedipus complex in himself, and had recognized the will of the gods and the oracle as glorified disguises of his own unconscious; as though he remembered in himself the wish to do away with his father and in his place to wed his mother, and must abhor the thought. The poet's words seem to him to mean: "In vain do you deny that you are accountable, in vain do you proclaim how you have striven against these evil designs. You are guilty, nevertheless; for you could not stifle them; they still survive unconsciously in you." (ibid.: 290–91)

It is clear that in Freud's analysis, things need not be what they appear to be—that they can represent something else, even their opposite. In consequence, the accuracy of Freudian interpretations of myth is virtually impossible to determine.

Psychoanalysts often compare myths to dreams; indeed, Roheim postulated that myths originate in dreams, which are then retold (Dundes 1962: 1043). However, while dreams can be told and may even become sources of myth, a general relationship between the two has not been demonstrated and therefore should not be assumed. A crucial difference between the two is that while dreams are experienced only by the dreamer, myths or traditional stories are communicated. Myths are not only told; they are listened to and repeated for generations. Myths, not dreams, imply an audience. The essential question is why such stories are told and listened to—what makes a myth worth the time and interest of an audience?

The Psychological (Intellectual) Explanation:
Claude Levi-Strauss

Levi-Strauss has dominated the anthropological study of myth for a half-century. However, though much in his writings may be brilliant, there is a good deal that is confusing. Leach, who writes that he has "been greatly influenced by Levi-Strauss's work," suggests that Levi-Strauss wraps up "profundity in verbal obscurity. Some passages of Levi-Strauss when translated into English seem almost meaningless." Nevertheless, Leach concludes, "Levi-Strauss often manages to give me ideas even when I don't really know what he is saying" (Leach 1967: xv–xvii).

Levi-Strauss writes that the purpose of myth "is to provide a logical model capable of overcoming a contradiction (an impossible achievement if ... the contradiction is real)" (1963a: 229, parentheses in original). Interestingly, that idea may have come from Durkheim (although not cited by Levi-Strauss). When discussing the claim by Australian Aboriginal peoples that they are at the same time both human and their totem animal, Durkheim writes: "In order to give a semblance of intelligibility to this duality, so strange for us, the primitive has invented myths which, it is true, explain nothing and only shift the difficulty, but which, by shifting it, seem at least to lessen the logical scandal" (Durkheim 1961: 157).

Levi-Strauss uses the myth of Oedipus (see Note 1) as a "concrete example" of his method of myth analysis (Levi-Strauss 1963a: 213) and argues that the Oedipus myth is aimed at overcoming a contradiction involving the origin of humanity. He further implies that the myth has almost nothing to do specifically with Oedipus, but instead has to do with the belief that humans are autochthonous—that they emerged, were born, from the earth. This belief is contradicted, he argues, by the knowledge that everywhere humans are born from humans (ibid.: 216). He presents no evidence, however, that this contradiction is seen by the Greeks as significant enough to warrant the myth's creation and regular retelling. Nor does he suggest why it has captured the interest of audiences for more than two thousand years, regardless of their own particular origin myths.

As support for his interpretation, Levi-Strauss offers a translation of the names of three characters that he claims "refer to difficulties in walking straight and standing upright": Labdacus (Laius's father) = "lame," Laius (Oedipus's father) = "left-sided," and Oedipus = "swollen foot" (ibid.: 214–15). In regard to this evidence, he writes, "In mythology it is a universal characteristic of men born from the Earth that at the moment they emerge from the depth they either cannot walk or they walk clumsily" (ibid.: 215).

Based on his translations of these three names and this alleged universal characteristic, Levi-Strauss concludes that the myth of Oedipus focuses on the belief that man is born from the earth. He himself notes, however, that the translation of these names is questionable (ibid.: 214–15); indeed, Graves translates Labdacus as "help with torches" (Graves 1978: 12). Yet, even if it is assumed that the translations are accurate, and even if it is true that when mythological characters emerge from the earth they always either cannot walk or walk clumsily, it does not follow that whenever limping characters are encountered in myths, one can conclude that they have just emerged from the earth. Levi-Strauss's argument here is based on logical error; he has committed the Fallacy of Affirming the Consequent. Furthermore, his translation of Laius as "left-sided" suggests only vaguely an inability to walk straight or stand upright. It might just as easily refer to being left-handed, and thus translate to "sinister," a meaning, as we shall see, not inappropriate to the character of Laius.

Levi-Strauss goes further. He argues that the purpose of the Oedipus myth is not simply to express the belief that man is born from the earth but to emphasize a contradiction to this belief: the knowledge that humans are actually born from other humans: "The myth has to do with the inability, for a culture which holds the belief that mankind is autochthonous ... , to find a satisfactory transition between this theory and the knowledge that human beings are actually born from the union of man and woman" (Levi-Strauss 1963a: 216).

According to Levi-Strauss, the denial that man is autochthonous is represented by the slaying of two monsters: the dragon killed by Cadmus and the Sphinx killed by Oedipus. Cadmus killed the dragon that prevented humans from being born from earth. Of the slaying of the Sphinx by Oedipus, he writes only that it "is a monster unwilling to permit men to live." Since the monsters are overcome by men who are obviously alive, these two events represent the "denial of the autochthonous origin of man" (ibid.: 215). It is difficult, however, to see the significance of the Sphinx as a denial of autochthony; she merely ravaged Thebes until Oedipus solved her riddle and then conveniently killed herself. But Levi-Strauss continues: "Although the problem obviously cannot be solved, the Oedipus myth provides a kind of logical tool which relates the original problem—born from one [the earth?] or born from two [a man and woman?]—to the derivative problem: born from different [the earth?] or born from same [humans?]" (ibid.: 216).

Turning to Levi-Strauss's mind-boggling details: the myth seeks to overcome the first contradiction by confronting it with a second, which, by being "self-contradictory in a similar way" (ibid.), overcomes (or rather replaces) the first. It does this "by the [implied?] assertion that contradictory relationships are identical inasmuch as they are both self-contradictory in a similar way" (ibid.). This second contradiction involves an emphasis on "the overrating of blood relations," which is opposed by the "underrating of blood relations." The evidence cited for the overrating: "Cadmos seeks his sister Europa, ravished by Zeus"; "Oedipus marries his mother, Jocasta"; "Antigone buries her brother Polynices, despite prohibition." The evidence cited for the underrating of blood relations: "[T]he Spartoi kill one another"; "Oedipus kills his father, Laios"; "Eteocles kills his brother, Polynices" (ibid.: 214–15).

Levi-Strauss summarizes his argument:

[T]he overrating of blood relations is to the underrating of blood relations as the attempt to escape autochthony is to the impossibility to succeed in it.

Although experience [knowledge of reproduction?] contradicts theory [belief in autochthony?], social life [kinship relations?] validates cosmology [the belief in autochthony?] by its similarity of structure [meaning that both the kinship and the belief in autochthony contradictions are contradicted in a similar way]. (Ibid.: 216)

By "a similar way" Levi-Strauss could mean that the overrating of blood relations is an overrating of birth from humans (blood relations imply such births), whereas the underrating of blood relations could be the denial of such birth. This contradiction would be identical to the first (that involving autochthony) but with the emphasis reversed. But Levi-Strauss's cryptic writing often confuses, and the pursuit of what he "really" means can be almost infinite, as a number of analysts attempting to follow his approach seem to demonstrate (for example, Burridge 1967; Douglas 1967; Yalman 1967).

Levi-Strauss's explanation of myth, if not itself a contradiction, is almost meaningless. He argues that the purpose of myth is to overcome contradictions, and yet real contradictions (are there any other kind?) cannot be overcome. His possibly brilliant, but certainly confusing, approach, like that of Freud, is difficult if not impossible to challenge by data; it is not subject to falsification (Strenski 1974). The mere identification of oppositions in myths demonstrates neither that the purpose of myth is to overcome contradiction nor that any particular myth is aimed at that particular opposition. When Oedipus's killing of the Sphinx is said to deny autochthony (even though Oedipus's name is said to affirm it), the flexibility of the categories used seems almost infinite. Anything can be anything else—even, so it seems, its own contradiction. Such an approach appears consistent indeed with the proposition that the purpose of myth is to do something it cannot do.

Myth as Communication: An Alternative Analysis

Regardless of Levi-Strauss's argument, the major problem recognized by most analysts is to account for the suffering of Oedipus, for he seems to suffer undeservedly. To get some feeling for the controversy and incredible range of explanations offered, one need only read the nine articles and seventeen "viewpoints" in *Twentieth Century Interpretations of Oedipus Rex* (O'Brien 1968). Plutarch, for example, stated that Oedipus suffered because of an "itch of curiosity" (ibid.: 99). Voltaire wrote that the play was so contrary to probability that it, and hence the suffering, was absurd (ibid.: 99–100). For Frazer, because of Oedipus's incest, his blinding and banishment were necessary to restore the country's fertility (ibid.:

100–101). For Shorey, Oedipus's suffering is no more than to show the worst that can happen to a man (ibid.: 101–2). According to Webster, Oedipus suffered because he and Jocasta criticized the oracles (ibid.: 102). For Fromm, rather than a Freudian desire to sexually possess his mother, Oedipus was driven to rebel against the authority of his father and suffered because of it (ibid.: 107–9). For Jaeger, Oedipus suffered for humanity (ibid.: 103). Waldock argues that the significance of the suffering is that it is so rare (ibid.: 103–4). For Gould, it is because Oedipus, like Jesus, is innocent, and who thereby reprieves "the rest of us from guilt. We are more innocent for his having suffered innocently" (ibid.: 106). For Thass-Thienemann, it is because, by guessing the riddle of the Sphinx, Oedipus gained sexual knowledge and, hence, anxiety (ibid.: 109). For Thompson, Oedipus suffered to relieve the social frustration caused by the transformation of the Athenian social order (ibid.: 110–11). For Hathorn, Oedipus's guilt was a result of his "failure to recognize his own involvement in the human condition, a failure to realize that not all difficulties are riddles, to be solved by the application of disinterested intellect … but that some are mysteries … to be coped with … [by] the whole self" (ibid.: 111–12). For Sewall, the reason Oedipus put out his eyes was to stand as "his culminating act of freedom … independent of any god, oracle, or prophecy" (ibid.: 113). And finally, for McLuhan, the blindness of Oedipus was the penalty for his creativity in solving the riddle of the Sphinx (ibid.).

The basic problem with these interpretations is that none is consistent with the facts of the story. Surely, the accuracy of an interpretation, a hypothesis, put forward to account for a myth or traditional story must be measured by the extent to which it accounts for all the elements in the story.

To some critics the "play's meaning is embroiled in seemingly hopeless controversy" (ibid.: 2), but the most widely held literary interpretation seems to be that the play demonstrates a person's lack of control over his or her own destiny. No matter what he does, Oedipus cannot avoid the fate the gods have set for him. Thus, Gould writes: "The effect [of the play] is to make the audience fear that perhaps the efforts of human beings to create lives for themselves may be devoid of meaning" (1970: 2). Similarly, Bowra concludes that "the gods display their power because they will" (1944: 175). And, for Ehrenberg, "it is Chance as the expression of the inscrutable will of the gods that eventually destroys Oedipus" (1968: 80). The predictions of the oracles come true no matter what steps Oedipus takes to prevent them.

Is the aim of the story to convince the audience that behavior is irrelevant—that no matter what they do, humans can influence nothing? If this is the case, how can we account for the writing of the play itself, which surely implies the possibility of influencing an audience? Could the message of perhaps the greatest tragedy ever composed be nothing more than that behavior is pointless?

Not all literary critics accept the interpretation that the play is a "tragedy of destiny." Dodds, for example, writes:

> What fascinates us is the spectacle of a man freely choosing, from the highest motives, a series of actions which lead to his own ruin. ... The immediate cause of Oedipus' ruin is not "Fate" or "the gods"—no oracle said that he must discover the truth—and still less does it lie in his own weakness; what causes his ruin is his own strength and courage, his loyalty to Thebes, and his loyalty to the truth. (1968: 23)

Thus, Oedipus is more than simply the innocent dupe of the gods. The actions that lead him to disaster—to killing his father and marrying his mother—result from his own choice. Because he exiles himself from Corinth in order to avoid killing his apparent father and marrying his assumed mother, he ends up on the road to Thebes where he, unwittingly, kills his real father. By daring to answer the riddle of the Sphinx, an action foretold by no oracle, he saves Thebes and is offered its kingship and queen. Based on his concern for the people of Thebes (for example, in *Oedipus Rex,* lines 58–61, 322, 629, 1449–50) and seen in his statement "to help another is man's noblest labor" (line 315), Oedipus seeks relentlessly to discover the murderer of Laius, even when he is aware of the possibility that it might be himself. When he learns eventually whom he has killed and married, he blinds himself, again an action not determined or foretold by any god. As Dodds notes, he does not simply suffer *in spite of* what he does, he suffers *because* of what he does.

But there is a deeper problem with the "fate" explanation: the attempt by Laius, and later by Oedipus, to thwart the prediction is illogical. If Laius and Oedipus believed in the oracle, they would have to assume that they could do nothing to thwart it and therefore should do nothing. If the prediction were true, it could not be thwarted, and if it were not true, there would be nothing to thwart; the fate predicted would either be impossible to influence or irrelevant. The oracle did not say in regard to Laius that, *unless* he killed his son, his son would kill him. And for Oedipus, the oracle did not say that, *if* he left Corinth, he would avoid killing his father and marrying his mother. Neither prediction was contingent on any action. Thus, with respect to the oracle, there was no appropriate behavior for either Oedipus or Laius; the only rational behavior would have been to ignore it.

Why, then, does Sophocles have Laius and Oedipus respond to the oracle? We suggest that one important use of oracles in myths is as a literary device used to facilitate the plot. Oracles are used to set events into action without making any particular character responsible for what happens. The use of such supernatural phenomena prevents the complications that would have to be introduced into the story if events were only naturally influenced. Is there a better way to make Laius fear his innocent baby son sufficiently to try to kill him? Is there a better way to get Oedipus both to leave his Corinthian parents and, at the same time, demonstrate his love for them? Later, it is the oracles' prediction that if Thebes is to be saved Laius's killer must be found that eventually leads Oedipus to the discovery that he himself is the killer. Thus, oracles can be useful, particularly when they are an acceptable idiom. Gould writes: "There is nothing whatsoever to support the suggestion that Oedipus was impious to have turned away from Corinth and to have tried to avoid a fulfillment of the oracle in its baldest, literal form. His earnest intention to avoid patricide and incest is disapproved of neither by man nor god" (1970: 136; see also 91–92).

The behavior of Oedipus and Laius, as well as everyone else in the play, implies the assumption that behavior makes a difference—that it has consequences, regardless of predictions of destiny. Sophocles' writing of the play itself presumes this. Far from influencing the audience to accept fate and do nothing, everything about the play encourages the opposite.

The immediate reason for Oedipus's suffering is clear. He blinds himself because he has violated his parents, piercing his eyes the moment he realizes he had killed his father and married his mother. It is also true, as the quotation at the beginning of this chapter shows (when Oedipus discovers the reason for his name), that his unwitting patricidal and incestuous acts against his parents are a consequence of his father's attempt to kill him. Sophocles wrote his plays for an audience that already knew both the Oedipus myth and the meaning of the name (Watling 1947: 11). To the Greek audience, Swollen Foot (or "Feet") was not simply a personal name; each time it was uttered, they were reminded of the treachery of Laius, the ultimate cause of Oedipus's mutilation and tragedy. Although Oedipus himself does not discover why he bears this name until late in the play (indeed, the entire play focuses on his gradual acquisition of the details surrounding his name), the Greek-speaking audience, unlike those of today, was well aware of its significance. To the Greek audience, the name of the myth, the play, and the hero symbolized the consequences of a selfish, treacherous father. The Greeks knew why Swollen Foot suffered.

The fundamental cause of his tragedy is recognized by Oedipus himself when he asks the question at the beginning of this chapter: "God! Was it my father or my mother who did it?" This question refers to the riveting of his ankles (Gould 1970: 124) and to his biological, not adoptive, parents. He recognizes it again, explicitly, after blinding himself, when he entreats Creon to banish him to that mountain where, as a baby, he was sent to die, saying, "[My] mother and my father ... made it my destined tomb, and I'll be killed by those who wished my ruin!" (lines 1452–55). That Oedipus clearly identified the cause of his tragedy can be seen also in Sophocles' play *Oedipus at Colonus,* when he seeks permission to stay in a sanctuary near Athens. Oedipus points out that there is nothing to fear from him, that his only

> *strength has been in suffering.*
> *Not doing—as you should hear, could I but tell it;*
> *Could tell all that my father and my mother did—* ... *I did not know the way I went. They knew;*
> *They, who devised this trap for me, they knew!*
> (lines 262–75, Watling 1947)

Interestingly, Jebb (1904) translates this last line as "they who wronged me knowingly sought my ruin."

Oedipus Rex takes place years after Laius's attempt to kill his son, and the play does not discuss why Laius was confronted by the oracle. However, from the plays *Seven against Thebes* (742ff.) by Aeschylus and *The Phoenician Women* (18ff.) by Euripides, it is clear that the audience knows that the curse is a punishment against Laius for abducting and seducing Pelops's son Chrysippus. *Because* of this deed, Laius was told that *if* he had a son, then he would be killed by that son (Gould 1970: 92; Jebb 1966: x–xii).

Laius, despite the oracle, went on to have a son, but, rather than accepting his punishment, he attempted to save his own life by having his son killed. Thus, in his effort to evade punishment, he committed a crime greater than the one for which he was to be punished. Laius, in sharp contrast to Oedipus, does not suffer innocently or unselfishly. His death is the result of his own crime, and the ultimate destruction that comes to his wife and descendants is the result of his attempt to avoid his punishment. For a father to lose his son is a tragedy, but for a father to selfishly kill his son to save his own life must rank among the greatest of evils. Nothing forced Laius to try to kill his son. He could have responded to the oracle: "As a father I shall sacrifice for my son, even at the risk of my own life." Oedipus, in contrast, did not knowingly kill his father; he was not in any sense an evil son. Both Oedipus and Laius tried to thwart the oracle, but the difference between the two was that Laius tried to kill his son to save his own life while Oedipus blinded himself because he had (unwittingly) violated his parents.

Oedipus, in contrast to his father, is not selfish. He is the epitome of a respectful son, a concerned and loving father, a good king. He values his kinsmen and his people more than himself. When he first hears of the prophecy, rather than allowing the possibility that he would kill his father and marry his mother, Oedipus exiles himself from Corinth to avoid harming the parents he loves. And even years later, when he learns of his (adoptive) father's death and is offered the kingship of Corinth, he declines it because of his fear that by returning he may fulfill the prophecy and marry his mother (lines 976–86). As the Theban king, Oedipus demonstrates his concern and willingness to sacrifice himself for his people. When he discovers that he himself is the cause of the plague affecting Thebes (because he had unknowingly killed King Laius), he begs to be exiled (lines 1449–51). Indeed, in his first attempt to save Thebes, he risks his life to answer the riddle of the Sphinx. As a father, Oedipus is equally virtuous; his final line in the play voices his concern for his young daughters: "Do not take them from me, ever!" Oedipus sacrifices himself for others, for both his kinsmen and his subjects, whom he calls his "children." Far from being lustful and treacherous, Oedipus's behavior is noble.

The tragedy of Oedipus is that despite his selfless, virtuous, courageous behavior, he was caught in the consequences of his father's selfishness. What the audience learns from the story is that the significant consequences of a person's behavior are not limited to that person alone. This is an important message for both kings and fathers. Both children and subjects depend on parental sacrifice. Laius refused to make such a sacrifice and destroyed, ultimately, his family and very nearly his kingdom. He was not only a bad king and father but, in addition, his behavior threatened the basis of society.

Recognition of this crucial relationship between Oedipus's suffering and Laius's foul deed throws light on an intriguing problem. To whom the "Great Song" of the chorus of Theban Elders refers has been the subject of much controversy. The song is presented at the moment Oedipus first suspects he may be the killer of Laius, but before he or anyone in the play realizes that he is also Laius's and Jocasta's son.

STROPHE 1	LINES
	May there accompany me
	the fate to keep a reverential purity in what I say,
865	in all I do, for which the laws have been set forth
	and walk on high, born to traverse the brightest,
	highest upper air; Olympus only
	is their father, nor was it
	mortal nature
870	that fathered them, and never will
	oblivion lull them into sleep;
	the god in them is great and never ages.
ANTISTROPHE 1	
	The will to violate, seed of the tyrant,
	if it has drunk mindlessly of wealth and power,

875   without a sense of time or true advantage,

mounts to a peak, then

plunges to an abrupt ... destiny,

where the useful foot

is of no use. But the kind

880   of struggling that is good for the city

I ask the god never to abolish.

The god is my protector: never will I give that up.

STROPHE 2

But if a man proceeds disdainfully

in deeds of hand or word

885   and has no fear of Justice

or reverence for shrines of the divinities

(may a bad fate catch him

for his luckless wantonness!),

if he'll not gain what he gains with justice

890   and deny himself what is unholy,

or if he clings, in foolishness, to the untouchable

(what man, finally, in such an action, will have

strength

enough to fend off passion's arrows from his soul?),

if, I say, this kind of

895   deed is held in honor—

why should I join the sacred dance?

ANTISTROPHE 2

No longer shall I visit and revere

Earth's navel, the untouchable,

nor visit Abae's temple,

900   or Olympia,

if the prophecies are not matched by events

for all the world to point to.

No, you who hold the power, if you are rightly

  called

Zeus the king of all, let this matter not escape you

905   and your ever-deathless rule,

for the prophecies to Laius fade ...

and men already disregard them;

nor is Apollo anywhere

glorified with honors.

910   Religion slips away. (Gould 1970)

For Ehrenberg "the song, and in particular the denunciation of the tyrant are relevant to Oedipus and [J]ocaste. ... Between the first and the last stanzas, the chorus describes the man who is born of hybris, such hybris as is displayed by ... the tyrant, mentioning his pride, greed, and irreverence. Not every feature fits the character of Oedipus; but to expect that would not only be pedantic, it would be mistaken" (1968: 79–80).

Why it would be mistaken to expect that every feature fit Oedipus is not clear, but Ehrenberg implies clearly that the Song describes Oedipus (and even Jocasta). Jebb, too, argues that this "prayer against arrogance" refers to "the King's [arrogance] towards Creon"; the impiety refers to Jocasta's "mistrust of oracles" (1966: xiv). Gould, however, writes almost the opposite: "[T]he depraved tyrannos described here [in the Great Song] has almost no resemblance to Oedipus at all" (1970: 109), and he is not alone in this interpretation (Dodds 1968: 19; O'Brien 1968).

The Song cannot be a criticism of Oedipus, for the chorus has nothing but praise for Oedipus throughout the play, even when they realize that he has committed incest and patricide. When they know the worst of Oedipus, the chorus sings: "For he [Oedipus], outranging everybody, shot his arrow and became the lord of wide prosperity and blessedness, oh Zeus, after destroying [the Sphinx] ... and against death, in my land, he arose a tower of defense" (Gould 1970: lines 1197–1201). Earlier in the play, just after the prophet Tiresias has accused Oedipus of killing Laius, the chorus sings that they will not accept the accusation (even though they had just spoken of this prophet as "one gifted with the truth as no one else"). They sing: "[U]ntil I see the word made good, never will I assent when men blame Oedipus. Before all eyes, the winged maiden [the Sphinx] came against him of old, and he was seen to be wise; he bore the test, in welcome service to our state; never, therefore, by the verdict of my heart shall he be adjudged guilty of crime" (Jebb, 1904: lines 504–11).

Later (in lines 964–65), the chorus refers to King Oedipus as the one "who, when my cherished land wandered crazed with suffering, brought her back on course" (Gould 1970). Indeed, just prior to the Great Song, when Oedipus is condemning himself for killing Laius, the chorus counsels Oedipus, saying: "[T]hese things seem fearful to us, Lord, and yet, until you hear it from the witness, keep hope!" (ibid.: lines 834–35).

In Greek tragedies it is the chorus, particularly, that emphasizes the characteristic religious element in the dramatic theme (Watling 1947: 11). Clearly, the Great Song is concerned with religion—the importance of worshipping the ancestral gods and accepting their laws. As they have done throughout the play, the chorus of Theban Elders lament for Thebes, grieving that men and kings no longer follow the moral, religious laws. They sense that the killing of Laius by Oedipus is but another terrible event in the series that has afflicted Thebes.

But the Song means more to the Greek-speaking audience, for it knows that Laius tried to evade his punishment by killing his young son. Almost from that moment, Thebes began to suffer, culminating in the plague of the Sphinx and the death of their king. Oedipus dramatically reversed this misfortune, and Thebes thrived—but only for fifteen years or so, when a new plague threatened Thebes, the plague initiating *Oedipus Rex*. But what the audience knows, and the Elders do not, is that Oedipus is the son of Laius and Jocasta. The audience knows that what troubles the Theban Elders is related to the treachery and selfishness of Laius. Hence, it appreciates what the Elders cannot.

To the audience, "the will to violate, seed of the tyrant ... mounts to a peak, then plunges to an abrupt ... destiny, where the useful foot is of no use" refers directly to Laius, for it is Laius who violated the moral law, first by abducting and seducing Chrysippus and, second, by ordering the death of his son, Oedipus, to avoid his own punishment. The segment referring to the foot is translated by Jebb as "wherein no service of the feet can serve." Gould notes: "[T]he mention of the foot ... makes the fall of the tyrannos here somehow right for Oedipus" (1970: 109), presumably because of Oedipus's name. This "somehow" appropriate reference to the foot or feet being of no use to the pride-swollen, depraved tyrant is, in fact, an instance of Sophoclean irony: it forcefully reminds the audience that Laius tried to save himself by having his son's feet skewered. Thus, as Sophoclean irony, like the name Oedipus itself, the Great Song reminds the audience, "because of its superior knowledge of the facts, of the real situation" (ibid.: 171).

Sophocles' use of the word *arthra* is yet another example of such irony, for it too reminds the audience of the connection between Laius's attempt to kill his son and Oedipus's ultimate tragedy. *Arthra*, meaning literally "ball-joint" or "socket" (seen today in the word "arthritis"), is used in the play for both the eyeballs of Oedipus (when he pierces them) and his ankles pierced by his father Laius (lines 718, 1032, 1270). *Arthra* does not mean eyeballs, and surely Laius would not have had a pin driven through Oedipus's actual ankle joints when the soft area between the joint and the Achilles tendon would serve as well, as many commentators have noted. The unparalleled use of this word by Sophocles, therefore, uniquely emphasizes a connection between Oedipus's self-inflicted blinding and his father's treachery. Gould senses this relationship when he notes that "the piercing of the eyes continues and completes the piercing of the ankles" (1970: 145, see also 123). Jebb, without citing support, merely asserts that the *arthra* pierced by Oedipus "can only mean the sockets of the eyeballs" (1966: 133).

To the audience, the last lines of the Great Song refer clearly to Laius. The audience knows already that the tragedy of both Oedipus and Thebes is a result of the fact that Laius did indeed have the "will to violate" both God's law and his own son. Indeed, the Great Song itself focuses on the consequences of Laius's wickedness. It is he who disdained justice and religion; it is he who did not deny himself what is unholy; and it is he who did not "fend off passion's arrows from his soul."

The play *Oedipus Rex* turns on the contrasting behavior of Laius and that of his son Oedipus, between a selfish parent and a son who is the epitome of selflessness. But whence comes the virtue of Oedipus? In one sentence Oedipus reveals the answer: "[My] father ... Polybus, to whom I owe my life" (Watling 1947; line 827). Oedipus's morality must be related directly to the influence he received from his foster parents. Their parental care was not only crucial to his survival; it was their love for Oedipus that led him to love them and others—his loyalty, bravery, and willingness to sacrifice himself. Human behavior is influenced profoundly by the behavior of others; indeed, traditions themselves presume this.

The behavior distinguishing Oedipus is kinship behavior—that sacrifice which occurs regularly between close kinsmen. It is filial love for his Corinthian parents that leads Oedipus to exile himself from Corinth, and it is a willingness to sacrifice himself for others that leads him to challenge the Sphinx. Indeed, Oedipus uses a kinship idiom to justify his search for the murderer of Laius, a search to save his Theban "children": "I mean to fight for him [Laius] now, as I would fight for my own father" (ibid.; line 265). It is his parental love for his two young daughters that makes him implore Creon, their uncle, to promise to cherish them forever. And it is his concern for kinsmen that leads him to plunge the needles into his eyes when he learns he has violated his parents.

As emphasized throughout this book, kinship relationships result not simply from the fact that relatives share genes, but that they sacrifice for one another. That birth alone is insufficient to establish kinship relationships is seen in the relationship between Oedipus and Laius. Because the parental behavior of foster parents toward an adopted child, like that of the king and queen of Corinth toward Oedipus, is not necessarily different than toward a true offspring, the resulting relationship may be identical. As it is the behavior that is crucial, and not necessarily the number of genes shared, social relationships identical to those between kinsmen can occur between nonkinsmen.

Thus, behavior normally directed toward close kinsmen can and does create social relationships between individuals, whether or not they are identifiable kin. And a person does not behave like a kinsman automatically—a child comes to behave in this way because he or she is influenced to do so by others, especially by those who raised him or her. Kinship behavior, crucial to human existence, is extremely modifiable by the behavior of others and must be seen as the product of both a particular human nature and the behavior of other individuals. The lack of either results in the failure of individuals to behave like kinsmen.

Returning to our myth, while neither Laius nor Jocasta, Oedipus's biological parents, behaved like parents toward him, his Corinthian parents did. The consequences of such behavior were Oedipus's love, loyalty, and willingness to sacrifice himself for them, and for anyone he identified as a kinsman—including his biological parents. Through parental behavior, and the responsiveness to it, social relationships referred to as kinship develop. It is such behavior that normally results in the most enduring, trustful, cooperative relationships in every society in the world. Indeed, the parental behavior on which social relationships are based appears the ideal for a good king. It is for this reason that kinship terms are so widely used to identify and encourage social relationships between nonkin, and why the first words in *Oedipus Rex* are "my children," as King Oedipus addresses his people. We submit that the aim of the Oedipus myth is neither that it expresses our alleged unconscious guilt nor a contradiction between normal and autochthonous birth. Nor is it aimed at convincing us that fate—itself usually a post hoc claim—is inevitable (see Cicero's *On Divination*). We choose to tell and listen to the Oedipus myth because of what we gain from it: in particular, an understanding of the contrasting consequences of parental selfishness and love.

Conclusion

The major assumption underlying the story of Oedipus is that it is behavior that creates social relationships—not human nature alone—and it is behavior that can destroy them. The story of Oedipus encourages kinship behavior in both fathers and kings. It is not without significance that Aristotle observes that in most good tragedies the "suffering" is a result of deeds done among *philoi* (kinsmen), "as when the murder, or whatever, is carried out or intended by brother against brother, son against father, mother against son, and son against mother" (*Poetics* 1453b: 19–22, cited in Gould 1970: 33). Interestingly, the Greek word for nonerotic love is *philo*, suggesting that it refers to the behavior found regularly among close kinsmen.

Traditional stories, by teaching vicariously the consequences of social behavior, transmit social knowledge. We propose that it is this effect that can account for the persistence of traditional stories, for such knowledge is the basis of kinship and, hence, social cooperation. When traditional stories include supernatural claims of such unverifiable things as supernatural cannibals, or oracles who can foresee the future, the traditional communicated acceptance and repetition of these "myths" greatly magnify this effect.

Note

1. Following Watling (1947: 23–24, 69–70) and Graves (1978: 9–15), here is a summary of the Oedipus myth:

Oedipus was the son of Laius and Jocasta, the king and queen of Thebes. Laius, the son of Labdacus, was a direct descendant of Cadmus, the founder of Thebes. King Laius, because of a crime he had committed against a prince of a neighboring kingdom (Gould 1970: 72; Jebb 1966: x–xii), was told by an oracle that if he had a son, that son would kill him and marry his wife, Jocasta. Laius and Jocasta did have a son. But then Laius, in an attempt to thwart the oracle, ordered a shepherd to kill their baby (some say that Laius himself did it—see Graves 1978: 9) by abandoning him on a mountainside after cruelly piercing his ankles with an iron pin to prevent him from crawling to safety.

This was done. But in a moment of compassion, the shepherd gave the injured child to a passing shepherd from Corinth to raise as his own. This Corinthian shepherd, a servant of the king and queen of Corinth, was asked by them for the child, for they were childless and wanted to raise him as their own. Oedipus grew to manhood, loved and honored as their true son. By chance, however, Oedipus heard a rumor that he had been adopted. Although his parents denied the rumor, Oedipus was not satisfied and traveled to Delphi to find the truth. But the oracle there did not answer his question, asserting instead that he would kill his father and marry his mother.

Like his biological father before him, Oedipus attempted to thwart the oracle. In order not to violate his beloved Corinthian parents, he resolved never to see them again. While traveling on foot on the road to Thebes, he had a sharp encounter with a small group of men, one of whom was in a chariot. After some angry words and actions (Oedipus resisting their demand that he give way, saying that he acknowledged no betters except the gods and his own parents), Oedipus slew several of them. Continuing along the road, Oedipus approached Thebes and found it to be in the grip of a deadly monster, the Sphinx. Risking his own life, he attempted to save the city by answering the Sphinx's riddle. He was successful, thereby destroying her power, and so was received joyfully into Thebes. Because their king had recently been killed while traveling, the grateful Thebans made Oedipus their king and gave him their queen, Jocasta, as his wife. During the next fifteen years Thebes prospered, and Jocasta bore Oedipus sons and daughters. But the pestilence and famine struck again, threatening Thebes with utter extinction. And the citizens cried out to their beloved king for help.

The play *Oedipus Rex* (*Oedipus Tyranus* in Greek) begins when Oedipus answers, inquiring, "My children, what ails thee?" During the course of the play, Oedipus, trying to discover the source of Theban affliction, gradually uncovers the hideous secret of his unwitting sins. The man he had killed in the chariot was his own father, Laius, and the wife whom he had married after rescuing Thebes, and who had borne him children, was his own mother, Jocasta. In his horror at this discovery, and at the self-inflicted death of Jocasta, he chooses not to kill himself and thus continue to plague his violated parents in the afterlife. Rather, he destroys the sight of his own eyes and asks Creon, his mother's brother (or brother-in-law), to banish him forever from Thebes. At the conclusion of *Oedipus Rex,* Oedipus implores Creon to protect and cherish his young, vulnerable daughters and begs, "Do not take them from me, ever!"

The Oedipus narrative is carried forward in the play *Antigone.* In this episode, Oedipus leaves Thebes forever. But then discord again rends his family, for while his daughters remain faithful to their father—Ismene remaining home, while Antigone, the younger, joins him in his wanderings—his two sons, Eteocles and Polynices, fight and kill each other in their struggle for power. Because Polynices had attacked Thebes, Creon orders that he not be buried. Antigone, in defiance, chooses to perform the burial ceremony for her brother and is sentenced to death by Creon. As a result, Creon's son, Haemon, who loves Antigone, kills himself. Finally, Haemon's mother, Creon's wife, commits suicide upon hearing of her son's death.

Chapter 7

Shamans

Shamans ... see all the gods, the first human beings, and come to understand the establishment of their social order.

—*Shultes and Hofmann (1992: 123)*

[The shaman] is doctor as well as priest, psychologist as well as magician, the repository of tradition, the source of sacred knowledge.

—*Von Furer-Haimendorf (1993: 81)*

"My white brother," said one Apache shaman, "you probably will not believe it, but I am all powerful. I will never die. If you shoot me ... it will not hurt me. ... If I wish to kill anyone, all I need to do is to thrust out my hand and touch him, and he dies. My power is like that of a god."

—*Eliade (1964: 299)*

As IMPORTANT AS TRADITIONAL MYTHS ARE, they are subject to certain limitations as a means by which ancestors can guide the behavior of their descendants. First, there is the possibility of losing cultural information through improper copying. Such "cultural drift" can occur because "transmission from elder to junior is in perpetual danger of being lost" (Barth 1987: 27; see also Diamond 1978). That is why Barth (1987) emphasizes the importance of having specialists, commonly referred to as shamans (see below), to remember certain elaborate myths and rituals. Balicki, too, states that "although the knowledge of myths was not limited to shamans, it is probable that they knew more traditions than the simpler folk" (1967: 205).

Second, myths and rituals deal with basic and fundamental values that lay down only *general* rules about what ought to be done in situations experienced or anticipated by long-dead ancestors. Myths do this by telling a specific story that illustrates basic values, but the details of the story will not be the same as the actual situations encountered by the descendants. The inheritors of these myths will, therefore, be constantly forced to make decisions about how to behave in *novel* situations, the details of which differ from the mythological stories and could not have been anticipated by ancestors. This means there will be a constant need for the general rules and values of myths and rituals to be *interpreted* in light of specific circumstances. If such interpretation was casually left to those involved in a conflict, self-interest and a possible lack of knowledge about tradition could lead to disagreement, social chaos, and the deterioration of traditional values.

Evidence for the importance of religious specialists to maintain and interpret ancestral traditions comes from traditional societies where traditional religious leaders—shamans in this case—appear to be functioning in a less than optimal manner. For example, Knauft (1985) suggests that the failure of Gebusi "spirit mediums" to maintain peaceful relations within Gebusi villages is contributing to depopulation and the systematic encroachment of the neighboring Bedamini. This might be an example of the kind of evolutionary process that selected for effective shamanic traditions.

We suggest that the importance of religious specialists in maintaining and interpreting the traditions that encourage cooperation is why ancestors throughout the world supported traditions of designating and training certain individuals to be both the guardians and interpreters of the religious traditions that make social life possible.

There are three main kinds of religious leaders: priests, shamans, and prophets. Priests occupy an established position in a cult or church. Shamans also hold a recognized position, but unlike priests are said to exhibit supernatural powers. Prophets, like shamans, are also said to be supernatural, but they do not occupy established positions: a prophet creates a new religious cult and recruits priests who, by conveying the prophet's message, continue it. This chapter focuses on shamans; prophets will be discussed in Chapter Twelve. Although the degree to which the "position" of shaman is formally recognized varies cross-culturally, shamans in the sense of traditional religious leaders were almost certainly universal in all traditional societies. Not only were shamans probably the first religious leaders, until the last few thousand years they may have been the only religious leaders.

The Behavior of Shamans

What needs to be explained about shamans is their behavior, and the influence of their behavior on others. Unfortunately, most approaches to shamanism have attempted to explain the supernatural things they are *claimed* to do, or at least explain the *belief* that shamans do the supernatural things they are claimed to do (Eliade 1964: 499, 5; see also Haviland 1978: 656; Kottak 1974: 45; Lowie 1952: 173; Nadel 1946: 25).

Fortunately, Eliade pointed out four identifiable things that a young person wishing to become a shaman is required to learn from a master shaman:

1. The traditional shamanic techniques.
2. The names and functions of the spirits.
3. The mythology and genealogy of the clan.
4. The secret language. (Eliade 1964: 13)

Eliade notes that the "secret language" may, like that of the Yakut shamans, have a vocabulary three times larger than that of the only language known to the rest of the community (ibid.: 30). We can understand why Eliade writes the following: "A shaman's practice is very, very fatiguing" (ibid.: 28).

Little more is stated, however, about the education and importance of the shaman to the community. Instead, Eliade focuses on the shaman's alleged mystical activities. Point 3 (above) of the neophyte shaman's requirements— learning the "clan genealogy"—is hardly mentioned again, and nowhere does Eliade attempt to account for it. Eliade sometimes uses the term "clan" to refer to the community (ibid.: 17–18, 147), which indicates that it is the community's genealogy that must be learned. What can be derived from this information is that a shaman's job not only has to do with a community but also includes knowledge of how the individuals within the community are related to one another. We shall return to this point later.

Rasmussen gives us a detailed description of the performance of an Inuit shaman, instead of simply the supernatural events claimed to take place (1972: 388–91). During the ceremony, the shaman is said to travel down under the sea to visit Sedna, the sea spirit (the Inuits' alleged *ancestress,* according to Franz Boas in *The Central Eskimo* 1964: 175, first published 1888), to persuade her to stop sending misfortune to the people. The performance of the shaman occurs either at the request of an individual beset by sickness in his or her family or bad luck in hunting, or on behalf of the whole village when scarcity of game threatens famine. All the adult members of the community attend the ritual, which takes place in a darkened house. The shaman produces sound effects to illustrate his alleged journey, such as the noises of sea animals or the sighs of the spirits of the dead. Using ventriloquism, he often produces a conversation between himself and Sedna, who tells him that the bad luck in hunting is caused by someone's breach of a taboo. An example of this would be "the secret miscarriages of the women and breaches of taboo in eating boiled meat bar the way for the animals" (Rasmussen 1972: 390). The shaman then placates Sedna until she finally agrees to have mercy on the people. He then requests the congregation to confess any breaches of taboo they have committed, and everyone does so: "[M]uch comes to light that no one had ever dreamed of; everyone learns his neighbors' secrets" (ibid.). The shaman remains unsatisfied until "all sins have been confessed," and finally identifies the individual whose misbehavior "caused" the problem (for example, it may be a young woman who confesses to having had a secret miscarriage). With this discovery, the ritual ends, and "all are filled with joy at having escaped disaster" (ibid.: 391).

Explaining Shamanism

Explanations of shamanism have been directed by the assumption that shamans, and particularly their followers, *believe* the supernatural claims concerning shamans. Further, the role of shamans as the custodians and interpreters of religious traditions has been largely overlooked because of the attention focused on the more exotic and seemingly bizarre behavior (for example, trances, sleight-of-hand trickery, ventriloquism, and the ingestion of hallucinogenic drugs) that is often part of a shamanistic performance (Douglas 1978; Furst 1972; Harner 1973; Maddox 1923). As a result of this focus, researchers have argued for more than a century over whether the peculiar behavior of a shaman—visions, trances, and so on—is a result of mental illness (Eliade 1964: 24). Kroeber, for example, suggested that primitive societies reward their psychotics with the socially acceptable role of shaman (1952, from Torrey 1972: 41). To the contrary, shamans are not only intelligent and responsible; they also display the qualities of a leader. Torrey observes that shamans "appear to be among the least disturbed members of the society" (1972: 42; see also Turner 1964). Although a shaman's intense performance is distinguished by appearing frenzied or out of control, the very predictability of his or her performance demonstrates remarkable skills and knowledge acquired methodically during years as an apprentice. This fact, combined with the demonstrated importance to the community of the shaman as a religious leader, contradicts the proposition that he or she is a psychotic.

Eliade, in his supernatural idiom, notes that, in contrast to a person who truly appears to be possessed, "the shaman controls his spirits, in the sense that he, a human being, is able to communicate with the dead, 'demons,' and 'nature spirits,' without thereby becoming their instrument" (Eliade 1964: 6). Further: "[The shaman] can control his epilepsy. ... [T]he shamans, for all their apparent likeness to epileptics and hysterics, show proof of a more than normal nervous constitution; they achieve a degree of concentration beyond the capacity of the profane; they sustain exhausting efforts; they control their ecstatic movements, and so on" (ibid.: 29). Eliade cites Nadel's perceptive comment: "No shaman is, in everyday life, an 'abnormal' individual, a neurotic, or a paranoiac; if he were, he would be classed as a lunatic, not respected as a priest" (ibid.: 31).

To understand a shaman's behavior we must look well beyond his or her own particular psychological makeup, and focus on his or her traditional, identifiable behavior. We must examine the shaman's impact on the individuals in his or her community—those who support him or her, and toward whom his or her unusual performance is directed.

What is clear immediately is that a shaman has a difficult, demanding, and important job, valued highly by the members of the community. It cannot be explained as a mere psychopathological phenomenon. Nor can it be accounted for by the shaman's alleged ecstatic experience. People in shamanistic societies know that what shamans actually do is significant, for, as Eliade has shown, when the shaman does not perform properly, he or she will not be accepted by the community. The initiation requirements demonstrate this: if they do not learn the proper techniques, myths, language, genealogical knowledge, and so on, they will be rejected, no matter how frenzied or out of control is their "supernatural" behavior.

Behavior said to be supernatural, but which is identifiably only out of the ordinary, usually falls into one of two categories:

1. *"Magical" tricks.* The entire subject of magic will be discussed in detail in the next chapter, but in short, what is done is the production of an illusion: ventriloquism, climbing up an unconnected rope, sawing someone in half, extracting an object from someone's body. People actually see the extraordinary outcome, but not the behavior leading up to it. The techniques required for these spectacular results are carefully learned and guarded. These spectacles are seen as extraordinary only to a naive observer. Thus, one who performs such tricks may be seen as extraordinary and described as supernatural, although from the performer's perspective, such tricks are simply business as usual.

2. *Trance.* This is described by many terms—possession, ecstasy, convulsion, semiconsciousness, a hypnotic state—but seems to be distinguished by an apparent loss of control over one's own body, achieved perhaps by intensive concentration, self-hypnosis, or the ingestion of hallucinogenic drugs (Douglas 1978; Furst 1972; Harner 1973; Maddox 1923). It may include falling, swooning, convulsing, or babbling incoherently.

Several authors have asserted that the ingestion of hallucinogenic drugs is the very basis of shamanism. For example, Harner states not only that the use of hallucinogenic drugs "strongly reinforces a belief" in the alleged supernatural experiences of shamans but also that such experiences "may have also played a role in the innovation of such beliefs" (1973: xiv). La Barre (1972) argues that the drug-induced hallucinations of shamans are the origin of all religious beliefs (see also Shultes and Hofmann 1992).

Such arguments neglect the fact that shamans continue to behave in traditional ways even when intoxicated. As Crapanzano and Garrison note: "[E]ven the aspiring Yąnomamö shaman, functioning under drug-induced trances, must be able to exercise control over himself, and present stereotyped 'proper' possessed behavior, otherwise he will not be permitted to continue his shamanistic apprenticeship" (1977: 77).

Magical tricks and trances do not exhaust "supernatural" behavior. Having a particular kind of dream, or being "spared" in a natural catastrophe such as a flood, fire, or storm, unusual behavior of mystics, perhaps even the modified speech of preachers, and speaking in tongues may all be asserted to be supernaturally caused. Most of the remaining behavior claimed to indicate supernatural power cannot be experienced as having occurred: journeys to the sky or underworld, visits and consultations with dead ancestors, fighting with evil spirits, finding lost souls, being supernaturally saved, and so forth. But whether a claim of supernatural behavior is based on real events, however unusual or extraordinary, or whether it is based on events only alleged, the existence of supernatural influences cannot be demonstrated. Such an assertion, therefore, depends not on actual evidence, but on people's willingness to communicate acceptance. To communicate acceptance of the assertion that an individual has supernatural power is to accept his or her influence. The crucial question in regard to such claims is why people would be willing to accept a shaman's influence.

It is a fact, not always appreciated, that people regularly seek the influence of others. We are arguing that to understand religious behavior depends on recognition of this fact. Parents generally want not only to influence their children but also to be influenced by them—told when they are in distress, hungry, uncertain, and so on. Indeed, the effectiveness of much of their influence on their children depends on the parents' responsiveness to their children's communications—crying, smiling, speaking, and so on. And if children were not responsive to those around them, particularly parents, they would not acquire a human language, or, indeed, any traditional behavior. Because of the importance of such behavior to them, children have been selected to have a nature that seeks such influence.

Similarly, because others accept their guidance, leaders are those whose task is to influence followers. A preacher's job is to influence the behavior of his or her congregation; when a congregation seeks a preacher, they are seeking a particular kind of influence. The same is true when people seek an education, even though that education may be used, in turn, to influence others. In modern societies, people regularly seek the influence of doctors, psychiatrists, marriage counselors, and leaders in such organizations as the Boy Scouts and Alcoholics Anonymous.

To be influential, an individual usually must demonstrate a concern for the interests of those he or she is trying to influence; he or she must be responsive to them. The behavior distinguishing a successful leader, like that of a parent, is not only guidance but also responsiveness.

How can we account for the acceptance of a shaman's influence? It is clear that a shaman is no mere religious mystic; he or she is a vital and influential member of his or her community. Shamans treat people who are sick, and they encourage them to accept suffering—taboos, sacrifice, and pain (see Chapter Ten). But the shaman's magical "curing" cannot be shown to influence disease physically, he or she cannot demonstrably divine (see Chapter Nine) the future, and he or she cannot, in fact, verify the alleged supernatural consequences of broken taboos (see Chapter Ten).

The shaman, above all, diagnoses social problems, problems involving the interaction between the members of the community, who basically are kin to one another. The requirement to learn the "clan" genealogy implies this. We suggest that the social significance of the shaman's performance and the reason why it is encouraged by the ancestors and supported by the community lies in its encouragement of close kinship behavior between more distant kinsmen— Eliade's "clan." It is just this behavior, and not his or her supernatural journeys, that makes the shaman the center of the "magico-religious life of society" (Eliade 1964: 4).

The other requirements of the shaman's apprenticeship—the traditional shamanic techniques, the knowledge of the spirits, the secret language and so on—can be seen as contributing to his or her communication about so-cial relationships. Magical tricks, along with the other parts of shamanistic performance—elaborate costumes, drums, music, special language, and so on—communicate not only the shaman's alleged power of influence on the world but also his or her concern for his or her audience, and responsiveness to their interests.

Much attention also has been given to the use of sleight-of-hand trick-ery by shamans during their performance or séance. Such discussion often focuses on the question of whether shamans are sincere believers in their powers, or charlatans exploiting their followers (Boas 1930; Frazer 1951; Levi-Strauss 1963b). As has been stressed throughout this book, the question of whether shamans or the other members of society actually believe in the shaman's claims is as difficult to verify as whether the shaman's soul actually performs the tasks attributed to it during trances. What can be identified is that ethnographic data do not support Frazer's view that shamans arise because they "perceive how easy it is to dupe their weaker brother and to play on his superstition for their own advantage" (1951: 350). Shamans almost invariably are reported to be self-sacrificing and concerned for the well-being of their followers. Becoming a shaman nearly always involves sacrifice, often in the form of rigorous training and/or sexual and dietary taboos, while the actual performance of shamanistic duties often entails arduous work (see Brown 1993; Chagnon 1983; Eliade 1964; Grim 1983; Maddox 1923; Turner 1972). Perhaps most important, shamanic activities are almost always done for the good of other individuals. As Howells states: "[S]hamans are among the most intelligent and earnest people of the community, and their position is one of leadership" (1993: 88).

Although the various debates over shamanism have left some questions unanswered, they have demonstrated certain general findings. First, shamans are intelligent and socially adept individuals. Second, they are usually in control of their social behavior and behave in traditionally prescribed ways even during trances and drug-induced states. Third, far from being exploitative charlatans who take advantage of other people for their own gain, they are leaders who gain their position through self-sacrifice for others—a shaman's distinctive behavior is social behavior. A final characteristic of shamans that is often reported, but usually treated as being of only secondary importance, is *the claim that shamans visit and communicate with dead ancestors*. A focus on religious traditions as descendant-leaving strategies suggests that this effect is actually the key to explaining shamanism.

Shamans as Interpreters of Traditions

Talk about communicating with dead ancestors is so common in descriptions of shamanism that it is possible to speak of the "*classical* shamanistic voyage to nether regions for purposes of communication with the dead or the ancestors, to bring back divinatory messages, or to seek the cause of illness or misfortune" (De Rios 1984: 111, emphasis added). In addition to fascination with the more striking activities of trance, trickery, and drug use, the key reason for the lack of attention this aspect of shamanism has received is the previously described failure to appreciate fully the role of ancestors in traditional religion throughout the world. For example, even though Eliade reports that "the role of the *souls of the dead* in choosing the future shaman is important [in Siberia and] in places outside Siberia as well" (1964: 82), he rejects the claim that "shamanic election was connected to the ancestor cult" on the questionable assertion that the ancestors had to be chosen by a divine being (ibid.: 67). Although acknowledging the frequent role of dead ancestors in many examples of shamanism throughout the world, Lewis also refers to a category of nonancestral shamanism in which there are "more autonomous deities which are not simply sacralized versions of the living" (1971: 34). This also appears to be a questionable distinction because the shamans in this supposedly *non*ancestral category are said to communicate with "clan spirits" (ibid.: 149–77). For example, Lewis includes the Tungus in the *non*ancestral category despite stating that a Tungus shaman "controls the clan's own ancestral spirits" (ibid.: 51, 157).

Perhaps the clearest example of an intimate relationship between shamanism and dead ancestors in a society in which dead ancestors are not usually considered to play any role in religion is the Yąnomamö. As previously mentioned, Yąnomamö religion centers on shamans ingesting hallucinogenic drugs and controlling *hekura* "spirits," and "when the original people (the *no badabö*) died, they turned into spirits: *hekura*" (Chagnon 1983: 92). The close relationship between shamans and these spirits of the original people (the dead ancestors) called *hekura* is clearly demonstrated by the fact that Yąnomamö shamans themselves are called *hekura* (ibid.: 107). Although it remains to be demonstrated that shamanic activity always involves claims of communication with dead ancestors, the frequency with which this occurs suggests that it may be crucial to the role of shamans (Steadman and Palmer 1997).

We now examine how shamans use their alleged ability to communicate with dead ancestors to influence the living. Despite various cultural and geographic differences, shamanism has certain nearly universal characteristics. First, "shamanistic rites are 'non-calendrical,' or contingent upon occasions of mishap and illness" (Turner 1993: 73). This means that shamans are most frequently involved in curing physical illnesses, supernaturally attacking other villages, settling disputes, and divining the cause of deaths or other misfortunes (see Eliade 1964). Grim points out that, regardless of its specific manifest function, "shamanic activity is generally a public function. The tribal community witnesses the dramatic encounter with the spirits and benefits from the ritual communications" (1983: 11). Hence, the shaman's performance has effects on living members of the community that should be identifiable. Reports from various parts of the world indicate that the clearest and most common of these effects is the encouragement of social behavior and the maintenance or repair of social relationships, especially between kin. Bichmann states that for shamans, "illness does not mean so much an individual event but a disturbance of social relations" (1979: 177; see also Brown 1993; Chagnon 1983; Edgerton 1993; Eliade 1964; Grim 1983; Howells 1993; Lewis 1971; Middleton 1960; Rasmussen 1972; Siskind 1973; Turner 1972).

The shaman's ability to reduce social tensions and uphold tribal morality depends on the ability to master and integrate two sources of knowledge: the general values of the particular religious tradition and the nature of the social relationships that form the context of the specific event he or she is dealing with. First and foremost, shamans are guided "by an intuition into what is just and fitting in terms of ... [the local] moral values" (Turner 1979: 374). This intuition comes from "a period of instruction, during which the neophyte is duly initiated by an old shaman ... to learn the religious and mythological traditions of the tribe" (Eliade 1964: 110–11). These moral values are, however, quite general, such as the Ndembu "concept of the 'good man' ... who bears no grudges, who is without jealousy, envy, pride, anger, covetousness, lust, greed, etc., and who honours his kinship obligations ... [and] respects and remembers his ancestors" (Turner 1979: 374), or the Lugbara's statement that to sin is to offend kin (Middleton 1960: 22). Although this knowledge enables the shaman to perform ceremonies whereby "he exhorts the people of his neighborhood to shun such evils as incest, adultery, sorcery, and homicide, and emphasizes the value of harmony in social relations" (Lewis 1971: 137), it is insufficient for dealing with specific social problems.

Knowledge of moral values can direct a shaman to certain basic questions in the attempt to divine the cause of some misfortune. For example, Edgerton reports that in any case of illness, a Hehe shaman "asks five preliminary questions: Did the patient commit adultery? Did he steal? Did he borrow money and refuse to repay it? Did he quarrel with someone? Did he actually have a fight with someone?" (Edgerton 1993: 161). Although such questions can serve as a starting point, they are not sufficient for determining a successful solution to the particular situation. That is because, unlike the grand visions of prophets, the divination of shamans are "mechanical and of a case-to-case kind" (Nadel 1954: 64). In other words, "the diviner clearly knows that he is investigating within a social context of a particular type" (Turner 1979: 374). This need to know the structure of the social relationships of the members of the community can account for why the traditional training of shamans often includes the memorization of not only the mythology of the tribe but also the genealogy of its members (Eliade 1964: 13).

Turner states that the interaction between the general religious values and the specific social context is "represented in the symbolism of divination ... mnemonics, reminders of certain general rubrics of [the local] culture, within which the diviner can classify the specific instance of behaviour that he is considering" (1979: 375). The key point is that the symbols are general, while the situation is specific: "Here the vagueness and flexibility of the series of referents of each symbol leave him [the shaman] free to make a detailed interpretation of the configuration of symbols corresponding to the diagnosis he is making of the state of [social] relationships" (ibid.).

This observation is relevant to the discussion concerning whether shamans control the spirits they encounter or are controlled by those spirits (see Bourguignon 1976; Evans-Pritchard 1937; Firth 1964; Howells 1993; Turner 1993; Von Furer-Haimendorf 1993). We support Crapanzano and Garrison's (1977) conclusion that this is too rigid a distinction. On the one hand, the shaman, unlike the prophet, "is not a radical or a reformer" (Turner 1993: 73). The shaman's behavior and divinatory decisions are clearly guided by religious tradition; indeed, credibility as a leader depends on adherence to these values. On the other hand, the generalness of traditional values and the symbols that represent them give the shaman freedom and power of interpretation, which metaphorically entail some limited control over the will of the ancestors. This situation is clearly seen in Siskind's description of the limited freedom of Sharanahua shamans: "[D]ream and vision symbolism among the Sharanahua does not involve a one-to-one relationship of meaning and symbol, but neither is there complete free rein for idiosyncratic dreaming or hallucinating" (1973: 37). Instead of being a hindrance to the smooth inheritance of traditions, this limited freedom of shamans is better seen as an ancestral strategy that allows traditional values to be properly applied to novel and unique events (see Rogers 1983). At least, that is what the traditional selection, training, and performance requirements of shamans are aimed at.

If the social effect of shamanism is actually its function, why do shamans so often engage in acts of trance, drug use, and trickery? We suggest that the key to answering this question is the realization that all of these aspects of shamanism are closely related to the supernatural claim that shamans visit the land of the dead and converse with dead ancestors. Hence, the first question to be asked is, Why are shamans claimed to have supernatural power instead of simply being seen as nonreligious sociopolitical leaders? The answer lies in the uniquely powerful influence of supernatural claims on the behavior of others. To be a successful shaman one must be "an expert at intense direct communication" (Siskind 1973: 36). Rappaport points out that "communication is effective only if the recipients of messages are willing to accept, as being in at least some minimum degree reliable, the messages which they receive" (1979: 261). He adds that people must often accept statements when "there may be no known operations of verification" (ibid.). Therefore, he proposes that the traditional encouragement of accepting unverifiable supernatural claims establishes the "sanctity" of the shamans' statements (ibid.: 262). This sanctity, defined as "the quality of unquestionable truthfulness" (ibid.), obviously increases the ability of shamans to influence their followers through their claims, such as the typical shamanic statement that "the ancestors are alive and well in the other world" (ibid.).

Such behavior as trance, ecstasy, and so on, also communicates the willingness to give up control over his or her own body for the benefit of the audience. We suggest that such a "gift," when it is accepted as sincere, is seen as selfless. Indeed, the authenticity of the trance is often described in terms of whether the shaman is "honest" or "dishonest" (Spiro 1967: 209; see also Davies 1963: 67). Sincerity, of course, is determined not by the shaman's intentions (which are unobservable) but by what he or she exhibits. A charlatan shaman might be defined as one pretending to be out of control, but one who in fact is perceived by the audience as very much in control, with such control *serving his or her own interests.* The effect of "out-of-control" behavior seems to demonstrate the discarding of self-interest.

The next question: Why do the supernatural claims of shamans so often involve traveling to the land of the dead, communicating with dead ancestors, and returning with instructions? In addition to establishing the "sanctity" of the shaman's pronouncements, this particular supernatural claim further increases the shaman's ability to influence followers. The claim directs attention to the shaman's *traditional* nature, knowledge, and role in society. To reject a shaman's influence, therefore, is not just to reject one individual but to reject *tradition*; to reject what is crucial to kinship relations and social life in general. This greatly increases the "unquestionable truthfulness" of the shaman's instructions because, as was previously mentioned, "although one can argue to a point with an elder, no one questions the wisdom and authority of an ancestor" (Lehmann and Myers 1993: 285; see also Fortes 1976: 2).

The use of drugs, trancelike states, and trickery can all be seen as behavior supporting and elaborating the supernatural claims made by and about shamans. In regard to trancelike states, Lewis claims that "religious leaders turn to ecstasy when they seek to strengthen and legitimize their authority" (1971: 34). There are several possible reasons why entering such states should increase the influence of the shaman. First, such states appear to be distinguished by an apparent loss of control over the body. Because this loss of control occurs as part of an attempt to help others in the community, it is one of the ways the shaman communicates a willingness to sacrifice for his or her followers. Claims that the shaman (or the shaman's soul) is involved in dangerous activities during the trancelike state also communicate the willingness to sacrifice. It is an appropriate symbol that reinforces the verbal claim.

Although debates over whether shamanic tricks cause supporters to believe in the claimed supernatural powers of shamans are fruitless, sleight-of-hand tricks and ventriloquism are other appropriate symbols that also elaborate the shaman's supernatural claims. They make the performance more interesting and dramatic. This may lead to an increased arousal level among the participants, which has been shown to increase the effectiveness of communication (see Nuttin 1975). Further, the shaman speaks for the dead ancestors. That is a supernatural event. Acceptance of all of the other supernatural claims, concerning sleight-of-hand tricks and other dramatic acts, implies acceptance of the fundamental claim that the shaman is speaking for dead ancestors.

The role of hallucinogenic drugs is less clear. In addition to the hallucinations themselves, other relevant psychological effects may include increased suggestibility and a focusing of concentration on relevant stimuli (Harner 1973; Slotkin 1955). There are, however, social effects of drug use that may account for its widespread use in shamanic activities. Drug use often increases the communication of sacrifice inherent in the trancelike state by increasing the shaman's loss of control over his or her body. This may help to communicate that the shaman can be trusted because the loss of bodily control makes the shaman appear incapable of manipulating followers for his or her personal gain. To the extent that the drug is considered dangerous, simply ingesting it also communicates a willingness to sacrifice. Brown reports an Aguaruna shaman in Peru who "took pains to emphasize the intensity of his intoxication ... [because] willingness to endure the rigors of a large dose of *ayahuasca* is a sign of his good faith as a healer" (Brown 1993: 94; see also Chagnon 1983).

Drug use, however, is not universal among shamans (Harner 1973) and may play primarily a symbolic role when present. For example, Chagnon states that Yanomamö "shamans have to take hallucinogenic snuff—*ebene*—to contact the spirits, but adept shamans with great experience need very little" (1983: 108). Hence, drug-induced hallucinations may best be seen as another appropriate symbol to reinforce and communicate claims of visiting the land of the dead. Indeed, this symbolism is often very explicit, as when there is a close association between dead ancestors and the hallucinogen itself. For example, not only do some West African shamans use the hallucinogenic plant *Tabernanthe iboga* "to make contact with the spirits of their ancestors, and thus preserve a direct relationship with their own cultural origins" (Shultes and Hofmann 1992: 115), the plant itself "is frequently anthropomorphized as a supernatural being, a 'generic ancestor'" (ibid.: 112; see also Fernandez 1972).

Shamanism: An Example

As a concrete example, a curing ceremony described by Turner makes clear both the duties of a shaman and the impact of his or her behavior. Turner's description demonstrates the influence of a shaman—here called "doctor" or ritual specialist—on the social relationships of individuals living in an Ndembu community in the Democratic Republic of Congo. The shaman, speaking for dead ancestors—here called "shades"—uses a curing ceremony to improve a complex web of strained social relationships. He thereby produces behavior that is both cooperative and in accordance with the basic traditional values of Ndembu culture.

According to Turner, although the Ndembu say that every disease is caused by supernatural forces, a curing ceremony is performed only when there is some disturbance in the patient's network of social relationships (Turner 1964: 231). Although the doctor's purpose in performing the curing ritual is ostensibly to rid the patient of physical symptoms, doctors "are well aware of the benefits of their procedures for group relationships, and they go to endless trouble to make sure that they have brought into the open the main sources of latent hostility in group life" (1964: 237).

"Doctors" are trained by means of initiation into various special cults (see ibid.: 232–33) and are said to have mystical powers. The doctor in our example was not only well known but, like most Ndembu curers, was "capable, charismatic, [and] authoritative" (ibid.: 241). He was called in at the request of a number of relatives and neighbors of the patient. The doctor diagnosed the supernatural cause of the illness, but during the process of divination he questioned the relatives until he had "a complete picture of the contemporaneous structure of the village, and of the position in its relational network occupied by the victim" (ibid.: 243). The doctor examined the "social relationships in order to diagnose the incidence and pattern of tensions and to attempt to reduce them in his handling of the rites" (ibid.: 242).

The patient in this case was Kamahasanyi, who in addition to his various aches and pains—including fatigue, heart palpitations, and failure in hunting—was having serious difficulties with certain individuals in the village. In his village there was considerable conflict between two opposed factions. The old headman had died a few years before, but his brother, who should have inherited his position according to tradition, left the village. Kachimba, the uncle of the patient, was acting headman. Opposed to Kachimba's leadership were Makayi and his family, who felt that the old headman's brother should have taken over the position—resenting both his departure and Kachimba for taking over. Relations were so bad between Makayi and Kachimba that they refused even to sit down together at the same gathering. The patient, Kamahasanyi, was related through his father to one faction and through his mother to the other and, thus, was not clearly allied to either one; he heard grumblings and complaints from both sides.

Kamahasanyi had further problems with his personal relationships. He had not lived in the village all of his life and personally was not a very likable fellow. In addition, he was married to his cousin Maria, the daughter of Kachimba, the present acting headman. Maria was strong-minded and independent and was carrying on a rather open adulterous affair with Jackson, the son of Makayi.

The curing ceremony was attended by all of the villagers discussed. Through communication with ancestral spirits during the divination, the problem had been diagnosed to be due to an "incisor tooth" of a dead "hunter" that was inserted by the hunter's "shade" (ancestral spirit) because there had been a transgression of moral rules or customs (see ibid.: 234–35). The ritual revolved around the shaman's attempt to extract the alleged tooth from the patient's body. Cuts were made in the skin, and horns were attached that were then sucked and examined to see if the tooth had been extracted. As this was going on, all of the participants were involved in singing, drumming, and praying in the attempt to facilitate the removal of the tooth.

The doctor assigned particular relatives of the patient special roles in the ceremony. The patient's cousin and errant wife, Maria, was asked to collect some special leaves, which she then chewed, spitting the juice on her husband's body while tapping him with a rattle. Wilson, the son of the late village headman, was asked to place a piece of white clay on the fork of a tree as a token of his friendly intentions. The dead headman's brother was asked to invoke the shade (ancestral spirit) who was afflicting the patient. In assigning these tasks, the doctor encouraged everyone to cooperate and work together "to please the shade and thus to cure the patient" (ibid.: 260).

When the tooth was not found in any of the horns, the doctor explained the cause to the congregation in a statement that followed a traditional form "which usually entails a fairly detailed account of the patient's life story and of the group's interrelations" (ibid.: 258). He then encouraged everyone to confess any ill feelings they had against the patient, as the shade would not be placated unless all such disturbances were eliminated. A number of people admitted to having borne bad feelings against Kamahasanyi or to having neglected him, and he confessed his resentment toward those he felt showed little concern for him (ibid.: 260). Finally, in a dramatic moment the doctor succeeded in discovering and extracting the tooth from one of the bloody horns. Turner describes the effects of the ritual: "[T]he women ... all trilled with joy. Men and women who had been on cool terms with one another until recently, shook hands warmly and beamed with happiness. Kachimba even smiled at Makayi, who smiled back. Several hours later a mood of quiet satisfaction seemed to emanate from the villagers" (ibid.: 261). When Turner returned over a year later, the patient "was enjoying life, was accepted by his fellow villagers, and was liked by his wife" (ibid.).

It is precisely this effect on the kinship relationships of the participants that can account for the behavior and the ancestral encouragement of shamans. The essential job of the shaman is to encourage cooperation among the codescendants of the ancestors who supported the shamanic tradition. Both the community's acceptance of the supernatural claims of the shaman and his or her acceptance of the ancestors' traditions promote this cooperation.

Conclusion

The claim that shamans obtain advice from dead ancestors on how to deal with current social problems is, in a sense, true. The identifiable communication between dead ancestors and shamans, however, takes place in ways other than visitations to the land of the dead during shamanic performances. Instead, it takes place over many generations in the repetition of certain traditional behaviors. First are the traditions about the criteria for selecting potential shamans, which often include the demonstration of a willingness not only to lead but also to sacrifice for others. Then, there is traditional training that includes the memorization of the traditional secret languages, rituals, and myths. The shaman is also required to attain an intimate knowledge of the social relationships of his or her followers, which often entails the memorization of genealogies. Perhaps most important, the shaman must meet traditional standards in the performance of the role. Although that often entails mastering various traditional tricks that make the performances more dramatic and effective, the shaman's most important task is to be able to apply general traditional values to specific events in a way that both solves the current problem and preserves the values. It is in this sense that shamans really are "mediums who act as the vehicles of . . . ancestors and express their wishes" (Lewis 1971: 140).

Eliade claims that during their trancelike performances shamans "can abolish time and reestablish the primordial condition of which the myths tell" (1964: 171). Indeed, the voyages to the land of the dead that shamans are said to make during their trancelike performances are most accurately conceptualized as trips, not through supernatural space but through time to when their dead ancestors were alive. Regardless of the truth of this voyage, the words of dead ancestors do identifiably travel through time from the ancestors to living shamans via the medium of tradition. By influencing shamans in this way, dead ancestors are able to influence their descendants for generations. The extent of this influence is considerable because "significant tribal activities . . . are often undertaken only with the guidance and support of spirits communicating through the shaman" (Grim 1983: 11). Therefore, the shamanic tradition can be seen as not only a major part of religion but also a major aspect of the strategy of humans to leave descendants.

Chapter 8

Magic

MAGIC IS DISTINGUISHED by the claim, and its communicated acceptance, that certain *techniques* have supernatural effects, effects that cannot be demonstrated. Hence, such behavior is religious. Magic can be performed by anyone, but, as mentioned in Chapter Seven, magic is often performed by shamans. That is because magic tends to be traditional, and shamans are often the guardians of religious traditions. Hence, it is often shamans who claim that certain techniques have supernatural effects, and other people who communicate their willingness to accept the shaman's influence by communicating their acceptance. Although some writers have excluded magic from religion because it does not refer necessarily to entities such as "spirits" (for example, Durkheim 1961; Evans-Pritchard 1940; Tylor 1958), magic does include religious behavior. Consequently, it is usually included in anthropological discussions of religion.

Previous Definitions and Explanations of Magic

As we might expect, previous definitions of magic almost always include belief. Thus, "a set of beliefs and techniques designed to control the supernatural or natural environments" (Hunter and Whitten's 1976 *Encyclopedia of Anthropology*); or "the art which claims or is believed to produce effects by the assistance of supernatural beings or by a mastery of secret forces in nature" (*Webster's Dictionary*); or a technique that uses objects in which mystical power is believed to reside (Evans-Pritchard 1937: 9). Nadel, recognizing the failure of magic to work as alleged, nevertheless speaks of belief when he writes: "By the word 'magic,' we always mean some procedure or manipulation believed to bring about effects which, by its physical properties, it is incapable of bringing about. In a word, magic attempts the physically impossible" (1977: 1). Had Nadel used the term "claimed" instead of "believed," his definition would be useful in the study of magic and also consistent with the one proposed here.

Those who are most knowledgeable about the failure of magic to work as alleged should be just those who have the most experience with it—the practitioners and their audience. Nadel notes perspicaciously that "inevitably, the believers in magic must be confronted, again and again, with evidence proving the failure of their magic efforts. How, then, does the belief in magic survive?" (ibid.). Indeed, the fundamental question in regard to magic is: Regardless of beliefs, why do people persistently make such claims and practice such techniques?

Although magic cannot be shown to have the effects alleged, both the talk and the technique can be shown to influence humans, but only when they become aware of the performance. In other words, the particular influence of magic that can account for its persistence occurs through its communicative effects.

But the claim that magic actually, physically works implies a denial that it is communicative. This denial is similar to the paradox we encountered with totemism in Chapter Five. The claim that magic actually works—like the claim that certain humans are actually kangaroos—is not literally (demonstrably) true. But such talk must mean something; it must make a difference, for why else do people make such claims and practice such techniques? Magic, like totemism, is responded to, identifiably, as metaphor. To be understandable to the participants, the claims of magic, like those of totemism, must be transformed into similes by the audience. For example, the simile of sorcery that is communicated by the metaphor is that the magical performance is *like* killing or injuring a person. This metaphor is made more powerful by the claim that it *actually* does kill or injure, but it remains still only a metaphor. Like all metaphors, however, it depends on, and thereby promotes, collusion, a form of cooperation. When magic is traditional (as it usually is) the acceptance of the claim that magic truly works implies collusion with ancestors, and hence with living codescendants. Thus, magic has the effect of promoting cooperation.

The most significant effect of magic demonstrably lies in its communication to receivers. The different kinds of magic (white, black, love, curing, sailing, gardening, and so on) transmit different similes and thereby encourage different kinds of cooperation. It is the effect achieved through communication, promoting the descendant-leaving success of those using and supporting magic, that can account for its ubiquity and antiquity.

Magical techniques are often divided into two categories on the basis of the effects they are said to achieve: white magic if the goal is protective or constructive, and black magic or sorcery if the goal is destructive. Thus we find, on the one hand, magical practices said to cure or prevent disease, attract a lover, ensure success in hunting, fishing, gardening, trading, and warfare, prevent accidents, and provide protection from sorcery. On the other hand, black magic or sorcery is said to cause the opposite: disease or death, bad weather, accidents, and failure in economic, political, or romantic pursuits.

The alleged influence of magic is sometimes said to be analogous to natural forces such as gravity, magnetism, and electricity. In order to use such forces, one simply follows the proper procedure for setting them into action. Just as the chemist expects to get a certain reaction by mixing particular chemicals together in a specific proportion and under specific conditions, the magician, too, claims that his or her techniques work automatically. However, there is a crucial difference between magic and gravity, magnetism, electricity, and chemical reaction—the latter are demonstrated by regular correlations between identifiable events. Such correlations, by definition, cannot be identified for magic. That is why magic is distinguished from science. For example, the *Encyclopedia of Anthropology* (1976) distinguishes magic by its "empirically untested belief(s)." In short, magical practices cannot be shown to have the influence they are said to have.

Some theorists attempt to circumvent this fundamental problem by arguing that belief in the efficacy of magic exists because sometimes, simply by chance, magical practices appear to work: the patient "cured" by countersorcery sometimes gets better; a successful hunt sometimes occurs after the performance of hunting magic; a safe journey sometimes follows the purchase of a St. Christopher's medal. Kluckhohn (1972: 102) argues that because Navajo individuals sometimes recover from a case of snow blindness after being "sung over" by a native curer, Navajos continue to use this method to treat not only snow blindness but also other illnesses. However, the reason such practices are identified as magical is precisely because they are no more associated with their stated goal than any other random event. Thus, it could be just as well argued that because Navajos sometimes recover from snow blindness when they are *not* treated by a curer, they should continue to avoid magical treatments. Random association is not sufficient to lead to the conclusion that something works. If magic cannot be shown to work—if its alleged correlations are not discernible—then this fact is true not only for the analyst but also for the people who use it.

Today there are two widely accepted explanations of magic: one identified most often with Frazer and the other with Malinowski, the latter apparently following James and Marrett (Evans-Pritchard 1965: 39–40, 48).

Frazer's *The Golden Bough* (1951) probably has been the most widely read and influential book ever written on the subject of primitive religion and magic. In this classic work, Frazer argues that magical practices are based on the Laws of Similarity and Contact, which are believed in by those who use them, but which are, in fact, false. Frazer (1951: 12, 15) argued that "primitive man's" belief in magic is based on a false understanding of cause and effect, and hence he attempts to influence various things—people, objects, weather, and so on—by following a "Principle of Sympathy." This principle consists of two "laws": the Law of Similarity in which "the magician infers that he can produce any effect he desires merely by imitating it"; and the Law of Contact, whereby the magician "infers that whatever he does to a material object will affect equally the person with whom the object was once in contact" (ibid.: 12). Because primitive peoples (in which category Frazer includes "cunning and malignant savages in Australia, Africa, and Scotland" [ibid.: 14]) are incapable of true scientific thought, their mistaken notions of cause and effect lead them to believe in Frazer's two "laws." A consequence of this belief is the practice of magic: "In short, magic is a spurious system of natural law as well as a fallacious guide of conduct; it is a false science as well as an abortive art" (ibid.: 13). Although such an argument may strike the reader as bizarre, it has been accepted widely by anthropologists (for example, Haviland 1983: 368; Haviland, Walrath, and McBride 2005: 354–56; Kottak 1974: 187). The reason for this state of affairs is that to date there is no other explanation offered to account for the virtually universal use of techniques that appear, superficially, consistent with Frazer's Principle of Sympathy.

Frazer uses the term "imitative" to refer to magic based on the "Law of Similarity." An example selected from Frazer's own abundant and charming cases illustrates this law:

> Perhaps the most familiar application of the principle that like produces like is the attempt which has been made by many peoples in many ages to injure or destroy an enemy by injuring or destroying an image of him, in the belief that, just as the image suffers, so does the man, and that when it perishes he must die....
>
> When an Ojebway Indian desires to work evil on anyone, he makes a little wooden image of his enemy and runs a needle into its head or heart, or he shoots an arrow into it, believing that wherever the needle pierces or the arrow strikes the image, his foe will the same instant be seized with a sharp pain in the corresponding part of his body; but if he intends to kill the person outright, he burns or buries the puppet, uttering certain magic words as he does so. (Frazer 1951: 14–15)

Frazer's other category of magic, which he calls contagious magic, is based on the "Law of Contact": things that have once been in contact remain mystically joined even when separated, so that what is done to one will affect the other. Of this law, he writes:

A curious application of the doctrine of contagious magic is the relation commonly believed to exist between a wounded man and the agent of the wound, so that whatever is subsequently done by or to the agent must correspondingly affect the patient either for good or evil.... In Melanesia, if a man's friends get possession of the arrow which wounded him, they keep it in a damp place or in cool leaves, for then the inflammation will be trifling and will soon subside....

Strained and unnatural as this idea may seem to us, it is perhaps less so than the belief that magic sympathy is maintained between a person and his clothes, so that whatever is done to the clothes will be felt by the man himself. (Ibid.: 47–50)

These examples (and countless others) appear indeed to exhibit Frazer's false Laws of Similarity and Contact. It is precisely for this reason that Kottak, like many authors of anthropological textbooks, writes that Frazer's two laws are "still accepted as valid today" (1974: 187).

A more penetrating, skeptical look at Frazer's argument, however, reveals striking contradictions. If the sorcerer were indeed convinced that action taken against one object would affect equally all objects that resemble it, he or she should be exceedingly careful to ensure that the doll bears no resemblance to himself or herself, his or her friends, or relatives. Yet, in the literature we find no suggestion that sorcerers take measures to ensure that their dolls uniquely represent their victim and no one else. Similarly, the sorcerer attempting to harm a man by burning his clothes ought to be careful not to touch the clothes himself, for he or she would be harmed through contact with them. But again, such a precaution is not taken. The man who places glass in the footprint of an intended victim in order to lame him or her is equally unconcerned about who else may have trod on that spot, as should be the case if he or she were convinced that harming that spot would harm anyone who had ever touched it.

But Frazer's argument is defective fundamentally. If his Law of Contact were accepted as true, it would have to be assumed that everything would be affected by every action, for everything on earth is, or has been, in contact with the earth: every magical ritual would not only affect everything on earth but also affect everything equally. If people were indeed convinced of the validity of Frazer's Laws, why would not a Nootka wizard simply eat the image of a fish rather than place it in the water to attract real fish? If he assumed that similar things were actually the same, eating an image of a fish should satisfy him as much as the real thing and save him the trouble of having to catch it. Obviously, people do not follow the mistaken notions of Frazer's so-called Laws of Similarity and Contact. Why would anyone bother to risk his or her own life in killing an enemy if he or she believed it could be accomplished simply by destroying the enemy's clothing or burning a wax doll? If one took these laws seriously, one should never do anything risky or difficult; magic should be used to accomplish everything.

It is not surprising to find that people do not use magic in these ways; indeed, they would not survive long if they did. To humans everywhere, stabbing a carving of a lion is not the same as stabbing a real lion, just as eating a picture of a pig is not the same as eating a pig, nor is imitating good health the same as having it. Further, the practices described by Frazer are usually highly traditional; they have been passed down from ancestor to descendant for thousands of years. They have not only been practiced for a long time, they have become extremely widespread, as Frazer's examples illustrate. So, what we have are particular magic rituals that have persisted over long periods of time, despite the fact that they cannot be shown to work as alleged. This suggests that the accuracy of magical claims is not itself what is significant, despite magicians' and ancestors' assertions to the contrary.

The major criticism of Frazer's work has come from Malinowski. In contrast to Frazer, Malinowski actually performed fieldwork and found that natives do indeed depend upon accurate knowledge (Malinowski 1931: 634), that the "savage" is no more superstitious than modern man (ibid.: 636), and that primitive knowledge, like knowledge everywhere, is "essentially scientific [in] character" (ibid.: 634). "Primitive man is capable of exact observation, of sound generalizations and of logical reasoning" (ibid.). Further, "the only association or connection [constituting knowledge] is the empirical, correctly observed and correctly framed concatenation of events" (ibid.: 636).

However, while Malinowski's depiction of the rational native certainly undermines Frazer's argument of "false laws," *Malinowski fails to account for Frazer's data*. Malinowski explains the apparent use of the "Sympathetic Principle" by no more than a specious claim that "the magician is haunted by imagery, by symbolism, by associations of the result to follow" (ibid.: 638). This claim that the ritual is the result of the magician's illusions, a kind of mental aberration or mystical apparition, cannot be tested by empirical data and hence is itself mystical. Further, such a claim goes directly against his own argument regarding the importance of accurate knowledge to the "savage."

Malinowski's own explanation argues that magic is used in situations where there is a gap in practical or scientific knowledge: no matter how much skill and hard work a person puts into his or her garden, the crop may still fail as a result of such uncontrolled influences as the weather. Malinowski points out that in the Trobriand Islands, every village has a garden magician whose job, along with supervising the labor, is to perform special rites at each stage of the garden's progress (Malinowski 1961: 59–60). Thus, he argues, magic is to be found wherever there is uncertainty or danger beyond the human ability to influence events.

The Trobriand Islanders build large sailing canoes that are sometimes used on long sea voyages. Sailing along the coast is easy and safe, and thus magic is not used, but distant voyages on the open sea can be both dangerous and uncertain. Before an open-sea expedition sets out, therefore, magical rites are performed to make the canoe swift, safe, and seaworthy: the magician utters a spell, urging the canoe to be speedy, a member of the crew rubs the canoe with medicated leaves, and prepared streamers are tied to the rigging and mast, as utterances are made imploring the canoe to be light and swift (see Malinowski 1954).

Malinowski argues that magic originated in such situations because of the tension and frustration individuals feel when faced with their inability to control the outcome of important events. The natural urge to "do something" results in a spontaneous burst of activity, which naturally imitates the results desired, leading to a release of tension and giving the individual a feeling of calm and confidence. Malinowski writes that such initial activities eventually became standardized and accepted because of the influence of the initiators, and were perpetuated because they gave people hope, confidence, and certainty in the face of uncertain situations.

Evans-Pritchard challenges this psychological explanation of magic: "[W]hat evidence is there that when a man performs agricultural, hunting, and fishing magic he feels frustrated, or that if he is in a state of tension the performance of the rites releases his distress? It seems to me there is little or none. ... [The rites] are a customary and obligatory part of the proceedings" (Evans-Pritchard 1965: 45).

Further, Evans-Pritchard writes, "Who ever met a savage who believed that by a thought of his he could change the world? He knows very well that he cannot" (ibid.: 47).

Malinowski assumes that magic gives confidence because the people *believe* it actually works. He argues that the original initiator of a magical practice somehow became convinced of its efficacy because, by the performance, he or she released his anxieties and tensions. And because he or she felt better, he or she gained confidence in the effectiveness of the ritual.

But magic cannot be shown to physically influence the garden, the weather, or the victim, and Malinowski nowhere suggests that it does. Indeed, when he emphasizes the importance of the accuracy of native knowledge, he threatens his own argument in regard to magic. Why should the native, who is concerned with the actual effect of his or her endeavors, resort to practices that have no discernible effect on the world? Let us keep in mind that the actual problem is a dangerous overseas voyage, or a ruined crop of yams, or a hostile individual, and not simply the anxiety stemming from such difficulties. Although anxiety can be reduced in a number of ways, it does not necessarily help the individual to cope with the problem that caused it. Does the alcoholic become convinced that alcohol is an effective means to success simply because he or she feels better when drinking? And whether he or she feels more confident or not, he or she is still more likely to have an accident when driving at high speed. Indeed, the proposition that performing an ineffectual activity in a tense situation makes one feel less tense is itself open to question; much more so is the assertion that this would convince the individual of the effectiveness of that activity.

Although Malinowski argues that magic rituals are aimed at decreasing anxiety, some rituals obviously increase it, and even appear aimed at increasing it, as Radcliffe-Brown has noted (1979). Talk of hell and eternal damnation should not make people feel better, nor should talk of ghosts, the devil, evil, and so on. That alone should disprove Malinowski's thesis. In addition, if all magic practices were indeed aimed at achieving the same simple effect—reduction of anxiety—then what can account for their great variety? One simple all-purpose ritual should be sufficient. Furthermore, anxiety, like pain, is not necessarily bad. Presumably humans have evolved to be anxious and wary in dangerous situations because that helped their ancestors survive such situations and leave descendants. What is fundamentally important is not feeling better or worse, but being able to cope, not only with physical problems but also with other humans. To account for how practices such as magic became widespread, we should seek to identify what the participants themselves can identify and respond to, what can influence them to repeat, modify, or abandon such activities. On the basis of Malinowski's own explanation of magic, it should not matter what the natives actually do, so long as they do something. As he observes, "[F]ear moves every human being to aimless but compulsory acts" (Malinowski 1931: 639). But the crucial question is this: If just any activity would be sufficient to reduce fear or anxiety, then why do magic practices so closely fit Frazer's Laws of Contact and Similarity? Any explanation of magic must satisfy that question. Neither Frazer's nor Malinowski's does.

Evolutionary Explanations of Magic

Recent evolutionary and cognitive explanations of magic have made the same basic assumption found in the earlier explanations just discussed: the practice of magic results from the *belief* that magical practices work as claimed. Although their explanations of this alleged belief differ from earlier explanations in the sense of being generated from evolutionary theory, they contain many of the same flaws found in the earlier theories. Some evolutionary psychologists have questioned "the apparent strangeness of these beliefs" (Bloch 2002: 129; see also Atran 2002; Boyer 2001; Sperber 1996) because of the previously discussed fact that sometimes, by chance, the magical practices have the predicted effects. Burkert (1996) also refers back to long-standing arguments by proposing an evolutionary reason for why the practitioners of magic believe in Frazer's Law of Contact. In some magical practices the sacrifice (cutting off) of a body part is claimed to have some beneficial effect. Burkert's explanation of why people believe this claim begins with the observation that "'part for whole' sacrifice can be plainly rational in its calculation of loss and gain" (ibid.: 40) and that "partial mutilation has its analogues in the world of animals" (for example, "spiders' legs break off easily ... to distract the attention of simple-minded predators, lizards tails ... easily break off in the grip of the pursuer while the lizard itself escapes, ... a fox caught with a paw in a trap will bite off its paw to escape)" (ibid.). Of course, the real question is why humans engage in similar magical sacrifices when there is no evidence that sacrifice of the part benefits the whole. Burkert's answer is that the pattern of actual benefit from sacrificing a part "explodes beyond what is functional and rational" as it "loses contact with reality and turns into ritual ... which may be called magical" (ibid.). Unable to explain further why the pattern "explodes" and the practitioners become irrational and believe in something for which there is no evidence, he simply asserts that they do: "At any rate, the nonobvious connection of cause and effect is widely acceptable, and it makes sense to those who practice it" (ibid.).

Boyer also claims that "evolutionary reasoning may well explain certain forms of magical beliefs" (Boyer 2001: 133). He phrases his hypothesis in terms of psychological mechanisms that evolved because they helped us to better predict reality when used in certain "domains," but became applied to other domains where they failed to fit reality accurately. For example, humans accurately recognize that sometimes unseen contaminants spread disease via bodily contact. Therefore, according to Boyer, "Apparently strange beliefs about touching the hand of a blacksmith [causing one to become polluted] are only an application of these principles outside their adaptive domain, that of contaminants and toxins" (ibid.: 134). But if that were the case, humans would be led to "believe" that contamination follows any and all contact with anything. Just as Frazer's explanation cannot elucidate why people believe in the Law of Contact only in certain situations, Boyer's explanation cannot explain why people get fooled by their evolved psychological mechanisms only in particular situations. Once again, the assumption that people believe what they claim about magical practices leads evolutionists simply to rephrase the idea that people believe in magic because of some flaw or malfunction in their thinking, and then propose a possible evolutionary explanation for that malfunction.

Magic as Communication

The key to explaining magic without assuming beliefs is to remember that it is certain talk, not certain beliefs, that distinguish magic from other activities. The custom in the United States of hanging a football coach in effigy for having had a poor season can be identical to a magical performance, *except for people communicating acceptance of the claim that it injures or kills the victim.* Such a performance obviously can influence individuals: the coach, the students, and perhaps the university president. The same holds for political dissidents burning the picture of a despised leader. These effects are identifiable not only to the outside observer but also to the participants and audience, and may influence their decision to repeat that behavior in the future. Such customs are a form of communication. Since it is certain claims that distinguish magic from such customs, and such claims are obviously also communicative, we suggest that magic needs to be explained as a form of communication. More specifically, magic is a form of communication that combines the message sent in nonreligious symbolic acts, such as burning the effigy, with the communication of a willingness to accept a speaker's influence nonskeptically.

With this in mind, let us examine Australian sorcery, as described by Elkin (1964). Many forms of sorcery are practiced in Australia, including the damaging of a straw image of the victim and the stabbing of his or her footprint in order to cause sickness or death. But the "most powerful, most feared, and most widespread" magic is "pointing" combined with "singing," or "singing" alone (ibid.: 286). In pointing, a specially prepared bone is used. Ideally, this was obtained from a dead man, but a kangaroo bone, or even a sharpened stick, may be used. The sorcerer, in plain view of the victim, assumes the proper posture, chants the song, and points the bone in the direction of his victim (ibid.: 287). The bone is said to enter the victim's body and cause serious illness or death.

Sorcery is not performed casually, but requires careful and elaborate preparations. Special rituals and chants must be learned in detail, and special objects must be obtained and prepared. Much care is taken to perform the ritual. Indeed, because individuals are sometimes punished or killed for causing another person's death through sorcery (even, in some cases, where there is no actual evidence that they practiced sorcery), it is never done casually (ibid.: 293).

What is the evidence that Australian Aboriginal peoples are convinced of the efficacy of these magical techniques? Their practices are generally traditional:

acquired from their ancestors. It is said that they are learned and performed for the purpose of killing or doing injury, and they are claimed to work. Although deaths are often attributed to sorcery (especially when there is prior illness), Australian Aboriginals frequently use other methods for killing and injuring. Actual spear fights are common. When a revenging party is sent out after an accused sorcerer, he is killed with a spear, not by magic. If the victim of pointing does not die in two or three days, he or she too may be speared to death by the sorcerers. If these people were convinced that death could be caused at a distance, by magic, why would they take the risk of fighting their enemies face to face with real weapons? Why not always use sorcery?

If one were to argue that the aim of sorcery is merely to express the sorcerer's feelings, that the purpose or function of sorcery is to influence the sorcerer himself, the facts of Australian sorcery would contradict that proposition. In many cases, people seek to prevent sorcery from being practiced, and sorcerers are sometimes punished or even killed. Why should others be concerned with suppressing something whose only aim would be expression, whose only significant effect would be on the sorcerer himself?

Further, if the sorcerer's goal were simply self-expression, why would he not perform his activity in true privacy, where he could not be detected by the victim or anyone else and possibly criticized for his actions? In bone pointing, he faces his victim and actually points or throws the bone at him or her; he does not simply hide in the bush and perform the act in secret. The accompanying chants are sung out loud; they are not simply thought or secretly mumbled. Either method may serve to express; only the former communicates.

These facts are consistent with the proposition that the aim of sorcery is communicative. The sorcerer's actions are indeed visible and can be observed by his audience, who therefore can be made aware of the sorcerer's displayed intentions. The sorcerer does more than express his desire that the victim die; he exhibits behavior *said* by the ancestors to kill a person. The elaborate preparations, which include time spent in learning the proper techniques and songs, emphasize the seriousness of the communication and strengthen the message. His willingness to suffer during the performance further increases the impact of his message. From this point of view, the particular objects used in the ritual are simply appropriate symbols. The fact that they are prepared carefully increases the seriousness of the communication.

If the aim of sorcery is indeed to send a message, we should not be surprised that many individuals are interested in controlling and sometimes preventing the use of sorcery. At the very least, sorcery is a hostile act; it communicates a hostile message. It can stir up angry feelings and quarrels and fights between the sorcerer and the victim and their supporters. Sorcery can also intimidate.

Elkin mentions that in one Australian tribe "the old men are seizing upon it as a method of restoring their authority" (ibid.: 290).

But if we are to understand fully why sorcery is performed, we must also identify the actual consequences of the message. To do this we must distinguish the audience, including the victim(s), and how it is influenced. Individuals sometimes perform "singing" sorcery against members who have committed incest. It is clear that the message communicated to the wrongdoer, as well as to anyone else who becomes aware of it, is severe disapproval of incestuous behavior and the willingness to take action against it. The support shown by the number of influential individuals participating in this act of sorcery should discourage individuals from committing incest in the future. Such sorcery is a serious declaration of the intent to harm or punish, more powerful than criticism or gossip, but significantly less so than actually killing the wrongdoer.

It has been pointed out that individuals sometimes die as a result of being sorcerized, and Cannon (1942) has documented the physiological responses to the fear and anxiety caused by sorcery that can lead to death. The operation of the sympathetic nervous system in situations of stress, if continued over a period of time, can lead to a drop in blood pressure and oxygen deprivation of the organs. These symptoms are the same as those described as "shock" (which results from physical stress and is frequently the result of injury). Cannon argues that only a strong belief in the effectiveness of sorcery can explain these deaths: the belief causes the victim to feel afraid and, certain of his or her death, to make no attempt to recover from the resulting effects. He suggests also that the victim even contributes to his or her own demise by refusing food and water. How else can this be explained except by assuming a powerful belief in the effectiveness of sorcery?

In his 1942 article, Cannon, using Warner's (1937) material, focuses on the case of Australian bone pointing. It must be emphasized again that in this case, as in any case of sorcery, for the victim to be influenced he or she must become aware that he or she has been sorcerized. Every act of sorcery certainly does not result in death, and the conditions under which death occurs, at least in the instance of bone pointing, support the hypothesis that it is the message communicated that is crucial. Cannon reports that in some cases the close kin and friends of the victim gather around him or her and have countermagic performed. If that happens, he or she is *always* said to survive. When death occurs it is under different circumstances. In such cases, the family and friends of the victim choose to withdraw their support and treat him or her as if he or she were already dead.

So, the victim's kin have a choice. When they choose not to perform countermagic, it is clear that they have chosen to support the sorcerer (and his message of ill will) rather than the victim. If that is the case, the friends and family will return to the still living victim and perform mourning ceremonies, as if he or she had already expired, thus communicating their acceptance of the death. According to Cannon, this is the final blow and the victim soon dies.

It is not surprising that the victim should find such a message devastating. Those on whom he or she depends for aid and protection, for livelihood, even for life, have displayed rejection. An Australian Aborigine in this situation did not have the modern alternative of moving to a new town, finding a job, and making new friends. It is not surprising that the recognition of his or her total alienation, the loss of all social relationships, should produce fear and anxiety that might indeed lead to death.

That the practice of sorcery elsewhere is often said to occur in secret would seem to counter our hypothesis that its aim is to communicate. But the fact that it is actually performed at all means that it is potentially detectable. It almost always involves special objects, "medicines" and charms used by the sorcerer that are left in a place where they can be discovered by the victim or his or her relatives, even if their preparation and placement have been done anonymously. In addition, the victim may actually hear, or hear of, the incantation. Thus, the Azande man who finds a "bundle" of medicine in the thatch of his hut knows that someone has sorcerized him. This "secret" but discoverable activity obviously has a different impact than one done publicly. For one thing, the sorcerer, like the anonymous phone caller, may want his or her victim to know that an anonymous someone wants him or her dead. The effects of such anonymity, by making it impossible to know, and perhaps confront, the sender, could well increase the impact of the message.

Although in the example of bone pointing, just discussed, the result may be the victim's death, we do not want to suggest that the aim of sorcery in general is to destroy the victim. On the contrary, sorcery is a substitute for direct violence. We suggest that its basic aim is to influence the victim's behavior, and perhaps the behavior of those close to him or her, in regard to the sorcerer and those supporting him. The message of sorcery must influence the victim. The sorcerer, by communicating that the victim has done something serious enough to warrant death or injury, may influence him or her either to leave the community (if possible) or to discontinue the objectionable behavior. What is distinctive of a victim of sorcery is that he or she has behaved in a way that has deeply offended the sorcerer or the sorcerer's supporters (see Hogbin 1964: 55–58). By communicating acceptance of the supernatural claims of sorcery, the sorcerer's supporters have communicated their willingness to accept the sorcerer's disapproval of the "victim's" behavior, and hence, their willingness to cooperate in future acts of punishment against the victim. Sorcery is a powerful but nonviolent means of letting the victim know it.

Sorcery, like magic generally, is extremely traditional. Not only is the formula and knowledge of the paraphernalia learned from ancestors, but also when, by whom, and for what reason it should be performed. All of this reduces the likelihood that it will be performed casually. Furthermore, to the extent that the practice is derived from ancestors, they are part of, and give considerable force to, the message.

In small communities, where everyone is more or less related, the use of violence threatens these relationships. Where individuals share the same traditions and ancestors, sorcery can be seen as one kind of ancestral influence on descendants to cooperate with one another. Although it appears to be anticooperative, if not actually destructive, it must have enhanced the descendant-leaving success of ancestors.

Communication occurs also through curing magic, which may take the form of elaborate rituals, such as the well-known Navajo curing ceremony described by Kluckhohn and Leighton (1962). This ceremony is said to operate through the influence of supernatural beings, but its effects are said to be automatic. Failure is said to result only from a mistake in the performance, not from the will of the ancestors.

The Navajo curing ceremony requires hiring a specially trained professional "singer," and the ceremony, or "chant," may take several different forms involving a number of activities lasting two, three, or five nights. All those who participate in the curing ceremony must observe special restrictions on their behavior, including sexual abstinence. Ceremonies may include a sweat-bath or bath in yucca suds, making prayer-sticks, and singing throughout the night. A common feature is the making of a dry-painting. Such paintings are made by sprinkling powdered charcoal, minerals, or vegetable matter in various colors on a piece of buckskin; there are many traditional designs, ranging in size from miniatures to some over twenty feet long. They may require the work of two people for an hour or up to fifteen people for most of a day. If the chant lasts for several days, one painting may be made each day. When the dry-painting is finished, the patient sits on it and the singer treats him or her. The singer gives the patient herbs to drink and prays for his or her recovery while touching various parts of his or her body. The painting is then destroyed (ibid.: 217, 221).

An obvious feature of this ceremony is that it can be very costly. The professional singer and his assistants—trained specialists—must be paid, and all who attend must be fed. The length and elaboration of the ceremony is not determined by set rules, but by how much the patient's family is willing to pay. Kluckhohn and Leighton point out that "during the chant the patient feels himself personally ... being succored and loved, for his relatives are spending their substance to get him cured, and they are rallying around to aid in the ceremonial" (ibid.: 231).

We suggest that this is precisely the message that is the aim of the ceremony: to demonstrate that the patient is loved and cared for by those supporting the ceremony. The impact of the message is not only on the patient, but on all those who attend, some from long distances. Such behavior implants a memory that is likely to encourage social behavior among the participants, for they have all sacrificed for the patient, who is usually their kinsman.

Indeed, Kluckhohn also reports that the Navajo say the ceremony will not only cure physical illness but will "also 'change' [the patient] so that he will be a better man in his relations with his family and neighbors" (1972: 104). A Navajo who had just been released from jail for beating his wife and stepdaughter told Kluckhohn that "I am sure going to behave from now on. I am going to be changed just like somebody who has been sung over" (ibid.). Clearly, being "sung over" is not simply seen as curing the patient of a physical malady, but as improving the patient's behavior toward others. Kluckhohn indicates that the Navajo themselves recognize these consequences. In a myth of the origin of the ceremony, it is stated that "[t]he ceremony cured Dsiliyi Neyani of all his strange feelings and notions. The lodge of his people no longer smelled unpleasant to him" (ibid.).

It is this effect that can account for the persistence of this ceremony—why individuals choose to repeat it generation after generation—regardless of their belief and whatever the physical results. The particular explanation given by the participants (and accepted literally so often by anthropologists) appears to be no more than part of the ceremonies themselves—traditional metaphorical claims that justify and thereby encourage their practice. Kluckhohn's own explanation of the ritual has been discussed near the beginning of this chapter.

Other forms of magic can also be understood as communicative. For example, in sailing magic, the participants communicate their willingness to cooperate with one another, a quality essential in open sea sailing. This explains why the greatest amount of magic is found in fishing activities requiring the greatest cooperation among crew members (Palmer 1989). Love magic communicates to a person that she (or he) is sexually desired, and so on. It seems likely that all magic rituals can be shown to be communication aimed at influencing an audience.

After the Hewa men had killed the elderly woman as a "cannibal" they fled back toward their own hamlet cluster. However, they stopped at a predetermined spot to perform a ritual at a stream and engage in an activity claimed to have the unverifiable effect of making them invulnerable to their potential pursuers. They engaged in a magic ritual, which involved drinking water that washed over one of their arrows bloodied by their victim. We suggest that this symbolic act communicated that they all shared in the bloody deed and would support one another in case of retaliation. By communicating acceptance of the traditional supernatural claims about the technique, they were communicating their willingness to accept one another's influence, and of their common ancestors, in their cooperative defense.

Conclusion

Magic refers to techniques distinguished by a "supernatural" claim of their efficacy. Magic, like prayer, does not depend on its alleged physical results; indeed, the truth of such alleged effects is irrelevant. Magic can only influence individuals when they are aware of its performance and its message: of lust, anger, concern for a person's health, his or her garden, a military or sailing venture, and so on. Because the messages are not only symbolic but also usually traditional, they tend to be sent between individuals sharing the same traditions, individuals sharing the same ancestors. Thereby the various kinds of magic, as forms of communication, encourage cooperation among individual codescendants. The significant effect of magic is not that it expresses fear, anxiety, or any other emotion, but that it communicates: it influences an audience by the use of symbols appropriate to the message. Magic so often appears to follow Frazer's laws of similarity and contact because similarity and contact are obvious ways of symbolically specifying both the receiver and content of the communication. It is this communicative effect of magic that can account for its variety and for its regular encouragement by ancestors. Disproof of this hypothesis would consist in showing either that magic does not influence an audience in the way specified, or that such influence is not its most significant effect.

Chapter 9

Divination

It is my judgment that divination has no reality whatever.
—*Cicero, Member of the Board of Augurs,* De Divinatione, 44 B.C.

DIVINATION IS DISTINGUISHED, and identified, by the supernatural claim that certain techniques reveal the future. As a supernatural claim referring to a technique, it is similar to magic, but it differs from magic by its distinctive assertion that its techniques are supernaturally influenced by the future (while the techniques of magic are said to supernaturally influence the future).

Divination is treated like knowledge and used to make decisions. The crucial difference between the two is that knowledge, unlike divination, is based on identified correlations. Instead of assuming that people engage in divination because they believe that it works as claimed, and then speculating that evolved psychological mechanisms may have led to the *belief* in divination (see Boyer 2001; Burkert 1996), we suggest divination can be best explained by identifying its actual effects. This approach was illustrated in our analysis of Turner's description of the divination used by a shaman in Chapter Seven. The more general hypothesis about divination proposed in this chapter is that the acceptance of the claim of divination requires, and thereby promotes, collusion. This collusion explains the persistence of divination through time, for it reduces acrimony that can result from decision-making.

During the First Punic War, Admiral Clodius gave feed to some chickens that had been brought on deck in order to divine when to attack the Carthaginians. Not happy with the result of this "alectoromancy" because the chickens wouldn't eat, he roared, "If they won't eat, let them drink." He had the chickens thrown over the side and then ordered the attack. But the chickens were right, for he lost the battle. Cicero writes: "This joke, when the fleet was defeated, brought many a tear to him, and mighty carnage to the Roman people" (cited in Howells 1962: 71).

The techniques used in divination are not accurate predictors of the future. Astrology, for example, is classified as a form of divination because it uses the positions of the stars and planets to answer questions about future events and individual character traits; yet the position of heavenly bodies has never been shown to influence such things. In other words, there is no consistent, observable correlation between the position of stars and planets, and the character and fortunes of individuals. If such a correlation were shown, astrology, or any other form of divination, would then be classified as an empirical technique for answering certain questions, like the use of meteorological observations to determine whether it will rain tomorrow, or the prediction of the winner of a football game based on past performance. Divining techniques are used without such a connection ever having been demonstrated—either by an outside observer or by the people who use them.

Sometimes a person divines for him or herself, at other times he or she may use a specialist. The techniques used by diviners have often been divided into two categories, labeled "mechanical" and "dramatic." The first category, mechanical, involves the interpretation of an uncontrolled, sometimes random, event such as the pattern of chains, nuts, sticks, shells, or other objects thrown on the ground; the appearance of the bones or intestines of various animals, the patterns of tea leaves in a glass—the list is long. The interpretation, which provides the answer about the future, always appears to be influenced by the technique.

The second category of techniques, the dramatic, involves a performance by the diviner who, usually through behavior said to be supernatural, communicates that he or she knows the future. This category includes divination by means of spirit mediums and is sometimes used by shamans or witch doctors. The diviner may go into a trance, use "magical tricks" to demonstrate the presence of the supernatural, reveal information about his or her clients, or imitate spirit voices by ventriloquism. All these activities contribute to the appearance that some influence beyond the natural powers of the diviner is operating, whether it is attributed to a spiritual being or to the diviner's supernatural powers. Music, rhythmic drumming or singing, and special settings are commonly used, all heightening the impact of the diviner's performance.

Sometimes a combination of the two techniques is used, and for some forms of divination, such as dream interpretation or the use of a divining rod, categorization into one or the other is difficult. What all the techniques have in common is that the answers arrived at are claimed to result from the technique.

In spite of the fact that divination cannot be shown to be accurate, its answers are used to make decisions. Although this point may seem obvious, and has been pointed out by others (Gibson 1961: 29–30; Park 1967: 234; Vogt and Hyman 1959: 194), it deserves attention. The questions put to divination frequently ask about the likelihood of success or failure of some important plan of action such as a journey, marriage, change in occupation, a political venture, or the timing of an attack. The answer provided by the ritual sometimes is used directly in determining the course of action taken. But in other cases, the connection to decision-making is not as straightforward; often there is simply a request for information, such as when palm reading is used to make judgments about character traits, or when African witch-finders identify witches (see Chapter Eleven) and sorcerers. However, the key value of such information is that it can be used to decide some future action.

In this respect, divination is similar to certain other techniques used in making decisions, such as tossing a coin, drawing cards, or guessing a number. These techniques, too, cannot be shown to be correlated with future events and therefore do not reveal the best course of action. But divination, unlike these techniques, is accompanied by the assertion that it truly reveals the future. With astrology, for example, the positions of stars and planets are said to explain why a person has the character he has and what he can expect. When individuals communicate their acceptance of such claims, it is an example of divination.

More often, it is said that the future or unknown events have an influence on the outcome of the divinatory ritual. One's future, for example, is said to influence the pattern of the tarot cards as they are dealt, so that an interpretation of the cards can reveal that future. It may also be asserted that a supernatural being influences the divining ritual, as when a medium says that he or she is possessed by the spirit of a dead person who is supposed to know secret or future events. Or the diviner may be said to have supernatural powers, such as the ability to see the future or into people's minds.

The basic question in regard to divination is not why individuals make decisions based on techniques that cannot be shown to work, but why they *assert* that such techniques do work. It is this *talk* (not just the accompanying technique) that must be explained. The answer to this question most frequently offered by anthropologists is that in a situation in which the outcome of some action is uncertain or may be unfavorable, individuals feel anxious. Divination is said to relieve this anxiety by providing answers that make individuals feel more certain about their decisions. The obvious question is how can individuals be inspired with confidence when the technique used to influence their choice cannot be shown to be valid?

Water Witching

Vogt and Hyman (1959), in a careful study of water witching, propose this anxiety-reduction explanation. Water witching is a form of divination that identifies underground sources of water, and hence locations for digging wells, by the dipping movements of a forked stick, or similar instrument, held in the hands of the diviner as he or she walks over the area of potential well sites. The technique is sometimes even used on a map of the area.

Vogt and Hyman convincingly make four important points about this practice. First, water witching cannot be shown to be a scientifically valid technique for locating water and is therefore accurately classified as a form of divination (ibid.: 190). The technique itself is not correlated with the presence of water. Second, despite the absence of a correlation between the movement of the rod and the presence of water, water witching is in widespread use, especially in areas where water is difficult to locate. Third, the use of the rod is by no means confined to uneducated individuals unaware of scientific methods. Fourth, because geologic methods for locating water in these areas are only approximate and cannot determine for certain whether a particular spot will produce a well, there is no empirical method for locating water that is clearly superior to divination based on the success rate of wells dug.

Vogt and Hyman propose what they term a "ritual theory" to explain why the farmer seeks a water witch (also sometimes called a dowser). They write that in an uncertain and anxiety-producing situation (a dry hole can be very costly), divination provides "certain and very specific answers that tend to relieve the farmers' anxiety about groundwater resources [and] encourage them to go ahead and drill a well" (ibid.: 212–13). Thus, the ritual of divination gives the farmer confidence about drilling a successful well.

But is confidence even relevant here? The farmer wants water—not confidence—and, given his available resources, he gets it the best way he or she can. When an individual diviner has a higher success rate than geologists, or even as good a rate, a farmer would be foolish to hire a geologist, whose services are always expensive ($3,000 to $15,000, as opposed to $0 to $25 for a diviner; ibid.: 168, 212). Thus, farmers will often choose a water witch with a rate of success comparable to that of a geologist "even though they aren't sold on [the technique]," as one Nebraska agent put it (ibid.: 212). The actual, empirical success rate of individual water witches is of great concern to farmers and influences their decision about whom to hire (ibid.: 201–2). For example, "farmers tend to seek a diviner whom they respect," write Vogt and Hyman (ibid.: 161). The relative success of a diviner can "spread throughout the state" (ibid.: 160). One dowser was known to have "located hundreds of springs and wells, another is said to have dowsed 175 wells in seventeen years, and still another had 19 successful wells out of twenty trials" (ibid.). Thus, it is not difficult to understand why even well-educated individuals (with Ph.D.s and M.D.s) chose diviners (ibid.: 124). Given the great expense involved in having a well dug, the likelihood of finding water is surely far more important to the farmer than any so-called ritually induced confidence. Thus, the farmer's actions in choosing a diviner over a high-priced geologist when their success rates are approximately equal do not require further explanation.

Furthermore, it is difficult to see how the use of a nonprovable technique such as a divining rod would make anyone certain about the successful outcome of drilling. According to Vogt and Hyman, professed belief in the efficacy of water witching often occurs only *after* the well has successfully come in (see, for example, ibid.: 156). And even then many individuals, even diviners themselves, express uncertainty about why or whether the technique actually works. Confidence, as we would expect, appears to be based not on ritual, but on the frequency of observed successful outcomes, a perfectly logical conclusion.

What must be explained is not why the farmer would hire a water witch with a success record equal to that of geologists, but why the water witch chooses to use a technique that does not work, one that cannot be shown to be influenced by the presence of water. Why does he or she not admit to choosing the well site on the basis of his past experience with wells, or even a hunch? Or put another way, why do people make supernatural claims about dowsers and why do people communicate acceptance of these claims?

We propose that the reason why a diviner chooses to use a technique (in this case the divining rod that is claimed to locate water) is to reduce his or her responsibility in the choice of a well site. The movements of the rod appear to be, and may even be, out of the control of the diviner who holds it; diviners claim that is the case. Many individuals who test this claim report that they, too, can feel the rod move in their hands of its own accord. The movement of the rod, of course, may be caused by unconscious muscle movements; the diviner, therefore, may be unaware that he or she is causing the rod to move (ibid.: 121–52). But whether this is true or not, that the movement is uncontrolled is the message that he or she communicates to his or her client. The consequences of a dry hole are severe for the client—wasted time and often considerable money—and an individual who would admit to choosing, on his own, such a well site could surely be criticized by those depending on him. Thus, *to the extent* that the divining rod—an impersonal and seemingly independent agent—is accepted as determining the choice of a well site, the responsibility belongs to the rod and not to the diviner. The diviner's many explanations for the failure of the rod to locate water—interference by buried sources of iron or other ores, presence of sediments that the rod cannot "read," or diversion of the water supply during the process of drilling the well—are further attempts to reduce his or her responsibility for locating a dry well.

Further, to the extent that the farmer accepts the influence of the diviner's answers, and drills accordingly, he reduces his own responsibility. In the event of failure, he too may be able to avoid at least some of the criticism that would come from his friends and family, because part of the blame would lie with the diviner's technique. If there is no better method of finding water than the chosen water witch, it is unlikely that he or she will be criticized (which could cause some social dissension).

Scapulimancy

Let us now examine another explanation for divination. Moore (1957) has proposed that the main benefit of divination lies in its randomness. Moore focuses on the divination technique of scapulimancy, using Speck's data on the Montagnais-Naskapi of eastern Canada (Speck 1935). Scapulimancy involves an interpretation of the appearance of bones, taking its name from the shoulder blade, which is frequently used. This technique is used widely by aboriginal groups in North America and is also found in many parts of Asia, including China. One such technique of the Naskapi involved holding the bone over a flame until it cracked and burned spots appeared. The presumably random pattern of these cracks and spots was said to reveal where game would be found and therefore was used to decide where to hunt. Moore claims that such a technique was valuable because it helped individuals to "avoid unwitting regularities in their behavior which can be utilized by adversaries" (1957: 73). Thus, Moore argues that the Naskapi used scapulimancy to avoid hunting in those areas where caribou had become "sensitized" to the habits of hunters.

Moore's theory, of course, is limited to those forms of divination that use chancelike devices—the techniques referred to as "mechanical"—and, hence, cannot account for other forms of divination. In addition, however, while the use of randomizing techniques is extremely widespread, the types of decisions that could benefit from them appear to be very limited. If Moore's theory were correct, randomizing techniques should be used to determine such things as the locations and timing of battles and some types of political strategies. Yet the "dramatic" kinds of techniques (which do not reduce the human element in the decision) are also often used to make these decisions. For example, Gibson (1961) reports that in Greece, Rome, Peru, and Egypt political decisions, including decisions about warfare, were more frequently based on oracles—spirit mediums or priests claiming to speak for supernaturals—than on mechanical divination techniques.

Furthermore, Moore's theory doesn't even account for many aspects of Naskapi scapulimancy (Speck 1935). First, people used scapulimancy for decisions other than locating hunting sites, including ones that did not involve adversaries. Second, they used other divinatory methods that did not employ chancelike devices (for example, gazing at a pool of water or a decorated object until an image appears, or a dream) to select hunting sites. Finally, and most important, the random cracking of the shoulder blade did not directly guide the hunters, but required interpretations that could vary widely (this is also a problem with Dove's explanation of the augury of the Kantu'; see Dove 1993; 1996).

Moore's hypothesis also depends on the assumption that "human beings require a functional equivalent to a table of random numbers if they are to avoid unwitting regularities in their behavior which can be utilized by their adversaries" (1957: 73). Admittedly, there are many situations in which individuals do not want their adversaries to predict their behavior (such as in battle or when hunting), but is random behavior the best way to achieve this? Strategists of warfare recognize the benefit in catching the enemy unprepared, and try to make decisions based on what they infer the enemy will not expect—by *consciously* changing their pattern of behavior, switching strategies, and so on. Hunters, too, can choose such a strategy by picking hunting sites that have not been used for a while rather than continually returning to places where the animals have learned to avoid them. Randomization of these decisions would be of benefit only if the regularities of behavior were truly unwitting. The peculiar situation required by Moore is that, except by divination, the Naskapi hunters cannot change their habits in ways that cannot be anticipated by the caribou. In other words, Moore assumes that in this regard the caribou are smarter than the hunters: while the animals are capable of adjusting to the behavior of the hunters, the hunters are incapable of adjusting to the "gun shy" animals. Moore uses the phrase "success induced failure" to argue that hunters would return to a hunting site where they had once been successful despite continual failure ever since. Such an argument stretches credulity indeed (for additional criticism of Moore, see Park 1967: 239).

Divination rituals are either publicly performed or their results are made public. Although such techniques cannot be shown to be effective in arriving at accurate answers, they can indeed be effective in communicating that a decision has been made, or was influenced, by divination. The Naskapi diviner and the water witch, to the extent that their decision is accepted as being the result of a technique, should not be held responsible for the decision; to that extent, they should not be blamed for failure. Like choosing a well site, the decision about where to hunt can have important consequences for many individuals. The best of hunters and well site selectors can make decisions that turn out badly. Nevertheless, decisions must be made, and those most capable should make them. Divination reduces the individual's responsibility and hence the criticism that may be directed against him or her. To the extent the technique is ancestral, the technique and the decision will include the support of ancestors.

This reduction of responsibility can explain why a decision-maker may choose, and be encouraged to rely on, a technique that cannot be shown to be effective. In some cases, an individual may simply wish to avoid having to account for or justify his or her actions to others. For example, Evans-Pritchard (1937: 350) reports that Zande men often consult oracles about whether to allow their wives to visit their parents. Thus, when a man refuses his wife a visit on the basis of the oracle's prediction of misfortune, he can circumvent the objections of his in-laws. Since he is not responsible for the decision, they cannot accuse him of arbitrarily refusing to permit their daughter to visit them.

However, what we have suggested so far would apply equally well to non-divinatory techniques used to influence decisions, such as drawing lots, tossing a coin, or consulting an expert advisor. Why do people claim that divination reveals, and hence can actually predict, the future? What in particular does the supernatural claim add to decision-making? The communicated acceptance of a supernatural claim, requiring nonskepticism, requires and promotes collusion with the speaker or diviner and, if traditional, ancestors. It thus requires, and thereby promotes, greater cooperation in decision-making.

The Azande

Let us examine briefly one final case. Perhaps the most important and best-known study of divination in anthropology is Evans-Pritchard's study of Zande oracles in *Witchcraft, Oracles and Magic among the Azande* (1937). The Azande use several types of divination, the most important being the poison oracle. A specially prepared poison is fed to chickens whose death or survival provides answers to proposed questions. The poison oracle was consulted about a wide range of problems, including health, marriage, change of residence, planting crops—questions generally concerning the success of important proposed ventures. It was also used to identify witches (see Chapter Eleven), sorcerers, and adulterers. To make an accusation of witchcraft or adultery without divination was practically unheard of. In regard to other questions, individuals varied a great deal in how frequently they consulted oracles; some used them for many aspects of their daily lives, while others used them only for the most important decisions. Because the use of the poison oracle is costly in both time and resources, since the special poison and fowl must be provided, one can assume that there must be an effect that makes such costs worthwhile.

The use of oracles for identifying witches and adulterers can be understood if we examine the consequences to an individual who makes an accusation of witchcraft or adultery. Such an accusation is always seen as criticism, since it implies immoral and antisocial behavior, and, in the past, witches were sometimes killed. At the time the Azande were studied by Evans-Pritchard, individuals accused of being a witch usually publicly accepted the accusation and apologized for any unwitting harm they might have done. But sometimes they became angry and took aggressive actions against the accuser. It is difficult to support an accusation of witchcraft or adultery with convincing evidence; an accuser, acting on his or her own, would have little more than an assertion to support such a claim. The Azande witch exhibits no distinctive behavior that can substantiate an accusation; he or she is merely alleged to have a motive of ill will against the accuser. Although the Azande claim that a witch can be identified by an autopsy, this procedure, of course, can occur only after the witch is dead; in most cases it was never performed.

Evans-Pritchard points out that adultery is almost as hard to demonstrate as witchcraft: "In a case of adultery there might be circumstantial evidence, but in fact simple cases of this kind were rare. The chance discovery of lovers during a few minutes' congress in the bush or during the absence of a husband from his homestead was small. ... [E]ven if a wife repented of her infidelity and told her husband the name of her lover he [the lover] might deny the accusation" (1937: 267).

In such situations, where the accusation's accuracy is essentially nondemonstrable, the use of a poison oracle makes the accusation less arbitrary, and the accuser less vulnerable to criticism. The names of suspected individuals are put to the oracle, and there is apparently about a 50 percent chance that the accusation will be denied. Usually the question is put to the oracle a second time to confirm or deny the original verdict. The consultation of the poison oracle is performed in front of witnesses, thus making it clear that the accuser did not manipulate the outcome. To the extent that a person is seen as making the accusation based on the oracle, then his or her personal responsibility for the accusation is reduced. If the accused attempts to deny his or her guilt, he or she must deal not only with the accuser but also with the oracle. Frequently, he or she will propose that the question be put to another test by divination; the oracle of a prince or other member of the ruling class is then consulted, with both parties agreeing to abide by its verdict. In the past, accused witches or adulterers were sometimes given the poison to drink themselves. Thus, responsibility for the accusation is seen as at least partly the result of the impersonal procedure of divination. If a second judgment fails to confirm the original accusation, the first accusation is seen as false, responsibility for which is also the oracle's.

Other situations in which questions are put to oracles—proposed marriages, residential moves, economic ventures, and so on—also involve some risk of a bad decision, but in general involve less serious consequences than those resulting from an unsubstantiated accusation of witchcraft or adultery. Less expensive methods of divination than the poison oracle (such as the use of "termites" or a "rubbing-board" oracle; ibid.: 321) may be used in these decisions. Depending on the particular situation, one would expect there to be varying incentives for reducing responsibility for these sorts of decisions. In those cases where the outcome has potentially bad consequences, such as choosing a particular spot to plant a crop, the decision-maker may wish to avoid criticism for his or her actions in case of failure.

In situations in which the individual is fairly certain about what course of action to take, there is always some risk in consulting divination, since that course of action may be denied. For example, the oracle might predict favorable outcomes for the wife's proposed visit to her family discussed earlier; if the consultation is made public, the husband must either let her go or take complete responsibility for denying her, and thereby refute the oracle that he himself consulted. Although an individual may ignore the advice of the diviners or techniques he consults, if he does so regularly, it will become known that these answers do not actually influence him, and thus, by ignoring the advice of the oracle, he limits its effectiveness in reducing his responsibility in the future. An individual who wants to continue to use oracles must, to some degree, be committed to following their advice.

Conclusion

In a perceptive article written some years ago, Park recognized that "a diviner does not, in fact, divine" (1967: 233). Noting that divination is used in a situation that calls for a "decision upon some plan of action ... not easily taken," he wrote that divination "has as its regular consequence the elimination of ... disorder in social relationships" (ibid.: 234). He emphasized "the diviner['s] ... universal exemption from reproach" (ibid.: 253). His main thesis, however, is that "divinatory procedure has the effect of stamping with a mark of special legitimacy a particular decision" (ibid.: 241).

But legitimation does not distinguish divination from anything that is traditional. In a sense, all things traditionally encouraged are legitimate; it is not divination, but ancestral encouragement that legitimates.

To the extent that divination—whether traditional or not—is accepted as making the decision, the technique, and not the person (like Admiral Clodius) voicing the decision, will bear the burden of responsibility. The reason why divination does indeed eliminate this "important source of disorder in social relationships" is not that it legitimates, but because it disarms both criticism and praise, and, hence, the dissension they may engender. We suggest that it is this consequence that accounts for why ancestors may choose to encourage its use and thereby make it legitimate. Since divination is a ritual that reduces individual responsibility over the answers it provides, it encourages a form of decision-making that reduces dissension among the individuals who accept it. Thus, while it is not clear that water witching legitimates, it is clear that when the rod (or whatever) is accepted as making the decision, the water witch is not to blame. It is this effect that leads a water witch to choose to use the technique and ancestors to encourage it. It is this same effect, we suggest, that leads two friends to flip a coin to decide which road to take or film to see. It is not that it makes the choice legitimate but that it reduces the responsibility of those who accept the coin's decision. The crucial difference between the coin flip and divination is only the nonprovable claim (the religious metaphor) that the latter actually divines the best course of action, which thereby requires, and encourages, collusion.

Chapter 10

Sacrifice: Voluntary Suffering

PREVIOUSLY, WE HAVE DISCUSSED how traditional religious leaders, typically referred to as shamans, memorize genealogical relations, transmit traditional myths, make claims about how certain techniques have supernatural effects, and other techniques are supernaturally influenced. Shamans also encourage, often by example, their followers to sacrifice for one another. We suggest that the sacrifice encouraged by religious leaders is best seen, as in religious behavior itself, as a form of communication.

Before presenting the details of our explanation of sacrifice, we briefly discuss three alternative approaches: the cultural materialist explanation put forward by Harris, the "pollution" explanation put forth by Douglas, and the more recent evolutionary explanation based on costly signaling theory.

One popular explanation of food taboos is offered by Harris, in *Cows, Pigs, Wars and Witches* (1974). The essence of this explanation is that patterns of behavior that appear to be sacrifices really aren't sacrifices over the long term (that is, an individual's lifetime). Harris begins his discussion with the Hindu prohibition on eating beef—a result of treating the cow as sacred—and suggests that, in contrast to the popularly held opinion that the Indian prohibition is economically irrational, this taboo actually gives significant economic benefits. Dung is collected and used as fertilizer, as well as fuel for cooking. Remarkably, the quantity of heat produced by burning cow dung in India is the equivalent of 35 million tons of coal per year (ibid.: 18). Although the milk yield of these cows is low, what is produced is always used or sold. When cows die, they can be eaten by the "Untouchables," and their hides are used to produce leather products, one of India's largest industries. Although many benefits are derived from cows, there is little investment required to support them. They are fed very little food that could be used by humans (ibid.: 24) and are generally allowed to simply scavenge for what they get, "eating every morsel of grass, stubble, and garbage that cannot be directly consumed by human beings, and converting it into milk and other useful products" (ibid.).

But the most important function of cows is in their production of oxen, for although India may have an excess of cows, they actually have too few oxen (ibid.: 14). Every farmer needs a pair of oxen to plow the fields and to haul farm products. But while India has 60 million farms, it has only 80 million oxen and male water buffaloes, the two principal traction animals. A farmer who loses his or her draft animals may have trouble surviving, since borrowing animals is difficult during the plowing season and he might have to go into debt to buy new ones. Although some of his cows may seem useless, there is always the possibility that they will produce an ox.

Given these facts, one might wonder why a religious prohibition against eating cows is necessary, for cows, apparently, are more valuable as milk, dung, and the producers of oxen than as meat. Harris's answer is that in times of famine, resulting from the failure of the monsoon rains, a farmer might be tempted to kill his livestock, to eat it or sell it to a slaughterhouse. But if he did so, although he might temporarily satisfy his hunger, he would be worse off in the long run: "[T]hose who succumb to this temptation seal their doom, even if they survive the drought, for when the rains come, they will be unable to plow their fields" (ibid.: 21). Thus, "cow love with its sacred symbols and holy doctrines protects the farmer against calculations that are 'rational' only in the short term" (ibid.). Harris argues that the religious prohibition helps people to resist the temptation to slaughter their animals and, as a result, benefits them in the long run by preserving the draft animals necessary to operate a farm. This makes a certain amount of sense, but leaves one to wonder why water buffalo are not considered sacred and taboo as well?

For the Jewish taboo against eating pork, Harris gives a similar explanation. Pork is a nutritious and tempting food, but for the farming and pastoralist communities of the ancient Middle East, raising pigs was a luxury they could not afford. Unlike cattle, goats, and sheep, pigs are not a source of milk, but are useful only for their meat. More important, the pig is not well adapted to the semiarid climate of the Middle East. Pigs do not sweat and, in order to cool, must roll in water; if that is not available, at very hot temperatures they will use their own urine and excrement to cool themselves.

In biblical times, herding of cattle, goats, and sheep was an important activity, but pigs are difficult to herd over long distances. In addition, pigs have difficulty in digesting the grass and leaves that cud-chewing animals eat and survive best on "nuts, fruits, tubers and especially grains, making it a direct competitor of man" (ibid.: 41–42).

As in the case of the Indian cow, Harris argues that religious prohibitions against eating pork are useful in overcoming the temptation to do something that is economically and ecologically harmful. Although the pig is difficult to raise, competes with man for food, and produces only meat:

> pork remains a succulent treat. People always find it difficult to resist such temptations on their own. … It was ecologically maladaptive to try to raise pigs in substantial numbers. Small-scale production would only increase the temptation. Better, then, to interdict the consumption of pork entirely, and to concentrate on raising goats, sheep, and cattle. Pigs tasted good but were too expensive to feed and keep cool. (Ibid.: 44)

Harris does not *specifically* state that all food taboos can be accounted for by their economic consequences, but he does argue that the other foods prohibited in Leviticus are either insignificant sources of food (such as ospreys and hawks) or would have been unavailable to the farming-pastoralist populations of the Middle East (such as shellfish) (ibid.: 45). "There is obviously nothing irrational about not spending one's time chasing vultures for dinner, or not hiking fifty miles across the desert for a plate of clams on the half shell" (ibid.). But why, then, are such items taboo? Are they aimed at preventing people from doing what they would not do anyway?

Further, Harris does not account for why the taboo against pork is maintained in areas outside the Middle East, where raising pigs is not economically irrational. Jewish people have lived in Europe for more than a thousand years, yet still maintain the prohibition on pork. Here, Harris suggests that taboos may have functions other than economic, "such as helping people to think of themselves as a distinctive community" (ibid.). But surely anything distinctive—a hat or badge, for example—could do that rather than the specific prohibition against pork, which, at times, must have been a serious deprivation. More to the point, if Harris's noneconomic explanation is sufficient to account for the persistence of the pork prohibition in Europe for more than a thousand years, why is it not sufficient to account for its persistence in general? The European example shows that the prohibition need not be economically beneficial; indeed, such prohibitions may be economically irrational.

In fact, *most* taboos are economically irrational and hence cannot be explained by their economic benefits. Taboos really do involve sacrifice. Although the economic, political, conceptual, or physical effects of a taboo may be significant, what must be determined in each case is whether such effects are sufficient to account for the occurrence and persistence of the taboo. A prohibition against sexual intercourse during the nursing period, or against eating a poisonous food, may be accounted for by its consequences. But the fundamental problem of taboo is not to account for the deprivations that make sense, but for those that do not. What must be accounted for are prohibitions such as not eating meat on Fridays, fasting from sunrise to sunset during the month of Ramadan or one Sunday per month, or European mourners wearing dark clothes, while Apache mourners shave their heads and destroy the property of their recently deceased relative. To discover some minor economic benefit in some of these instances does not approach the problem. The basic question is why individuals are encouraged, usually by ancestors, to refrain from doing things that would promote their survival and personal well-being.

Douglas (1968) proposes another widely accepted explanation of food prohibitions, an example of her "pollution beliefs" theory. She argues that the significance of taboos is to help maintain the structure of ideas by forcing people to avoid things that are ambiguous, things that threaten the conceptual system. Taboo, thus, represents a "reaction to any event likely to confuse or contradict cherished classifications" (ibid.: 338). Pollution rules, "insofar as they impose order on experience, support clarification of forms and thus reduce dissonance" (ibid.: 339). Thus, "not only marginal social states, but all margins, the edges of all boundaries which are used in ordering the social experience, are treated as dangerous and polluting" (ibid.: 340).

The most familiar example used by Douglas is the pig, which is listed as taboo because, while it has a cloven hoof, it fails to chew its cud (Leviticus 11: 7); animals such as cattle, sheep, and goats, which exhibit both characteristics, are acceptable for eating (ibid.: 3). Douglas argues that because the pig exhibits only one of these characteristics—a cloven hoof—it confuses the animal categories and was, therefore, forbidden. Her point is that the combination of cud chewing and having a cloven hoof defines an important conceptual category, one worth protecting, and any animal that exhibits one and not the other threatens this category and is thus taboo.

Douglas admits that not even she can come up with a creative way to fit some of the animals that are taboo into her argument (1968: 55), but there are more fundamental problems with the assumptions upon which her explanation is based. First, it has never been demonstrated that anyone has an orderly classification that embraces "the whole of experience," as Douglas proposes (ibid.: 341). Members of every society are capable of acquiring, and often willing to acquire, new and supposedly "category-threatening" items such as radios, matches, guns, airplanes, foods, animals, religious behavior, and new languages. If such things were less important than the preservation of categories, why are they not regularly placed on the taboo list? Even if there was a need to protect established categories, people can accomplish this by simply creating new ones. It seems incredible that Jewish people have not eaten pork for more than three thousand years, and have endured the difficulties related to that prohibition, simply because they did not have a conceptual category for those animals!

More recently, explanations of sacrifice have used the concept of "costly signaling theory" to propose "that expensive behavioral or morphological signals are designed to convey honest information benefiting both signalers and the recipients of these signals" (Smith and Bliege Bird 2000: 246). It is important to note, however, that this hard-to-fake signal hypothesis is not, as claimed, an explanation of religion or religious behavior per se. It is only an explanation of the *sacrifices* encouraged by religious behavior. Hence, it must be integrated with an explanation of religious behavior in general. Further, costly signaling theory typically sees the apparently sacrificial behavior as actually benefiting the signaler. In contrast, we see the sacrifices encouraged by religious behavior as actual sacrifices (see below). Hence, although the sacrifices encouraged by religions may be a form of costly signaling, the questions are these: Why is such encouragement accomplished via supernatural claims, and how does such communication influence the recipients of the message? How does it help them leave descendants and thereby increase the inheritable elements involved in the sacrifice to become more frequent through their descendants?

Standard conceptions of costly signaling theory see sacrifice as a way of conveying reliable information about "the signaler's competitive ability, genetic endowment, health and vigor, resource control, or the like" (ibid.; see also Irons 2001; Sosis 2000; Sosis and Alcorta 2003). Such behavior attracts mates and/or allies to the signaler. However, this explanation is inconsistent with traditional sacrifices found in religion because all members of a religion are often traditionally prescribed to make the same specific sacrifices. In such instances no individual gains a competitive advantage. More fundamentally, the sacrifices are not followed by the hedonistic enjoyment of greater rewards that might translate into increased fitness, but by a future of continued sacrifice. For example, the sacrifice required in lifelong celibacy clearly does not increase the celibate's reproductive success. Such sacrifices are at the expense of that individual's survival and reproduction, but they may increase the descendant-leaving success of that individual's ancestors.

Irons senses the fundamental nature of religion when he states that "[r]eligion basically is a commitment to behave in certain ways without regard to self-interest" (2001: 293). He is also correct in seeing the sacrifices encouraged by religion as hard-to-fake signals of *commitment* to behave in ways contrary to one's self-interest *in the future*. However, lacking the concept of traditions as descendant-leaving strategies, and religious traditions, in particular, as strategies to increase the number of distant descendants at the expense of more immediate reproductive success, Irons still feels compelled to require that religion serve an individual's self-interest: "An inflexible commitment to behave in a particular way can serve one's interests in the majority of cases even if in particular situations the behavior is contrary to self-interest" (ibid.: 292).

Thus, this commitment theory does not take the "contrary to one's self-interest" aspect of sacrifice far enough. It still tries to explain the sacrifice by an overall, or slightly delayed, benefit that comes back to the self-interest of the sacrificer during his or her lifetime. A concept of traditions as descendant-leaving strategies is required to explain the sacrifices encouraged by religion because individuals are encouraged to sacrifice *throughout* their lifetimes and to influence their descendants to do the same. We now present our descendant-leaving theory of religious sacrifice and contrast it with several competing explanations.

Taboo, Sacrifice, and Pain

Taboo, offerings, and initiatory pain are distinguished by voluntary suffering. The acceptance of encouraged suffering in regard to one's appetite, resources, and body communicates a willingness not only to accept the guidance of the encouragers but also to suffer for them, to endure pain, loss, and restraint for them. When the suffering is traditional, as it usually is, or may soon become, the encouragers include ancestors.

Cooperation implies a willingness to accept another person's influence and, hence, always involves some risk of suffering. Thus, a demonstration of the willingness to suffer for others should foster social relationships. Why should the acceptance of restraint and hardship that materially benefits no one be encouraged and accepted? The willingness to sacrifice for others is basic to enduring social relationships. Social relationships are distinguished by enduring cooperation, the acceptance of one another's influence, and therefore will not always be to one's own advantage. Accepting a taboo communicates to those encouraging it that they are worth suffering for and should influence them to be willing to reciprocate. Breaking or defying a taboo, of course, communicates the opposite.

But it is more than that. *To show a willingness to suffer for others not only influences individuals to reciprocate; it also influences them to exhibit such behavior toward others.* Some psychological studies have shown that witnessing "helping" actions influences observers to help others: "[E]xposure to others who act in a generous or helpful manner has been found to increase subjects' tendency to offer aid to [other] persons in need of assistance. Further, exposure to selfish[ness] has been shown to sharply reduce helping and generosity by observers" (Baron and Byrne 1977: 324–25). This is not a surprising finding, given the readiness of humans to copy the behavior of others (the basis of tradition). The important consequences of suffering for others are much more than reciprocity. Indeed, the very strategy of parental behavior itself (parental "sacrifice") has, as its most important consequence, not reciprocity, but its influence on offspring to be willing to suffer, in turn, for their own children. We suggest that the effect of taboos that can account for their persistence is that they encourage selflessness, the defining feature of social behavior and relationships. The hypothesis of this chapter is that the most important effect of the acceptance of encouraged suffering, the effect that can explain its persistence, is the encouragement of social behavior, and hence, the creation and strengthening of social relationships. We begin with taboo.

Taboo

In addition to the previously discussed food taboos, prohibitions on saying the name of a dead person, especially in front of his or her relatives, are fairly widespread. This taboo is found, for example, among all Australian tribes (Elkin 1964: 318) as well as many Native American ones. Opler (1972: 470) has described how this works among the Apache: the taboo on mentioning the name of a dead person was expected to be observed by everyone for a short time after a person's death. After even a long time it was expected to be observed by the dead person's close relatives, as well as by anyone within hearing distance of the relatives. Although this practice does not involve much cost or pain, it does require restraint and some concentration, and it demonstrates a concern for the deceased's relatives. There is no automatic time period for the application of this taboo, or a specified relationship that requires its use. Thus, the strictness of adherence to the taboo can communicate a clear message and have either a positive or negative impact on social relationships: "[N]othing is more insulting, provocative, and certain to precipitate conflict than to call out the name of a dead man in the presence of his relative" (ibid.). Such behavior shows a flagrant disregard for that relative, and communicates a lack of respect for him or her. On the other hand, "it is considered a graceful compliment to the family of the deceased and to the memory of the dead to take elaborate precautions that the name not be called. . . . Thus when a Mescalero leader named Beso (from the Spanish *peso*) died, everyone was obliged to say *dinero* instead of *peso,* especially when within earshot of the dead man's family" (ibid.).

This circumlocution communicates to the dead man's family the individual's concern for them and should therefore have an impact on his or her relationship with them. That it does so is suggested by the recognition that strict adherence to the taboo of a dead person's name is a "graceful compliment" to the family, according to Opler.

Several other practices that form a part of Apache mourning ritual would not normally be considered examples of taboo, but are clearly related to it. When a person dies, his or her close relatives cut their hair, "an act which will alone mark their bereavement for at least a year" (ibid.: 471). They wear as few clothes as possible, despite the cold, and for a certain period do not attend dances or other festivities. These practices share with taboos the feature of the abnegation of personal pleasure. The same practice is found in the Trobriand Islands, where mourners make themselves deliberately unattractive by cutting their hair, painting their faces black, wearing dirty clothes, and giving up scents and ornaments (Malinowski 1929: 291–92). Although all this is said to be done for the deceased, obviously he or she cannot be discernibly affected. But because these practices are public, the living can be influenced. By forgoing a number of pleasures after a death, the mourner shows everyone how important his or her social relationship with the dead person was, thereby demonstrating a willingness to undergo hardship for *existing* social relationships.

Another feature of Apache mourning rituals is the destruction of the goods belonging to the dead person. The house in which the person died is burned, and the family moves to another location. All of the dead person's possessions are destroyed, along with articles owned by other members of the family that were frequently used by the deceased, or that were gifts given by the deceased (Opler 1972: 469). In this case, members of the family of the deceased show their unwillingness to benefit from their relative's death by communicating selflessness. Such restraint on appetite is crucial for social relationships everywhere.

Sacrifice

Although Boyer (2001) tries to explain sacrifice as an *exchange* wherein people *believe* they are getting something back from supernaturals in return for what they give up, the term "sacrifice" implies a voluntary loss of something valuable. Firth points out that sacrifice "implies that ... the resources [sacrificed] are limited, that there are alternative uses for them, and that there is some abstention from an alternative use in making the offering" (1972: 325). When livestock are killed in many traditional societies, they are often killed only as a sacrifice, never just for meat; thus "sacrifice is presumably a killing which is not in the immediate food interest of the slaughterer" (ibid.: 327). Yet with such sacrifices, often only a small amount of meat is offered to the ancestors while the rest is eaten. How is that a real loss? By making a sacrifice, the slaughterer kills the animal in a public ceremony, and the meat is then distributed. Thus, even if the meat of the animal is not actually lost, the owner of it has given up the right to consume it alone with family at his or her leisure.

In other cases, the sacrifice seems to be so small as to be insignificant. For example, the Nuer sometimes claim that the sacrifice of a cucumber is actually that of an ox (Evans-Pritchard 1940). There is no evidence that anyone confuses the cucumber with an ox, despite this justification. When an actual ox is sacrificed, because it is a significant loss, it surely makes a much greater impact. This is evidenced by the fact that people sometimes criticize others for not sacrificing enough, or for sacrificing for selfish motives. As we have seen in Chapter Four, the Lugbara criticize a man who does not sacrifice enough for his ancestors, or who is stingy with his better animals. Similarly, the Ibo claim that spirits are annoyed and will cause a man to be bitten by a snake or to stumble when "the sacrifice [is] of a chicken when the man could have easily afforded a goat (which indicates some prudent calculation somewhere)" (Firth 1972: 329).

Such criticism of individuals for not sacrificing enough indicates not only that the amount sacrificed is significant but also that it is variable. Although an individual may be obliged to make a sacrifice, the actual loss he or she suffers depends at least in part on his or her own decision. Like the other examples of self-imposed suffering already discussed, sacrifice demonstrates/communicates an individual's willingness to give up valuable resources for the sake of others and, because of the human readiness to copy, should have the effect of encouraging those others to do the same.

Pain

Many religious rituals involve practices that encourage or require the acceptance of pain or other physical hardship, such as extreme discipline and endurance. An example of the latter can be found in the annual Zuni Shalako ceremony, involving great costs in time and money. Twelve men are selected one year in advance to perform the dances and to provide eight special ceremonial houses and food for the banquets. These expenses are not trifling, having "in some cases ruined for the whole of the year the families that have undertaken it" (Wilson 1972: 374).

The twelve dancers must learn difficult dances and long, precise speeches that must be recited by heart; one of these takes six hours, and all must be presented without mistakes (ibid.: 277). The dances, which require large, cumbersome costumes, last for many hours, and the dancers must not topple; if they do, it is said they will be struck dead by a god. Thus, dancing requires both costly and time-consuming preparation as well as great discipline and endurance.

By investing so much in their performance, the Shalako dancers demonstrate to the other members of the Zuni community their willingness to sacrifice for them. The impact of this message surely is to strengthen the willingness of the rest of the community to respect and support both the dancers and other members of the community. The importance of this yearly performance, the most spectacular ceremony of the Zunis, must be to create and enhance long-term and important social relationships within the community. Indeed, writes Wilson, of the small pueblo:

> Its strength and cohesion it seems mainly to owe to the extraordinary tribal religion: a complicated system of priesthood, fraternities, and clans. ... This cult includes the whole community. ... [A] very considerable proportion of the little town of twenty-six hundred has, at one time or another, a chance to play some role. With this, the Zuni religion imposes an effective discipline, involving periods of continence and fasting, and insisting on truthfulness ... and on civility and gentleness in personal relations. (Ibid.: 373)

Wilson concludes: "[T]he Zunis as a group are extremely self-controlled, industrious and self-reliant" (ibid.).

Two striking examples of rituals involving the acceptance of considerable pain are found in the Crow's *vision quest* and the *sun dance*. The Crow attributed success in life to the power received from visions during which supernaturals (that is, dead ancestors) were said to give the individual aid, protection, and advice. "To any major catastrophe, to any overwhelming urge, there was an automatic response: you sought a revelation" (Lowie 1935: 237). Although revelations, or visions (ibid.: 238), occasionally came to an individual without any effort on his part, they were usually sought out in an enterprise called *biricisam,* which is the Crow word for "not drinking water" (ibid.: 239). The individual would venture out alone to the mountains, wearing very few clothes and without food or drink. There he would wait for a vision, hungry, thirsty, and often unable to sleep because of the cold. Often he would cut off a joint of his left forefinger and offer it to the sun. According to Lowie, "[C]utting off a finger joint was so popular a form of self-mortification that in 1907 most of the old people I met were disfigured in this way" (ibid.: 240). Eventually, as a result of hunger and loss of blood, he would become unconscious and finally receive his vision. Other forms of self-mutilation were practiced, all said to encourage visions. Some individuals would pierce their breast or back with a skewer, tie this to a pole, and run around the pole until the skewer pulled loose (ibid.). Alternatively, they might tie the skewer to a horse, or attach it to a buffalo skull, which would be dragged around, again until the skewer was pulled out of the flesh (ibid.: 241).

The Crow sun dance was held by an individual "overcome with sorrow at the killing of a kinsman" (ibid.: 297). The dance was said to be "the most effective, if most arduous, means of getting a vision by which he might revenge himself upon the offending tribe" (ibid.). During the days in which the preparations were made (buffalo hunts to get large amounts of meat to feed the participants, preliminary ceremonies, building a special lodge, and so forth), the sun dancer would eat and drink very little, until by the time of the actual performance he was so weak and emaciated that he could hardly stand (ibid.: 322). During the actual ceremony, which might last several days, he would take no food or water (ibid.: 321), and had to dance continuously to drumming and singing, which went on all day with only four intermissions. During the dance, as many as twenty or more individuals would practice a form of self-torture, hanging themselves by the chest or shoulders from a pole. This continued until the sun dancer had a vision, which occurred when he finally passed out from exertion:

> [T]he women wanted to utterly exhaust him and began the first song over again, thus forcing him to go on dancing. The song was repeated twenty times. Then the Whistler [that is, the sun dancer], quite worn out, would go into a trance: he was like one demented, ... according to one informant, like an intoxicated person, according to another. ... [He] fell back panting, while the people cried: "Leave him alone! Don't touch him!" The "Owner" waited to see on which side the "Whistler" would fall, then whirled his rattle over him till the panting subsided, and dragged him to his bed. (Ibid.: 323–24)

Both of these forms of self-inflicted pain (the vision quest and the sun dance) were completely voluntary, and individuals varied in how often they participated in them. Thus, these practices communicated to others the willingness of the individuals to endure pain. Why was there so much emphasis on suffering by pain (rather than by restraint or material loss) among the Crow, as well as by other Plains Native Americans?

The answer may lie in the importance of warfare. Those who have been successful in warfare, who have demonstrated their bravery and courage, are the most honored and influential individuals among the Crow (ibid.: 215). According to Lowie, "War was not the concern of a class nor even the male sex, but of the whole population, from cradle to grave" (ibid.). Most warfare consisted of raids by a small group, initiated by an individual. They were conducted either for the purpose of getting horses, or for taking revenge on an enemy who had killed a kinsman, often as a result of a horse raid (ibid.: 219). The success of a raid obviously depended on the willingness of all the participants to cooperate and take risks for one another. The presence of an individual who was not willing to do this would be a danger to others. Thus, the effect of the sun dance and vision quest, no mere form of masochism, was to encourage willingness to suffer pain, indeed death, for one another, which thereby influenced their cooperation during the raids.

Ceremonies of initiation, often involving "supernatural" justification, occur widely and are often used for induction into social groups. In many societies there are semisecret or secret associations requiring the acceptance of pain for full membership. Social fraternities at many U.S. universities are a well-known example of such associations. Although the ordeal of initiation here should not involve dismemberment or permanent disfigurement, it often involves pain— both direct, such as being struck with a paddle, and indirect, enduring lengthy walks, long periods without sleep, lack of food, and so on. Such hazing may continue for days. At the completion of initiation, the initiates are often literally embraced into the group in an emotional union with the full members. Why the pain? The voluntary acceptance of pain inflicted by the full members demonstrates the willingness of the initiates to suffer for their "brothers"-to-be. It is this demonstration of commitment that the full members seek from the initiates.

One of the most dramatic eyewitness accounts of such initiation is given by Read (1965). The anthropologist spent almost two years with the Gahuku Gama, in the Central Highlands of New Guinea, near the Asaro Valley. The boys of this village are said to "die" during their initiation (ibid.: 156). The sacrifices the boys make during this ritual include thrusting razor-sharp leaves into their noses, causing blood to gush from them. The explanation we propose is that this behavior, and the others discussed, is not simply expression, but is, in fact, communication aimed at influencing onlookers. The blood-letting is a demonstration that the other males, and their ancestors, are worth such suffering. The performance obviously has a dramatic effect on the audience, which strongly encouraged it.

Conclusion

What is required to explain encouraged taboo, sacrifice, and pain is a general explanation rather than one focusing on the odd taboo or sacrifice selected because it is consistent with a particular theoretical approach. Social relationships are based on cooperation and, hence, the willingness of individuals to sacrifice for one another (selfishness always threatens social relationships). The hypothesis proposed in this chapter is that the acceptance of encouraged suffering encourages those aware of it to do the same. The identifiable effect of such suffering that can account for its persistence is that it encourages social behavior and its consequent social relationships. Disproof of this proposition could be made by showing that such effects do not regularly occur. One specific benefit of the cooperative social relationships built through the encouragement of sacrifice is the ability to trust one's allies under dangerous circumstances, including, for example, raids to kill someone accused of committing cannibalism.

Chapter 11

The Killing of Witches

In this chapter, we offer an explanation of the behavior observed among the Hewa that started our investigation into religion. In other words, we attempt to explain the killing of witches. We argue that the function of killing people said to be witches is to intimidate a category of people who actually threaten the social relationships (particularly the social hierarchy) of the killers. To make this case, we must identify what is meant by a witch, why certain individuals are accused of being a witch, and, finally, why they are killed.

The term "witch" has come to have two very different meanings. The first meaning describes an individual who actually practices sorcery; hence, the term "witch*craft*." The other meaning is an individual who is *accused* of being supernaturally evil. Although the first usage refers to an individual distinguished by his or her behavior, the second refers to an individual whose behavior is irrelevant; she or he is distinguished only by the behavior of the accusers. In this book, the use of the term "witch" is restricted to this second meaning—an individual accused of being supernaturally (nondemonstrably) evil. The term "sorcerer" is restricted to the person who actually practices sorcery, as already described in Chapter Eight on magic.

The confusion generated by these two meanings may stem from the fact that the accusation of being supernaturally evil often includes an accusation of sorcery. The practice of sorcery is not only said to be destructive; such an accusation may also be made without any supporting evidence. Thus, the accusation of sorcery, as well as of incest and cannibalism, is often used to specify the evilness of a witch. The important thing to note with a witch, however, in contrast to sorcery, is that it is the *accusation* of supernatural evilness, rather

163

than a technique, that is distinctive. Such an accusation is a metaphor whose implied simile is that the accused is "like evil." In short, the accused is used to represent evil behavior.

Patterson, in her survey of witchcraft in Melanesia, distinguishes a witch's actions, in contrast to those of a sorcerer, as being unobservable (1974: 140). This is consistent with our definition. Likewise, Douglas notes in her volume on witchcraft that "most of the contributors have used 'witchcraft' to refer exclusively to internal psychic power to harm, and 'sorcery' for bewitching by means of external symbols, whether by spells, charms, or potions" (1970: xxxvi). Internal psychic power is unobservable; its identifiable reality exists in the claim alone.

Malinowski makes the same observation:

> [A] sorcerer actually knows the magic of his trade; when called upon he will utter it over the proper substances; will go out at night to waylay his victim or visit him in his hut; and in certain cases, I suspect, may even administer poison. The witch, on the other hand, however much she may be believed to play the part of a *yoyoya,* does not—needless to say—really fly or abstract the insides of people, and she knows no spells or rites, since this type of female magic lives merely in legend and fiction. (1929: 47)

And finally, Middleton writes that "witchcraft may be distinguished from sorcery, although Lugbara often use the word *oleu* for both. Witches affect their victims by mystical means, but sorcerers use material medicines" (1960: 245, 247). For Europeans, he notes, both "are grouped together, as being evil and anti-social people" (ibid.).

The most important effect of talk of witches, as here defined, is not the description of what witches are alleged to do, or how to identify them, or even its use in accusing individuals of nonverifiable evil behavior. The most significant social consequence of a witchcraft accusation occurs when it is used to justify the execution of innocent individuals—innocent, at least, of the supernatural crimes of which they are charged. In an attempt to identify elements common to the killing of witches in general, we shall compare the killings that occurred among the Hewa of Papua New Guinea with those occurring in late Medieval Europe.

Europe

In Europe during the sixteenth and seventeenth centuries, the number of accused witches estimated to have been killed ranges from forty or fifty thousand individuals (Briggs 1996) to as many as 1 million (Cohn 1970: 12). Many of these slayings occurred along the area divided by the Rhine River, which has long been an important European boundary. During the Roman occupation, it marked the major segment of the northern frontier of the Roman Empire. Today the Rhine still coincides with the basic division between the Latin and Germanic languages, and, more or less, divides Catholicism and Protestantism. During the two centuries in which witch-killing was so prevalent, the Protestant Reformation and Catholic Counter-Reformation raged along this border. The Protestant reformers—Luther, Osiander, Calvin, Zwingli, and the humanist Erasmus—all lived near the Rhine. The historian Eric Midelfort (1972) studied the court records of more than twelve hundred cases of witches who had been killed during this period along a segment of the Rhine in southwestern Germany. His carefully collected and described data will be a focus of the analysis presented here.

In virtually all of the cases Midelfort examined, the threat of religious revolution is evident. For some two hundred years, people in this part of Europe lived daily with religious and, by association, political instability serving as a constant presence in their lives. The first *extensive* witch-hunt in the region occurred in 1562 in the community of Wiesensteig. Whether this community was Protestant or Catholic is so uncertain that it has been a point of controversy among historians (ibid.: 90). In 1555, as a result of "popular pressures for reform," certain reformers were invited to present lectures. These lecturers "split into factions, arguing among themselves the merits of Luther, Osiander, and Zwingli" (ibid.: 88). Despite this contentiousness, the Catholic authorities were eventually overthrown in favor of the Protestants. Seven years later (in 1562), sixty-three witches were killed. Five years after that, the town returned to Catholicism, with accompanying authority changes. Fifteen years later, at least twenty-five more witches were burned by the community (ibid.: 90).

Another example of the relationship between religious strife and witch-killing is provided by Offenburg, a city that remained formally Catholic during the Reformation, despite Protestant sympathies among the citizenry. "To guard against infection of the populace with noxious notions ... the town ... [closed] its gates on Sundays ... to prevent citizens from walking the short way to Weingarten, where services were Protestant" (ibid.: 127). Eighty-six witches were killed by this community during this period.

The historian Trevor-Roper emphasized the social and religious turmoil in European communities during the two witch-killing centuries, writing that "thus, if we look at the revival of the witch craze in the 1560s in its context, we see that it is not the product either of Protestantism or of Catholicism, but of both: or rather of their conflict" (1968: 139–40).

Although some writers have attempted to attribute witch-killings to mass hysteria or fanatical behavior, that would be a mistake, for there is considerable evidence showing that witch-killings were approved and rationally defended as necessary in those revolutionary times. Trevor-Roper notes that "the more learned a man in the traditional scholarship of the time, the more likely he was to support the witch-[killers]" (ibid.: 154).

Illustrating this rationality is the argument between two lawyers in the city of Schwaebisch Gmuend. A distinguished and respected lawyer and scholar, Dr. Leonhard Kager, strongly criticized the killing of witches and noted that people were being killed without evidence, solely on the basis of accusation and confession made under extreme torture. The argument made *against* Kager is summarized by Midelfort:

1. Witchcraft is primarily a spiritual crime and need not involve harm to require the death penalty.
2. Witchcraft is a special crime; therefore, the ordinary rules of law do not apply.
3. Judges must be concerned with the safety of society and should therefore be ready to sacrifice individual rights. (1972: 120).

We shall have more to say about the "safety of society" later on. The large number of witches subsequently killed in the next few years indicates that the argument *against* Kager won the day.

The facts presented by Midelfort make clear that European witch-killers were well aware that the kind of evidence used to justify the execution of alleged witches was never decisive. For example, the Jesuit Fredrich von Spee wrote that despite "years of experience as confessor to witches about to be executed" (ibid.: 28) he "had never seen one who really had done the things she confessed" (ibid.). Bodin, often called the "medieval Aristotle," explained at the time that "proof of such evil is so obscure and difficult that not one out of a million witches would be accused or punished if regular legal procedure were followed" (ibid.: 19).

The feature distinctive of the European witch, the feature used to publicly justify her death, was her relationship to the Devil. (We use the pronoun "she" because the vast majority of accused witches were female.) Midelfort cites Robbins: "[T]he main crime [of the witch] was knowingly invoking the Devil and opposing the Church; quite secondary was causing disease or death" (ibid.: 16). "Witches, [Luther] declared, should be burnt, even if they do no harm, merely for making a pact with the Devil" (Trevor-Roper 1968: 137).

Let us keep in mind that "the Devil" is the Christian symbol used by each Christian community to symbolize the behavior that most threatened their community. Pope Innocent VIII was obviously concerned with such challenges to the Church when he issued what turned out to be an exceptionally important bull against witchcraft. In 1484, on the eve of the two centuries of witch-killing, he "sorrowfully reported that he had heard of widespread witchcraft in Upper (that is, southern) Germany. ... Unmindful of their own salvation and deviating from the Catholic faith many persons of both sexes were supposedly abusing themselves with evil spirits" (Midelfort 1972: 20).

By definition, witches cannot be shown to be guilty of the crimes for which they are charged. They also appear guiltless of *any* threatening or antisocial behavior. Indeed, witches tend to be chosen from among the least threatening people. Vulnerability in their lack of social support seems to have been the only quality distinctive of the European witch. Midelfort discovered that 82 percent of the more than twelve hundred slain witches were female. He noted also that within this category "widows and spinsters were most commonly accused of witchcraft, far out of proportion to their numbers in society. Certainly it was against them that many hunts were initially directed; ... persons without families were ... unprotected" (ibid.: 185).

Several other points should be noted in regard to European witch-killing. Virtually all witches killed in Europe were killed by members of their own community: "[W]itch trials [in Europe] were essentially a social internal matter" (Trevor-Roper 1968: 160; see also Douglas 1967: 78; Mair 1969: 9–10).

When witch-killings occurred, they always had wide community support, including backing from magistrates, priests, ministers, and other high-ranking officials. But influential people alone were not the cause of witch-killing. Trevor-Roper emphasizes this fact: "[No] ruler has ever carried out a policy of wholesale expulsion or destruction without the cooperation of society. ... Great massacres may be commanded by tyrants, but they are imposed by peoples. Without ... the people, social persecution cannot be organized. Without the people, it cannot be conceived" (1968: 114–15).

Indeed, authorities were sometimes virtually forced to burn witches. Midelfort describes "the helpless position of the magistrates" when "the wrath of [the] populace, unwilling to abide by the rule of law [demanded that witches be killed]. Witch-killing was not mass madness to be sure, but it most certainly was not the madness or delusion of a small class of bureaucrats either" (Midelfort 1972: 191). Other witch trials broke out "not because the magistrate felt compelled to find a reason, a scapegoat, but because popular pressures demanded one" (ibid.: 190). Preachers sometimes vigorously cautioned magistrates not to "believe all the denunciations of the vulgar rabble" (ibid.: 39). In Offenburg, "[l]ocal pressure for witch hunting ... seems to have come almost entirely from the guilds, against the moderating, cautious attitude of the council" (ibid.: 127).

In short, those killed as witches in Europe do not appear to have been guilty of any crime or antisocial behavior, but rather tended to be nonthreatening, vulnerable individuals. They were not strangers or enemies, but were known by the accusers, and their killing enjoyed wide community support.

Why did European witch-killing finally end? Midelfort, assuming that people killed "witches" because they believed the witch accusations, argues that people became suspicious of the machinery involved in identifying witches. But why did they not become suspicious a century or two earlier? Some historians, including Trevor-Roper, have argued that witch-killing ended because the "stereotype" of the witch broke down. But that leaves the question of why this "stereotype" was not simply replaced by another. The hypothesis we propose, which does not require the unverifiable assumption of belief, is that witch-killings occur only when there is a significant threat to the social hierarchy of the killers and those supporting them. Therefore, it is of great significance that European witch-killing began and ended with the Reformation and Counter-Reformation. In other words, religious revolutions and witch-killings began and ended together. After two centuries of intense religious strife within individual European communities, especially along the Rhine, witch-killings finally ceased when the authority structures of the communities became stable once again. This striking correlation between witch-killing and religious revolution is crucial to any understanding of European witch-killing.

Witch-killing, of course, is not confined to Europe. Reports of such killings are common in the anthropological literature, but virtually all such studies were made after the killings had been banned by European colonial administrators. Evans-Pritchard's famous study of witchcraft among the Azande (1937), for example, was conducted long after the last witch was killed. Between 1966 and 1969, one of us (Steadman) spent twenty-two months living with and studying the Hewa of Papua New Guinea, a society virtually uninfluenced by Europeans. Additional fieldwork was conducted for five months in 1988 and 1989. At the time of those studies, and even up to 2008, individuals continued to be killed as witches. The episode described toward the beginning of this book was one such killing. To understand this example of religious behavior more fully, we examine the Hewa in more detail.

The Hewa

The Hewa live in one of the most inaccessible areas of the Western Highlands of Papua New Guinea. Occupying a mountainous region about a half-mile above sea level, they practice slash-and-burn agriculture and live in widely dispersed single-family houses. Population density averages only about three to four people per square mile.

The remoteness of the Hewa from one another, as well as from neighboring societies, is a major factor that has kept them isolated from European influence. When Steadman first entered the area in 1966, the only sign of European contact was the occasional steel ax, obtained through trade from individuals in neighboring tribes, but ultimately from the coast where interaction with Europeans was more common. Up to the time of his last fieldwork in 1989, there still were no administrative officers or missionaries in the area. Thus, in contrast to most other peoples of Papua New Guinea, the Hewa are virtually independent politically. This remarkable lack of administrative, missionary, or other outside influence means that the Hewa, at least when Steadman lived with them, can accurately be described as an aboriginal society (Steadman 1971; 1975; 1985; Steadman and Merbs 1982).

There are three main types of residential groups among the Hewa, each of them consisting basically of a set of codescendants and their spouses: the household, containing an average of seven people; the neighborhood cluster or hamlet, usually identified by a clan name, containing two to four dispersed households; and, finally, a very dispersed set of two to four neighborhood clusters called the hamlet cluster, characterized by cooperation that includes the roofing and flooring of one another's new houses. Each of these groups has its own identifiable hierarchy of leadership. The head of the household is called *wai-luais* ("house husband-father"), and the head of the two larger groups is called *mopi twa* ("big man"). The largest group, whose leadership is usually well defined, may contain forty to sixty people dispersed over a large territory and is somewhat amorphous because (based on kinship ties) individuals, and sometimes whole households, move between such groups. These moves are sometimes related to conflicts within their own group, but they also reflect an interest in moving to live with or near particular relatives. As a consequence of the Hewa prohibition on marriage between many identified relatives, including all members of one's own and one's mother's patrilineal clan, marriages tend to be distant, leading to the wide dispersal of relatives.

During the period in which Steadman stayed with the Hewa, he was able to gather detailed information on eighty separate killings occurring over more than ten years. These homicides reflect a killing rate of almost 1 percent of the population per year, which may be one of the higher known rates of continuous killing in the world. In about half of these homicides, the victim was killed as a witch, the great majority of whom were female. When males were killed, the killings occurred usually during the retaliatory fighting that sometimes followed a witch-killing.

Each witch-killing is preceded by accusations of witchcraft that may be made at any time by almost any adult, but a killing neither immediately nor necessarily follows. In cases where it has been "determined" that a dying person's viscera have been eaten by a witch (although their absence is never actually checked by autopsy), the alleged "victim" is encouraged to name the witch responsible for his or her impending death. If he or she fails to identify the witch, she may be identified by divination (as described in Chapter Nine), in this case reading leaves placed on the victim's chest.

Steadman discovered no cases in which close relatives of, or people closely associated with, the alleged witch agreed with the charge; they invariably and disdainfully dismissed the accusation as a lie. Witchcraft accusations are seen as threats not only to the witch but also to those associated with the alleged witch (especially the leaders) through either kinship or residence. The accusations thereby represent a challenge to their power and courage. Three choices are open to those associated with an accused witch: (1) they may challenge the accuser by fighting him, (2) they may move away from the accuser's area, or (3) they may ignore the accusation. Should the choice to fight the accuser(s) be made, it is normally done with a staff or cane rather than a bow and arrow (the usual weapon of choice for killing). If the group challenging the accuser(s) displays strength, the accusation will usually not lead to a witch-killing. On the other hand, when an accusation is ignored, there is always danger, for the accused is living under a kind of sentence of death, which may be executed at any time. In short, the group that does not react aggressively to an accusation is seen by everyone as weak and vulnerable.

The precipitous moment occurs usually at a funeral, when the decision is made to kill the person accused of eating the viscera of the person being mourned. An influential man, usually a leader of the deceased's hamlet or hamlet cluster, may then attempt to form a band of about eight or ten men to go and kill the accused witch. These men are related—politically, economically, and by kinship—to a number of people whose support is crucial to the killing. Thus, the killing is never automatic; the decision made at a funeral is always influenced by the adults attending, and the killing party never leaves on its mission without their general support. The men travel through the forest at night and, just before dawn, attack the accused witch with arrows while she sleeps. When she tries to escape, her attackers shoot arrows into her fleeing body until she falls, each member of the killing group striving, usually successfully, to shoot her with at least one arrow, or to strike her with an ax. Steadman was unable to find one adult man who had not participated in a witch-killing, and recorded no instance of a woman ever being involved in such a killing.

As stated previously, accusations do not always lead to killings. In a number of cases in which someone would suggest the killing of a particular person as a witch, the talk was met with either indifference or an outright refusal to accompany the killing party. Continued indifference or repeated refusals invariably would end the talk of the killing. In addition, prior accusations had almost always been made months, or sometimes years, before the killing and not necessarily only by the group contemplating the killing. Criticism by adult females may also stop the killing. Females have impeded the killers by leaving the funeral early, gathering on the trail leading toward the person to be killed, and shaming the killing party when they came along by lifting their skirts and exposing their genitals.

As previously described, the Hewa claim that the distinctive behavior of a *pisai* (witch) is that she is a cannibal, and that she somehow opens up a living person, eats the viscera, and then closes the person up again without leaving a trace. Her victim does not die immediately but gradually, sometimes taking weeks. As far as Steadman could determine, no alleged, surviving victim of a witch has ever been confident that his or her viscera were actually eaten. Being eaten is often determined by a diviner, not by the actual experiences of the victim, and is usually established as the victim lies dying, in an almost comatose state.

Thus, the determination of having been eaten is post hoc. Everyone knows that they themselves have never actually seen a witch performing her "cannibalistic" behavior, and also, so far as Steadman could determine, no one has ever been caught in the act of actually eating anyone's viscera or, indeed, any part of a human. As mentioned, when Steadman asked men who had killed witches for the evidence they used to justify their accusations, there was always uncertainty. Indeed, when discussing this problem in detail, several men pointed out that, after they had killed a person as a witch, they wondered whether the accusation was true, and even how they could be certain of it. Such doubts, however, apparently failed to deter them from subsequently killing other witches.

Further, no one ever seemed interested in identifying whether the viscera were missing, or even in seeking the opening by which the viscera were allegedly extracted. Although everyone knows that people may lie about such matters, no one ever sought to determine the truth by evidence. What this means is that *the actual behavior of a witch is irrelevant to the charges made.* Instead, *people are concerned primarily with the social consequences of the killing, such as past grievances with the group, the likelihood of retaliation, their own particular kinship relationship to the witch, whether it might eventually have to be settled by a "blood" payment of pigs, and so on.*

The evidence indicates that a Hewa "witch," like her European counterpart, is generally as innocent of wrongdoing as anyone in the society. Although there has been much effort spent by anthropologists emphasizing and attempting to identify some antisocial behavior by those accused of being witches (see, for example, Mair 1969: 22–23, 102; Patterson 2000: 132), Steadman could find none among the Hewa. The witch, as far as any Hewa was *certain,* did not do the supernatural things of which she was accused. If she had committed actual crimes or misdeeds, she would have been dealt with appropriately. For example, when a married woman runs off with a lover, she is likely to be pursued by her brothers and her husband and, if caught, killed. She is not called a witch.

Thus, the features common to both European and Hewa witch-killing, and perhaps witch-killing in general, appear to be the following: the accusation of being a witch is, by definition, one that cannot be either proved or falsified. It is an accusation of supernatural, and hence unidentifiable, behavior. The feature distinctive to both the European and Hewa individuals killed as witches is their vulnerability. The witches are individually known by the accusers, and their killing has wide support.

Explanations

Both old and new explanations of witch-killing assume that the killers *believe* in witches, even though the accuracy of such assumption cannot be verified. This assumption of belief leads to the same assertions of irrationality (or nonlogic) that have characterized the entire study of religious behavior. For example: "[A]ccusations of witchcraft grew out of *beliefs* that we no longer share. Accordingly, the depositions reprinted in this book are full of statements that seem *irrational* and bizarre" (Hall 1991: 8, emphasis added; see also Kors and Peters 2001). Although anyone can assert the existence of Hewa beliefs, the accuracy of such talk cannot be established.

Perhaps the most popular explanation for witch-killing is that witches provide a scapegoat for frustrated or anxiety-ridden individuals. The term "scapegoat" usually refers to a person who is made to bear the blame for others. Its meaning is derived from an ancient Jewish ceremony that involved "a goat upon whose head were symbolically placed the sins of the people, after which he was suffered to escape into the wilderness" (*Webster's Dictionary*); hence, "escaped goat" (see Leviticus 16: 20–22).

Howells gives such a scapegoat explanation: "[It] seems to be a fact that witchcraft works in several ways as a safety valve through which may escape the accumulations of anxiety, irritation, envy, and neurotic tensions that arise in all human groups, and which are particularly painful in a small, closed, primitive society from which there is no escape" (1962: 109–10).

Trevor-Roper also uses such an explanation. He argues that witch-killing in Europe must be seen as the social consequence of what he calls the *ideological* war between Protestantism and Catholicism. In the climate of fear accompanying this ideological struggle in their minds, the people sought a scapegoat in the witch (1968: 114, 140).

Levine (1973) offers yet another scapegoat explanation for the witch-killing in England. He argues that when poorhouses were built, people could justifiably refuse beggars, but because the old system had emphasized sharing, they still felt guilty when refusing them. The person feeling guilty projected his guilt onto a beggar by calling him or her a witch; the beggar was then tried and executed, making the accuser feel better by allaying his or her guilt (ibid.: 254–70). This explanation is defective on two important counts. First, it is not convincing that a person would feel greater guilt in refusing food to a beggar than in having that innocent beggar killed. Second, the accuser is not the person doing the killing; rather it is the magistrates, supported (or provoked) by the community. Thus, such killing cannot be explained by the "guilt" of the accuser, even if it could be identified. If the community members did not want to kill such innocent people, they would simply ignore the accusation, perhaps even ridicule the accuser. Accusations are always socially cheaper than killings.

The explanation for European witch-killings proposed by Harris is similar. He examines data presented by Midelfort and others and argues that the "principal result of the witch-hunt system ... was that the poor came to *believe* that they were being victimized by witches and devils instead of princes and popes" (1974: 237, emphasis added). In those economically troubled times, the rich convinced the poor that their economic troubles lay with imaginary witches. The anxiety and frustration felt by the poor, caused by the greed of princes and popes, was then dissipated by slaughtering innocent people as scapegoats: "You could actually see the authorities doing something to make life a little more secure; you could actually hear the witches scream as they went down to hell" (ibid.: 238).

On the basis of more than two years with the Hewa, however, Steadman found that witch-killing has just the opposite effect: it invariably created anxiety and fear. When innocent people are slaughtered, other equally innocent people are vulnerable to being accused and killed. Indeed, after arguing that witch-killing seemed to make life more secure, Harris more accurately characterizes the situation when he writes that "the witchcraft mania ... made everyone fearful, heightened everyone's insecurity" (ibid.: 249). Indeed, we shall argue that the aim of witch-killers is to achieve exactly that: to cause anxiety and fear and thereby to intimidate a category of people.

An Alternative Explanation

To account for the killing of people said to be witches, we must account not only for why the killings are justified by a supernatural accusation but also for why innocent people are killed in the first place. Public punishment has two important effects: it punishes the offender, but it also communicates what is likely to happen to future offenders. The second effect should be the most important: while a crime cannot be undone, its future incidence can be influenced. Although one killing cannot cancel the fact of another killing, and punishment of a thief cannot eliminate the fact of the robbery, public punishment of a crime can decrease the likelihood that individuals in the future will commit that crime. Thus, public punishment communicates to the offender, and also to potential offenders, the cost of the crime. Publicly backed capital punishment not only eliminates the punished and hence any threat that he or she poses; it also tends to intimidate those aware of the punishment who might behave in a similar way.

But why are individuals killed as witches? Because the reality of the alleged crime is irrelevant, a person killed as a witch is not killed for the behavior of which he or she is accused. The punishment of witches cannot be aimed at intimidating potential witches.

Hewa witch-killings invariably reflect grievances based on past hostilities. These hostilities include killings, adultery, and even, ultimately, one's garden being ruined by another person's pig. Members of adjacent hamlet clusters usually pose the greatest threat, and it is in those groups that witches are often "identified" and killed. One feature of a hierarchically defined Hewa group is that the most extreme form of violent competition—killing—almost never occurs within it. Other than a few females killed by their brothers and husbands for adultery, and the extremely rare killing of a cowife, no evidence of a person being killed by members of his or her own group was found—certainly not in his or her household or hamlet, or, so far as Steadman could determine, his or her hamlet cluster.

The reason for the lack of violent competition within groups may be at least partly related to the behavior of influential members—the social hierarchies. The continuous influence of parents generally reduces competition among their children and actively promotes their cooperation; siblings are raised to cooperate with one another. In the hamlet, the men, especially household heads, tend to suppress violence within them and encourage cooperation. Thus, fathers and mothers diminish competitive and hostile behavior among their offspring; household heads, among their household members; and the leaders of hamlets and hamlet clusters, within their respective categories. Although there is competition between individuals who come into frequent contact, such competition tends to be limited by the presence of influential leaders. And the behavior of these influential individuals, in turn, was influenced by their ancestors.

On the other hand, although there is not necessarily less contact between members of different hamlet clusters, there is a much greater likelihood of violence when competition does occur, when they are not close kin, and almost all witch-killings occur between such groups. The leaders of such groups are not in a hierarchical relationship with one another. Cooperation is not regularly encouraged between members of different groups, other than with particular kinsmen. If someone steals the wife of a member of another such group, he will not often be strongly criticized by his own group. That is in sharp contrast to taking someone's wife within one's hamlet cluster. Further, if a man's pig ruins the garden of a man in another hamlet cluster, the owner of the pig will rarely be encouraged to give restitution.

So, the primary threats are influential men in different, but usually nearby, hamlet clusters—men prominent in decision-making, decisions that may include killing someone. Yet it is not those men who are killed as witches, but weak and vulnerable individuals, usually women, who reside with, near, or are otherwise identified with the influential men.

By killing someone, the witch-killers announce to everyone their willingness to use violence against people who threaten their hierarchy and the social relationships based on them. Hewa witch-killing is recognized as a threat to people associated with the witch through either residence or kinship, for if there is a retaliation to either the accusation or the killing it is those people who will carry it out. The consequences of such a threat are not always predictable, of course, and, as indicated, sometimes include retaliation against, and killing of, the witch-killers themselves. It may even lead, years later and after a change in relative power between the two groups, to retaliation in the form of a new witch-killing. Usually, however, because such a killing is discussed and calculated long beforehand, it is not retaliated and *does* tend to have the consequence of intimidation. Everyone in the area realizes that the killing group is strong, is unified, and is willing both to use physical violence and to risk their lives to challenge another group. The major consequence of intimidation should lie in influencing future conflicts. When future competition occurs over such things as women, pigs, fruit trees, and other resources, there is a readiness by those who have been intimidated to give in to the interests of the intimidators. They are much more likely to yield the object of competition and even to move to different areas when competition threatens.

Why are innocent, nonthreatening individuals killed rather than those posing the real challenges? Those killed as witches are politically insignificant—females, weak old men, sometimes orphaned children; they do not have *close* ties to strong men who would be likely to risk being killed in their defense. Killing strong men, or people who will be defended by them, is extremely dangerous. Hewa adult men almost always have their bow and arrows, their main weapon, at hand, even when they sleep. Thus, while killing anyone is the most dangerous activity among the Hewa, the easiest, safest people to kill are those whose death is the least likely to be retaliated, those with the fewest and weakest ties to influential men.

But why is a witchcraft idiom used to justify the killings? Why do they not simply say that they are killing a person as an enemy, or as a member of a category they have feared and now wish to intimidate? Why do they not simply state explicitly that a known weak, vulnerable individual belonging, perhaps somewhat marginally, to the category of people they wish to intimidate should be killed because she is an easier target than anyone else in that category? Why, instead, does this activity include religious behavior?

First, a witchcraft justification may be used when there is a possibility of future cooperation between the killers and those associated with the victim. This consequence is important when future cooperation can be anticipated, such as within a community (as in Europe) or where current opponents, because of shifting alliances, may become allies, as is common in the Hewa. The witch justification can later be cited by those associated with the victim as an excusable motivation, however mistaken. Since virtually everyone that anyone comes across in the Hewa is some kind of kinsman, a witchcraft idiom facilitates the reestablishment of relations. Feud, too, often involves the killing of vulnerable, innocent individuals. Here, however, the implicit justification is usually the same as that stated explicitly: the victim is killed simply as a member of the threatening category. Future cooperation between the opposing sides is not usually anticipated; they often speak explicitly of each other as implacable, enduring enemies. A witchcraft accusation is irrelevant.

Second, the killing of an innocent individual known to the community requires wide support, which is often difficult to achieve. The Hewa are killing innocent people whom they know and who are likely to be distant relatives of the killers and their supporters. The movement of families and the dispersal of people by marriage lead to people having recognized relatives living at great distances. The individuals in the killing group will almost certainly be related to the "witch" in some way and, therefore, some closer kin may not be happy with the choice; they may even suggest others whom they feel would be more appropriate. The selection would then be open to discussion, argument, and criticism by members of the group associated with the killers. Such a debate would make the selection difficult to achieve.

Because a supernatural assertion is not verifiable, it is not disprovable; it is not challengeable by evidence. The supernatural idiom forces the listeners either to

accept or to reject the claim. Rejecting the claim is to reject the speaker's influence and hence, to some extent, one's relationship with him. If he is valuable
(such as a parent or leader), the accusation and what it implies are not likely to
be rejected lightly. Hence, the acceptance of a supernatural assertion is likely only
when it is based on a prior relationship. A related point is that when a person is
finally killed as a witch, accusations against him or her have circulated for some
time, thereby permitting people to think about the social consequences of the
killing. But the most important effect of accepting such a supernatural claim is
that it allows people to communicate their commitment to those encouraging
the killing, to show their willingness to support the enterprise, unfettered by
the truth of the accusation. In short, it creates a conspiracy.

Thus the Hewa appear to support the killing of an innocent person because
he or she is seen as being associated with a category of people that threatens
them. Their victims are killed as symbols that communicate a willingness to use
violence to protect their own hierarchy and social relationships. The fundamental
aim of such a communication is to reduce the likelihood of being killed by, or
losing something of value to, someone in the threatening group, and to increase
the chances of future conflicts being settled in favor of the witch-killers.

In Europe, the argument *against* the lawyer Kager in Schwaebisch Gmuend
rationally emphasized the importance of witch-killing to the community: since
the killing of witches would save their "society" (meaning their hierarchy and
social relationships based on it), the guilt or innocence of the victim, his or her
"individual rights," was irrelevant.

Similarly:

> Benedict Carpzov, a Lutheran scholar, in 1635 ... admitted that torture was
> capable of grave abuse and had led to thousands of false confessions through-
> out Europe. But he concluded that ... it should still be used, even on those
> who seemed innocent. ... He maintained that even those who merely believed
> that they had been at the [witches'] sabbat should be executed, for the belief
> implied the will. ... [He] procured the death of 20,000 persons. (Trevor-Roper
> 1968: 15)

Clearly, many individuals are willing to forgo the requirement of evidence,
and ignore the normal protection of innocent people, when they perceive a great
internal danger to their community. Threatened by such danger, individuals
tolerated and even encouraged accusations against vulnerable individuals and
then supported their killing.

Thus, in the sixteenth and seventeenth centuries, members of individual
European communities were willing to kill innocent individuals, whom they
knew, in an attempt to protect their own hierarchy from religious revolution.

By destroying innocent individuals who were accused of association with the Devil—the symbol of behavior most threatening to Christian communities—they attempted to intimidate those who posed the true threat, those likely to be, or in support of, religious revolutionaries.

The individuals who actually posed the threat would be neither easily identified nor, in most cases, guilty of a crime. Often their observed behavior would be difficult to identify as clearly threatening. Further, those who might support or bring about a religious revolution probably already had considerable influence, and killing or punishing them without good evidence might be strongly resisted. Thus, nonthreatening, vulnerable individuals, without social influence, were selected to represent the potentially dangerous members of the community and then killed. The acceptance by the members of the community of the supernatural justification demonstrated a willingness to collude in their destruction, uninfluenced by the lack of evidence of crime. Vulnerable individuals were selected because they were the easiest to dispatch. Such killings of innocent, known individuals, however, should occur only in special circumstances. Because of the problems associated with forsaking rules of evidence within a community, witch-killings should be supported only when something extremely important to many individuals is endangered. That something is the social relationships, and the authority structure on which they are based, of the witch-killers and their supporters.

Salem, Massachusetts

The conditions elucidated in this chapter accounting for European and Hewa witch-killing suggest the possibility that witch-killing, in general, should occur only where there is a serious threat to a social hierarchy. Therefore, as a test of our hypothesis, we now examine briefly the 1692 witch-hunt of Salem Village, Massachusetts, and the McCarthy period in the 1950s (which also has been described as a witch-hunt).

There is no witch-hunt more fascinating to Americans than that of Salem Village, which occurred near the end of the two centuries of witch-killing in Europe. Twenty individuals were killed over a span of one and a half years. Explanations offered often focus on the delusions of the children who were the accusers (see, for example, Starkey 1969). There has even been an attempt to explain the delusions as resulting from what the children had eaten (Caporael 1976). It should be clear that the killing of witches in Salem cannot be explained by hysterical fantasies of children, however they were caused. Explanations proposed must account for the behavior of the adult members of the community, including the magistrates and preachers, who supported the killings, for it was the adults, not the children, who carried them out.

It is generally known that the Massachusetts Bay Colony was founded in 1630 by a group of religious dissenters for the expressed purpose of religious freedom. What is not so well known is that within less than ten years these same people were prosecuting a woman and her supporters for simply emphasizing their own religious views. In those few years, the Puritan colony had changed from an assembly of people who used a religious idiom to defy an authority structure (England), to a group that used such talk to protect one. These Puritans had become an established community with a powerful authority structure composed mainly of clergy, who created laws by interpreting the Bible, and magistrates, who punished violations of those laws.

In 1636, a newcomer to the colony, Mrs. Hutchinson, did no more than state what was then current Puritan doctrine in England. She pointed out that as each person was individually responsible to God, the clergy had no right to act as God's intermediaries and interpret his messages for them. The interpretation of God's messages, she argued, should be left to the individuals themselves. Mrs. Hutchinson was charged with a political crime, sedition, rather than heresy, tried (Governor John Winthop was both the prosecutor and the judge), and, along with some of her supporters, banished from the colony (Erikson 1966: 71–107). The court charged her with having "seduced and led into dangerous errors many of the people here in New England," and, interestingly, compared her to "others in Germany" (witches, perhaps, or religious revolutionaries) who "make some sudden eruption upon those that differ from them in judgment" (Massachusetts Records, 1, pp. 211–13, cited in ibid.: 92). Note the connection recognized here between European witches and threats to their communities.

This trial against religious-political dissent appears to have effectively muted further challenges for some time. It was not until 1659 (twenty years later) that the colony was again significantly threatened. In that year, some thirty years before the Salem witch-killings, four Quakers were hanged and many others imprisoned and beaten for allegedly doing no more than wearing their hats before authorities (including magistrates) and addressing the authorities by the *familiar* pronouns "thee" and "thou." When Charles II prohibited both corporal and capital punishment of Quakers (Erikson 1966: 124), the attempt by the colony to cope with the threat posed by Quakers came to an end. Even fifty years later, this incident still aroused the fury of the famous witch-hunter Cotton Mather sufficiently to reflect on the Quakers' actions as "an intolerable contempt of authority" (ibid.: 133). In that case, however, the community, relying on actual evidence, failed in their attempt to intimidate the category of people seen as threatening their authority structure.

In 1692, Salem Village supported and encouraged witchcraft accusations and used the accusations to justify the killing of twenty innocent individuals and the incarceration of many others. We suggest that partly as a result of their earlier failure to intimidate dissenters legally, this Puritan community was willing to charge hundreds of innocent people with collaboration with the Devil in order to intimidate those who might indeed display "an intolerable contempt of authority." For evidence of political and religious dissent at this time in Salem Village, one need only consider the series of events that surrounded the witch-killings, as given by Boyer and Nissenbaum (1974):

1626	Founding of the town of Salem.
1672	"Salem Farms," a region of Salem Town, becomes the separate parish of Salem Village; James Bayley hired as its first preacher.
1679	Bayley resigns amid criticism by some Salem villagers.
1680	George Burroughs hired as the new village preacher.
1683	Burroughs leaves Salem Village.
1684	Deodat Lawson hired to succeed Burroughs as preacher.
1686–7	Futile effort to ordain Lawson and form a village church.
1688	Deodat Lawson leaves the village; Samuel Parris arrives.
1689	April: Governor Edmund Andros overthrown in a coup at Boston.
	November: Formation of the Salem Village church and ordination of Samuel Parris as its minister.
1691	October: Opponents of Parris win control of Salem Village parish committee.
1692	January to May: Witchcraft afflictions, accusations, arrests.
	June to September: Witchcraft trials and executions.
1693	Parris's supporters and his opponents jockey for position.
1694	March: The pro-Parris group regains control of the parish committee.
1695	April: An ecclesiastical council meeting at Salem Village under the leadership of the Reverend Increase Mather hints that Parris should resign; eighty-four of Parris's village opponents petition the council members to take a stronger stand.
	May: The council members recommend more forcibly that Parris resign; 105 of Parris's village backers sign a petition in his behalf.
	June: The Salem Village church endorses Parris, who agrees to stay on.
1696	July: Resignation of Samuel Parris (xvii–xviii).

Thus, evidence of political and religious competition for the religious-political hierarchy of Salem Village is clear. This dissension is strikingly similar to what occurred in the communities of southwest Germany described by Midelfort (1972). Such evidence supports our hypothesis that witch-killing is an attempt to intimidate a category of people seen as associated with the alleged witch, who do pose a threat to the hierarchy. The individuals killed as witches in Salem, as in Europe and the Hewa, were innocent and nonthreatening. Most of the twenty were vulnerable women.

McCarthy

The McCarthy period in U.S. politics, from 1950 to 1954, while often called a witch-hunt, was obviously quite different from the witch-hunts of sixteenth- and seventeenth-century Europe and Salem, as well as the Hewa: no one was killed.

The reason for the use of the term "witch-hunt" here, presumably, is that individuals were accused and, though not killed, were socially injured on the basis of either irrelevant or nonidentifiable evidence. What were the conditions that led to this willingness to abandon, if only temporarily, the normal legal requirements for evidence?

Virtually all adult Americans knew that in the five years or so prior to 1950 many Eastern European countries had been drastically affected by successful Communist revolutions, altering fundamentally their authority structures. Similar revolutions appeared imminent in Italy, France, Greece, Finland, Iran, Indochina, and the Philippines.

Not even the United States seemed immune to such a revolution, as it was clear that there were Americans who were Communists or Communist supporters in the labor movement, in the arts, and even in government. In response to this recognized threat, shortly after his inauguration, President Truman required more than 2 million government employees to submit to loyalty investigations.

In 1945, the editor of *Amerasia* had been discovered holding thousands of classified documents passed on to him by a State Department employee (Feuerlicht 1972: 45). In January 1949, eleven leaders of the Communist Party went on trial under the Smith Act and, in October, were found guilty of conspiring to overthrow the government. Accused in 1949, Judith Coplon, a political analyst in the Justice Department, was found guilty, in 1950, of passing secret documents to a Russian spy. In August 1949, the State Department announced that "the heart of China is in Communist hands." Five months later, Alger Hiss was finally convicted of passing State Department secrets to Communists (ibid.:

51–53). Two days after Hiss's conviction, Congressman Richard Nixon asserted that "this conspiracy would have come to light long since had there not been a definite ... effort on the part of certain high officials in two Administrations to keep the public from knowing the facts" (ibid.: 53).

Ten days later Klaus Fuchs was arrested in England and accused of spying. He admitted having passed information to Russian agents at various times between 1942 and 1949. This case eventually led to the arrest and execution of two Americans, Ethel and Julius Rosenberg, as atomic spies (ibid.: 54).

The fear of Communism was not simply a result of superstition or irrationality. There was tangible evidence indicating an internal Communist threat to the United States. In 1950, eighteen days after Hiss's conviction, Joseph McCarthy told a group in Wheeling, West Virginia: "'I have here in my hand a list of two hundred and five that were known to the Secretary of State as being members of the Communist Party and who, nevertheless, are still working and shaping the policy in the State Department.' These words ... were printed in newspapers throughout the nation" (Luthin 1973: 8).

McCarthy almost immediately became the spokesman for a substantial number of Americans. Even four years later, according to a Gallup Poll, "Fifty percent ... were favorable to the Senator against only 29 percent unfavorable" (Varney 1973: 170). In that same year, 1954, McCarthy was described by one journalist as "the articulate voice of the American people" (ibid.: 182).

From 1950 to 1954 hundreds of people were accused and dozens of reputations destroyed. The accusations began with "middle management" State Department employees and worked through scholars, movie writers and actors, librarians, high school teachers, and many others. McCarthy never formally accused business executives, senators, congressmen, cabinet members, or the president. He "was often careful to choose victims who were either timid or vulnerable or both" (Rovere 1973: 261).

Based on the almost instantaneous popularity of McCarthy, we must assume that many Americans were ready to accept nonverifiable accusations of Communist activities. People were singled out as Communist on the basis of such bizarre evidence as being cited in a biography in a study of Siberian folkways, having a library shelf containing detective stories written by a pro-Communist writer, a boyfriend's invitation to spend a weekend together, and promoting a dentist in the army (ibid.: 39–40). Such "evidence" of Communism was used to destroy the careers of many people because, in the words of McCarthy, "there is only one issue for the farmer, the laborer, and the businessman—the issue of Communism in government" (ibid.: 41). The identifiable effect of such witch trials was the widespread intimidation of Communists and their supporters.

Conclusion

The communicated acceptance of a supernatural claim (that is, religious behavior) is central to the subject of witch-killings because a witch is an individual accused of being supernaturally evil. Since the accuracy of a supernatural claim cannot be verified by the senses, the communicated acceptance of a witchcraft accusation uniquely communicates support for the killing or harming of an innocent, known individual used to *represent* those who actually pose a threat to one's social hierarchy. The essence of witchcraft does not lie in the alleged practice of witches, but in the use of assertion alone to justify injuring or destroying "the witch."

A fundamental problem in the analysis of witch-killing (or witch-harming) is to account for why harm is done to individuals who are identifiably innocent of the crime of which they are charged. Because the killing of such individuals is often disruptive, promoting fear and threatening anyone equally innocent, such killing should be resorted to and encouraged only in exceptional circumstances. The hypothesis proposed here is that these circumstances necessarily involve a situation in which the hierarchy on which social relationships depend is threatened by people within the society. The individual chosen as a witch is selected because he or she is, or will be recognized as being, associated with the category of individuals who pose the actual threat. The communicated acceptance of a witchcraft accusation, therefore, communicates the willingness to use violence against the threatening individuals. Killing the strong and influential (or those close to them) is likely to lead to sustained violence and social disruption, while killing vulnerable individuals is less likely to do this.

Further, the killing of a witch requires cooperation, for the person killed is known by the accusers and, on the basis of evidence, is innocent. Anyone, of course, can attempt to justify the killing or harming of someone by claiming that person is a witch, but such a claim is easily dismissed as self-serving, and the "witch" killer dealt with simply as a killer. Consequently, a witchcraft justification is almost always widely accepted before an innocent, known individual is harmed as a witch. Such a requirement thus has the effect of "testing the wind" in that it permits individuals to voice either their objection or commitment to the killing. A prior accusation thereby allows the killers and their supporters to anticipate the social consequences of a killing. Such a procedure helps to prevent the possible destruction of the existing social relationships, whose protection, we are arguing, is the aim of witch-killing.

In other words, one identifiable and memorable effect of witch-killing, like any killing, is that it can intimidate those associated with the victim. It is the attempt to intimidate a category of threatening people associated with the witch that constitutes the primary aim of witch-killing. Witch-killing, therefore, should not occur in the absence of this threat, and the identification of such absence would constitute a disproof of this hypothesis. The hypothesis would be disproved also by showing either that witch-killing does not intimidate those associated with the witch, or that the witch is not identified with a threatening category.

For the Hewa, the threatening category associated with the witch is usually a neighboring hostile, but related, hamlet cluster. This threat is indeed often reduced by the show of force communicated by the witch-killing.

For European witch-killing, the major threat to the communities was an internal religious revolution that threatened the existing authority structure. This threat lasted two centuries, during which time individuals agreed to kill innocent individuals and justified such killing not by evidence but by supernatural assertion of anti-Christian (Devil-like) behavior—the behavior said most to threaten a Christian community.

Although the Massachusetts Bay Colony was itself the product of religious strife in England, a major concern of the colony was threats to their own political, religious hierarchy: first, in 1640, posed by Mrs. Hutchinson and her followers; second, by the Quakers, twenty years later; finally, by the competition for control of the parish, as seen in Salem Village, culminating in the witch-killings.

In McCarthy's Communist "witch-hunt," the threat was revolution, and Americans were willing to harm members of their own country and community on the basis of "supernatural" accusations alone. The primary aim of the hunt was to intimidate potential revolutionaries and sympathizers.

In all of these examples, we see how the behavior of communicating acceptance of supernatural claims has life and death consequences for both the people involved in the communication and, in some cases, hundreds or even thousands of other people. The example of witch-killing also illustrates the difficulty of answering the question of whether religious behavior is good or bad in the sense of being a desirable or undesirable form of behavior, and how such an answer largely depends on one's perspective. We expect at least some readers to find altruistic, family-like cooperative social relationships, which we argue are the clearest identifiable consequence of religious behavior, desirable. Yet, we also expect many of those same readers to recoil at an innocent Hewa woman being killed on the apparent basis of nothing more than a supernatural claim, even though that act involved the promotion of altruistic family-like cooperative social relationships *among the witch-killers* through communicating acceptance of the supernatural claim that the innocent woman was a *pisai*. Whether or not the protection of cooperative family-like social relationships is desirable is a more difficult question to answer than it might first appear to be.

Chapter 12

Prophets and Modern Religions

THUS FAR, WE HAVE FOCUSED on traditional kinship-based religions, the only religion that existed for the vast majority of time. Now we take up the question of the relatively recent so-called world religions. "World," or modern, religions are so designated, not because they necessarily exist in every part of the world, but because they are not confined to a set of kin, a tribe. They do not see themselves as true codescendants of a common ancestor. The first question we address in this chapter is how such religions arise. We propose that modern religions are created by prophets and their followers.

Given that shamans were the only religious leaders for tens of thousands of years, it is not surprising that shamanlike "supernatural" activity is widespread in the more recent world religions. Like shamans, prophets are humans claimed to be supernatural or, at least, to have supernatural power. For example, the *Oxford English Dictionary* states that a priest's "office is simply to perform public religious functions," but a prophet is "one who speaks for God or for any deity."

What, then, is the crucial difference between a shaman and a prophet? They both engage in behavior said by their followers to be either supernatural or supernaturally influenced. Their acceptance as a supernatural renders their claims unchallengeable by evidence. Whatever the ultimate source of their alleged power, however, its observable source is the prophet or shaman. Either can be said to talk directly to a higher power and to perform miracles and magical tricks; either can go into trances and make others do the same; both encourage moral behavior. Indeed, in traditional societies those who have become prophets were often first shamans (see, for example, Kuper 1977: 301; Mooney 1965; Wallace 1958: 238).

One difference between the two is that a shaman, even a very successful one, is not followed by priests—individuals whose job is to repeat what the prophet said originally without being accepted as "supernatural" themselves. A shaman is followed by, or passes on, his or her supernatural practices to others who also become supernatural. Another difference is that a shaman must be trained; a prophet is not trained. However, the reason for these two differences is that *a shaman is traditional; a prophet, when successful, creates tradition*. A shaman is trained to fill a position in an established set of social relationships; a prophet creates new social relationships. A shaman exhibits the traditional functions of a priest with the supernatural qualities of a prophet.

From this perspective, the crucial difference between the two emerges: a shaman *acquires* an already existing set of cooperating individuals communicating acceptance of traditional supernatural claims; a prophet *creates* a set of cooperating individuals by making new supernatural claims. In this way, prophets create metaphorical kinship, whose members use family kin terms for one another. Specifically, the shaman's job is to enhance already existing social, kinship relationships, while the prophet creates new social, kinshiplike relationships.

Prophets and World Religions

Although it may be true that we cannot know the ultimate origin of religion, we can increase our understanding of the origin of *religions* by examining what is known about their creation. We will start with very brief descriptions of the prophets who are claimed to have started three world religions: Buddhism, Christianity, and Islam. The absence of solid historical information about the lives of these prophets limits our knowledge of their actual behavior. Therefore, we will restrict our discussion to only a few of the better-known supernatural claims attributed to them or made about them, and the behavior they encouraged in the people who communicated acceptance of those claims (that is, their followers). We shall then discuss several more recent prophets for which we have greater historical information. We shall find that "Follow me and love one another" is everywhere the prophet's message.

Buddha

Reliable historical data about the actual behavior of Siddhatta Gotama, the name of the person claimed to become "the Buddha," is so limited that we can only be "reasonably confident that Siddhatta Gotama did indeed exist" (Armstrong 2001: xii). He probably lived around 500 B.C., but there is great debate over the specific dates of his birth and death. More important, "there is not a single incident in the scriptures that we can honestly affirm to be historically true" (ibid.: xxi). As a result of this lack of historical information we focus on a few of the claims that have come to be associated with the Buddha (the "Enlightened One").

Although many people routinely refer to Buddhism as one of the world religions, Buddhism is sometimes claimed not to be a religion. That is because some forms of Buddhism do not include some of the supernatural claims commonly found in other religions (for example, the claim that a God exists). As far as we know, however, there is no Buddhist society without ancestor worship. Thus the worship of dead ancestors may be associated with Buddhism everywhere. Even if a Buddhist society without ancestor worship were to exist, referring to Buddhism as a religion is still clearly justified because Buddhists make, and communicate acceptance of, a variety of supernatural claims. In addition to the previously mentioned claims about nirvana, Buddhists, like Hindus, emphasize being reborn to the next life in a form that depends on their behavior in this life. Further, the very term "Buddha" is itself a supernatural claim, because it means an enlightened person, and the quality of being "enlightened" is not verifiable by one's senses. Many of the other supernatural claims concerning the Buddha are strikingly similar to the ones made about, and by, shamans. For example, according to Eliade (1964), when the Buddha returned for the first time to his own city, Kapilavastu:

> he exhibited several "miraculous powers." To convince his relatives of his spiritual capacities and prepare them for conversion, he rose into the air, cut his body to pieces, let his head and limbs fall to the ground, then joined them together again before the amazed eyes of the spectators. This miracle ... is so essentially a part of the Indian tradition of magic that it has become the typical prodigy of fakirism. (428)

Armstrong writes that the existence of many stories about "these myths and miracles show that even the Theravadin monks, who believed that the Buddha should simply be regarded as a guide and an exemplar, were beginning to see him as a superman" (Armstrong 2001: xxiii). Armstrong also states that "in modern historical criticism, it is usually a rule of thumb to discount miraculous events as later accretions. But if we do this ... we distort the legend. We cannot be certain that the more normal incidents are any more original to the legend than these so-called signs and wonders" (ibid.: xxi).

Thus, as "his disciples preserved the memory of his life and teachings as well as they could" (ibid.: xii), they repeated, and communicated acceptance of, a variety of supernatural claims.

Like a shaman, the prophet Buddha appears not only to have made supernatural claims but also to have attempted to influence his followers to engage in moral social behavior. "Morality (*sila*), which consists of right speech, right action and right livelihood" is the first of the Buddhist threefold plan of action (see ibid.: 82). Of course the forms of self-sacrifice the Buddha is perhaps best known for are similar to the fasting and other forms of taboo engaged in by shamans and often encouraged in their followers.

Although the Buddha is portrayed as being shamanlike in terms of the supernatural claims made about him, and in regard to the behavior he encouraged in his followers, the differences between a shaman and a prophet are also seen in the claims made about Buddha. Unlike shamans who promote cooperation among kin, prophets like the Buddha create kinshiplike social relationships among individuals who are not recognized as actual kin. Often this creation of social relationships with nonkin involves breaking the relationships with the actual kin who choose not to become followers of the prophet. For example, Armstrong writes that "right from the start, Siddhatta Gotama took it for granted that family life was incompatible with the highest forms of spirituality. It was a perception shared not only by the other ascetics of India but also by Jesus, who would later tell potential disciples that they must leave their wives and children and abandon their aged relatives if they wanted to follow him" (ibid.: 2).

Jesus

As was the case with Buddha, our knowledge about the historical figure of Jesus "can be at best partial" (Sander 1993: xiii). The supernatural claims made about Jesus, including "miracles" such as walking on water, transforming water into wine, curing people of lameness, leprosy, blindness, and bringing people back from the dead, are so well known that we will focus our brief discussion on some of the behaviors Jesus is claimed to have encouraged among his followers.

Jesus encouraged others to accept his influence and follow him by saying, "I am the way, and the truth, and the life; no man cometh unto the Father, but by me" (John 14: 6, KJV). Jesus encouraged his followers to give up their present way of life and to commit themselves to him completely: "If thou wilt be perfect, go and sell that thou hast, and give to the poor, and thou shalt have treasure in heaven: and come and follow me" (Matthew 19: 21, KJV). Jesus warned his followers that they would suffer persecution and even risk death, and that only by enduring such hardship could they be saved (Matthew 24: 9–13, KJV).

Like shamans, and the prophet Buddha, Jesus encouraged kinship behavior among his followers: they should be generous, moral, and love their neighbors as themselves. This applied not only among his followers but also to their behavior toward others—they should forgive their enemies and avoid violence. Strict sexual morality was required—even the thought of adultery was a sin. Jesus encouraged his followers to cooperate by saying: "Thou shalt love the Lord thy God with all thy heart, and with all thy soul and with all thy mind. This is the first and great commandment. And the second is like unto it, Thou shalt love thy neighbour as thyself. On these two commandments hang all the law and the prophets" (Matthew 22: 37–40, KJV).

As was previously mentioned, the shaman's essential task, in contrast to that of the prophet, is to enhance existing kinship relationships—it is for that reason he or she must know the genealogical relationships in the community. Because kin are created by ancestors, the cults led by shamans should always be ancestral. The prophet's task, on the other hand, is to *create* kinshiplike relationships. It is this phenomenon that distinguishes modern cults and religions. "Who is my mother or my brethren?" asked Jesus when told that his mother and brethren were outside seeking him. He looked at those about him and said, "[B]ehold my mother and my brethren! For whosoever shall do the will of God, the same is my brother and my sister, and mother" (Mark 3: 31–35, KJV).

Jesus also preached that a millennium (a prediction of the end of the world as it now exists, a radical change brought on by supernatural power, and a requirement for an immediate change in behavior) would come within the generation of his disciples and would bring the Kingdom of Heaven to earth, which would save his followers (Matthew 10: 7, 23, 24: 33–34, KJV; Mark 13: 29–30, KJV; but see Luke 17: 20–22, KJV). The words of Jesus suggest the explanation for such a prediction: "Verily, I say unto you, This generation shall not pass away, till all these things be fulfilled.... Therefore be ye ready: for in such an hour as ye think not the Son of man cometh" (Matthew 24: 34, 44, KJV). An interesting feature of such predictions is that, despite not coming true, the failures almost never result in the disintegration of the cult, in the followers' abandonment of the prophet. We suggest that the reason for such predictions is that the prediction of an imminent millennium adds urgency to the prophet's message; the followers must commit themselves *immediately,* or perhaps lose forever.

Muhammad

Muhammad, like Buddha and Jesus before him, "has left no personal account of his reflections, intentions, and activities. ... [W]hat the modern reader has received in the case of each religion is a rich tapestry of tradition, itself the product of many generations of embroidering" (Waines 2003: 10). Following Muhammad's birth around A.D. 570, "no more than the main events of the prophet's life will be known with certainty" (ibid.: 11). What is known includes, once again, a claim of supernatural experience and the encouragement of followers who communicated acceptance of this supernatural claim to cooperate with each other as if they were close kin. Thus, Waines describes: "[F]irst, Muhammad's encounter with God, and second, the formation under his leadership of the nascent community of believers" (ibid.). Muhammad's initial supernatural claim occurred when the soon-to-be prophet was probably around forty years old. At that time, he had a vision in which Allah "addressed him through the agency of the angel Gabriel" (ibid.: 12). Among the later supernatural claims Muhammad would make about Allah was one reminiscent of Jesus' claim of an imminent millennium. At the center of Muhammad's version of this type of prediction "was the claim of this god to raise up the dead at some moment of cosmic cataclysm and usher them before the throne of judgment. At this moment the individual's life would be weighed for its moral value and then rendered either an eternal reward or punishment" (ibid.: 14–15).

Simply making a new supernatural claim is not sufficient to become a prophet. A prophet comes to exist only when other people communicate acceptance of the new supernatural claim—and thereby the prophet. In the case of Muhammad, many of the people who initially heard this claim reportedly found "the notion of raising the dead ... absurd" and they "scoffed" (ibid.: 15). Because of this initial skepticism, "Muhammad did not immediately proclaim his message in public. Rather, he disclosed it at first only to a group of committed followers" (ibid.: 14). Part of the reason for this skepticism was the problem, potentially faced by all prophets, of having to influence people to sacrifice their relationships with their true kin in order to form new kinshiplike relationships with other followers. Waines writes:

> Muhammad's message appeared to question the honor of their ancestors and thus their total way of life. ... They charged him with dividing the people against themselves and, in the manner of a sorcerer, of separating "a man from his father, or from his brother, or from his wife, or from his family" [citing Guillaume 1955: 119]. It was asking too much to abandon the ways of the ancestors without replacing them with something as secure and familiar. (Ibid.: 16)

Muhammad persevered, and the number of his followers grew as more and more individuals chose to communicate acceptance of his supernatural claims and form kinshiplike relationships with his other followers. As the process continued, Muhammad was able to unite former warring factions, as when he traveled to the town of Yathrib, later renamed Medina, where he had been invited "by some of its inhabitants to act as arbitrator or judge in a bitter feud between rival factions" (ibid.: 18). Muhammad concluded his final public address to his followers "with these words: 'Know that every Muslim is a brother to every other Muslim and that you are all now one brotherhood; it is not lawful for any one of you to take anything belonging to his brother unless it is willingly given to you. So do not wrong yourselves!'" (ibid.: 21, citing Guilaume 1955: 651).

Today, "Every Muslim considers himself to be part of the *umma,* the community of living Muslims everywhere" (Eickelman 1981: 205).

Modern Cults/Religions

By examining newly created religions and, through comparison, identifying their common elements, these elements can reasonably be inferred for other religions, past and present. Those features most frequently encountered are likely to be important, if not essential. The word "cult," defined by the *Oxford English Dictionary* as "a particular form or system of religious worship," is used here to mean any religious group—ancestral or modern. Although the term sometimes suggests small size and recency, all religious groups begin small, and to restrict the term "cult" to a certain size or age would be arbitrary. A cult, then, is a set of individuals whose distinctive social relationships are based explicitly on their common acceptance of a religious leader's supernatural claim. Thus a cult is a religion.

As previously mentioned, the most obvious feature distinguishing modern cults from ancestral cults is that their membership is not limited to individuals identified as kin. Although members are often "born into" modern cults, in the sense of membership being acquired through parents, members are often expected to demonstrate their commitment to the church by passing through particular ceremonies, such as confirmation, first communion, or bar mitzvah. The crucial difference between ancestral cults and world, or modern, religions is that conversion is possible in the latter. Indeed, modern cults at their beginning, and often later, depend on conversion for their survival.

A kinship idiom seems to be used regularly to identify the relationships within cults, both modern and ancestral. Within the Roman Catholic Church, for example, priests and the pope are called "father" (making their followers their "children"), members of religious orders are "brothers," nuns are "sisters," and a head nun, "mother superior." In many churches, members of the entire adult congregation refer to each other by sibling terms: "brother" John, "sister" Mary. Worsley, speaking of New Guinean "cargo cults," writes of "the *fraternity* [that is, "brotherhood"] of [a] new cult" (1968: 252, emphasis and brackets added). People often speak of being "reborn" when they join a cult. Rebirth literally implies the acquisition of a new parent and (usually) siblings. By the claim of rebirth, individuals (including shamans, prophets, initiates, and reborn Christians) encourage family-like cooperation between individuals not in the same family. Individuals are sometimes given new names. This is significant because almost everywhere name-giving is a parental prerogative. When God is called the father (and even said to be involved in conception), the implication is that the followers, as his children, become siblings of one another. Hostetler and Huntington write of the Hutterites: "The individual must never pray 'My' Father but 'Our' Father" (1996: 11).

As stated in previous chapters, the use of "close" kinship terms does not simply reflect or express the importance of the various relationships; it helps to create them. Calling a person "father" or "mother" communicates one's respect for, and willingness to accept the influence of, that "parent," thereby encouraging fatherly or motherly behavior toward the speaker. To call someone "my child" communicates a promise to act parentally toward the person, to responsibly guide and help him or her, which thereby encourages the listener to respond *as if* he or she were the speaker's child. To call a person "brother" or "sister" communicates siblinglike concern, to helping him or her; hence the phrase "Brother, can you spare a dime?" Between opposite sexes the use of sibling terms often communicates sexual restraint.

When individuals join a cult, they are joining a family. Worsley, for example, speaks of Melanesian "cargo cult" prophets urging their followers "to practice a new moral code of brotherly love" (1968: 237). Indeed, it is such behavior that constitutes a cult. Thus, a fundamental difference between modern cults (including the world religions) and tribal or traditional (ancestral) cults is that in the former, the family-like social relationships are not based on actual genealogical identification. By accepting a prophet and the prophet's claim of a God who created them, followers accept the implication that they are codescendants, kinsmen, by virtue of descent from this supernatural ancestor. They are "supernatural"— metaphorical—kin. The kinship terms chosen are close kin terms, not terms used for distant kin. Thus, when individuals join a cult, new and enduring family-like relationships are both encouraged and expected, and their creation is often at the expense of actual family relationships. We now describe a diverse set of modern religious cults/religions, focusing on the behavior encouraged.

Alleged supernatural behavior characterizes prophets, including John Wesley, regarded as the founder of the Methodist Church, which developed in the eighteenth century. Davies, an ordained Methodist minister, using Wesley's own writings, describes Wesley's behavior and that of the early Methodists. Davies's 1963 account will form the basis of our analysis.

The movement that led eventually to the founding of the Methodist Church originated not in the preaching of Wesley, but in that of George Whitefield.

Whitefield's exuberant preaching was characterized by a "complete lack of emotional restraint," which had a spectacular effect on his audiences (Davies 1963: 67). His first sermon in Gloucester was reported to have sent fifteen people into madness (ibid.: 66). In Bristol, he attracted huge crowds and many converts, particularly among coal miners. When Whitefield decided to continue his work in the United States, he asked John Wesley to replace him "in the fields."

Wesley's success, however, was even more spectacular than Whitefield's, to the astonishment of them both. He drew crowds at least as large, and the reactions to his preaching have become legend. Wesley went on to spread the Gospel by "field preaching" through the length and breadth of England (ibid.: 69). Wesley himself describes the reaction of women to whom he preached in the Newgate Jail: "I was insensibly led to declare strongly and explicitly that God 'willeth all men to be saved'; and to pray that 'if this were not the truth of God, He would not suffer the blind to go out of the way; but, if it were, He would bear witness to His word.' Immediately one, and another, and another sunk to the earth; they dropped on every side as if thunderstruck" (ibid.: 70).

These women were not the only ones to be struck by Wesley's thunder. Typically, his listeners "became distressed ['cut to the heart']. . . . Distress turned to despair, which expressed itself physically in trembling and shrieking, and then in sinking unconscious to the ground" (ibid.). Wesley then prayed over these afflicted individuals until they were restored, full of "peace and joy in the Holy Ghost" (ibid.). Wesley attributed this "possession" to the direct intervention of God, who "suddenly and strongly convinced many, . . . the natural consequences whereof were sudden outcries and strong bodily convulsions" (ibid.: 71). As a result of this "supernatural" experience, many of those converted by Wesley continued to accept his guidance "for the rest of their lives in quiet and practical goodness" (ibid.).

Wesley claimed that he was himself "saved" twice by the direct intervention of God, a claim accepted and repeated by his followers. The first incident occurred at the age of five when he was trapped by a fire in the second story of his house. His escape from the fire was explained by his mother as being the result of God's direct intervention and was said to be a sign of God's particular interest in him. From then on, Little Wesley was "'a brand plucked [by God] from the burning,' in both the literal and metaphorical sense" (ibid.: 46). This story, a favorite object of "Methodist reminiscence," decorated the vestries of nineteenth-century Methodist chapels (ibid.).

Wesley's second "supernatural" experience took place at the age of thirty-four. He was an ordained Anglican minister, and a graduate of Oxford University, but had had little success in his preaching. He spent most of his time brooding about the state of his soul. One day, while attending a religious reading, Wesley was suddenly "assured" by God that he had washed away his sins (ibid.: 58). After this evangelical conversion, Wesley spent the rest of his life converting others and did so with great success. Despite criticism from the Anglican Church for his "enthusiastic" methods, Wesley continued his evangelizing, and by the time he died he had acquired seventy-two thousand followers in England and nearly that many in the United States (ibid.: 93). His followers were mainly from the working class, and the effect of his teaching was the encouragement of social behavior: industriousness, conscientiousness, frugality, and strict morality (ibid.: 92). What can account for Wesley's profound impact on his audiences? Davies explains that Wesley was working with highly suggestible people, hearing for the first time about the horror of their own sin and the glory of possible salvation. This news struck them violently "both with dismay and joy as they thought first of their sins and then of God's incredible grace and mercy" (ibid.: 71). We suggest that there may be a more objective explanation.

When Wesley began to preach he showed an intense concern for his potential followers: by his willingness to leave the pulpit and come to them in the fields; by bringing his great scholarly training, skills, and knowledge to bear directly on their problems; and by speaking to them personally, directly, with great intensity and sincerity. His message struck his listeners indeed like a thunderbolt and demonstrated a concern for these poor people that they had probably never experienced from anyone, other than perhaps their own parents.

This ordained Anglican deacon from Oxford, with his "immense spiritual and mental energies" (ibid.: 59), displayed respect and concern for these individuals who had been abandoned "by all human authorities, civil and ecclesiastical, and, to all appearances, by God" (ibid.: 67). Wesley showed desire and ability to help them, and they responded. It is not difficult to understand why they committed their lives to him. Falling to the ground as if struck, they gave him their bodies. By explicitly accepting his claim that he had been divinely saved—indeed, that they were divinely saved—they communicated this commitment.

The consequences of accepting his influence can be seen in the transformation of their lives. Davies reports: "[T]he effect of practicing the Methodist virtues was to send all of them steadily up the social scale, so that Wesley warns them frequently in his later sermons of the dangers of wealth. They were frugal, industrious, conscientious, sabbatarian ... staunch representatives of the Puritan tradition" (ibid.: 92–93).

Further:

This was indeed a transformation of abandoned souls. John Wesley, until he was seventy years old, ... traveled almost entirely on horse-back, covering four to five thousand miles a year, and sometimes seventy or eighty miles a day. He consistently preached four or five times each day; at every stopping place he set on foot, or inspected and improved, the organization required for caring for the souls of those whom he had influenced. He kept an eye on the financial and spiritual affairs of each Society. (Ibid.: 78)

Thus, Wesley, like all successful prophets, created a society, a community, or we might say broadly, a family. His followers continue it today.

To further understand the origin of modern religions one of the most fruitful areas of study is Melanesia, the home of "cargo" cults. Often emphasizing the acquisition of food or cargo (and hence, their name), a number of these cults have been analyzed by Worsley:

A prophet announces the imminence of the end of the world in a cataclysm that will destroy everything. Then the ancestors will return, or God, or some other liberating power, will appear, bringing all the goods the people desire, and ushering in a reign of eternal bliss. The people therefore prepare themselves for the Day by setting up cult organizations, and by building storehouses, jetties, and so on to receive the goods known as "cargo" in the local pidgin English. Often, also, they abandon their gardens, kill off their livestock, eat all their food, and throw away their money. (1968: 11)

As this description suggests, a typical, but not universal, feature of these cults is "millenarianism." This is typical of a number of religious movements in other times and places. For example, the prophet of the Ghost Dance, a religious movement popular among Native Americans in the late 1800s, predicted that the Native Americans' dead ancestors would return, bringing a new life "free from death, disease, and misery" (Mooney 1965: 19).

An example of a successful Melanesian religion is the Taro Cult, begun by the prophet Buninia in Papua New Guinea about 1914. Buninia claimed to have been possessed by the spirit of the taro plant, a spirit that had told him about certain rites that must be performed in order to ensure the growth of taro, a major source of food in the areas where Buninia attracted followers. The ceremonies of this cult consisted mostly of feasting, along with drumming, singing, and sometimes dancing. The taro eaten at the feasts had to be prepared, cut, and served in special ways. New forms of magic to encourage the growth of the taro, such as the use of special "medicines" placed in the garden to the accompaniment of drumming, were practiced. Offerings of taro, betel nut, and cigarettes were set out for the ancestors (Worsley 1968: 60–62).

A striking feature of the Taro Cult was the trance behavior exhibited by both leaders and followers. This has been described as a "shaking fit," characterized by jerking of the head, trembling of the body, and contorted expressions (ibid.:

61). Although thus possessed by various taro spirits or distant ancestors, or through dreams, participants claimed to receive messages from the spirits about ceremonies that needed to be performed (ibid.) or the making of special objects, such as forks for eating taro (Williams 1928: 39–40).

Initiates into the cult had to observe special taboos. For several weeks they were not allowed to bathe (ibid.: 32–33). There were many new food taboos, which included prohibitions on "red pandanus seed, sago, crocodile, different kinds of fish, frogs, eels" (Worsley 1968: 59), and even some species of taro. In addition, initiates generally made a payment or gift to the man who instructed them (Williams 1928: 33).

The leaders of the Taro Cult stressed friendliness and cooperation among the members of the cult, and no weapons could be carried in the garden. Although the cult divided into many sects that had slightly different practices, and which competed for members, this "good fellowship" was supposed to be maintained among members of all taro sects. A practice that "became the rage" among cult members was shaking hands, a custom that, according to Worsley, "was a symbol of the changed social relations between villages and tribes which had previously been discrete and isolated, often hostile, entities" (Worsley 1968: 65–66).

This "doctrine of amity" was common to all the Melanesian cults studied by Worsley. Mooney reports the same emphasis in the Ghost Dance religion of the Native Americans. Although some see this latter movement as hostile, culminating in the massacre of the Sioux at Wounded Knee in 1890 by the U.S. Army, in fact the predominant emphasis was on brotherly love: "[All] believers were exhorted to make themselves worthy of the predicted happiness by discarding all things warlike and practicing honesty, peace, and goodwill, not only among themselves, but also toward the whites so long as they were together" (Mooney 1965: 19). As is true of the New Guinean cargo cults, the Ghost Dance brought together peoples who formerly had no, or only hostile, relations with one another. The Ghost Dance prophet's message is clear. In Mooney's words:

> Now comes a prophet as a messenger from God to forbid not only war, but all that savors of war—the war dance, the scalp dance, and even the bloody torture of the sun dance—and his teaching is accepted and his words obeyed by four-fifths of all the warlike predatory tribes of the mountains and the great plains. Only those who have known the deadly hatred that once animated Ute, Cheyenne, and Pawnee, one toward another . . . are able to contrast it with their present spirit of mutual *brotherly* love. (Ibid.: 25, italics added)

The prophets of the Melanesian movements exhibit behavior very similar to that of a shaman. Worsley cites numerous examples of prophets claiming to have had a supernatural experience in which they had personal contact with, and generally received instructions from, a supernatural being (1968: 93–113). One Melanesian prophet said that he was in contact with Satan, who gave him supernatural powers (ibid.: 102), while another claimed to have received his instructions from Saint Peter during a visit to heaven (ibid.: 115). Many claims of supernatural abilities were made either by the cargo cult prophets or by their followers, such as invulnerability, or having died and returned to life (ibid.: 54, 215). Trances, in which the prophet or leader claimed to be possessed by spirits, were common, as was speaking in tongues, curing, and divining. One prophet would climb onto a roof in the dark and tell his assembled followers that he was flying over them (ibid.: 102).

As we have seen, such supernatural claims and performances are not limited to shamans and cargo cult prophets. Wesley, the founder of the Methodist Church, claimed to have been twice influenced directly by God. The miracles performed by Jesus—curing the sick, raising the dead, miraculously producing food and wine, walking on water, making a fig tree infertile, and returning from the dead—are asserted as true by Christians. Wovoka, the prophet of the Ghost Dance movement, claimed to have been taken to the "other world," where he saw God and the spirits of the dead (Mooney 1965: 14).

Worsley points out several features commonly found in the messages of the cargo cult prophets: people should be moral, honest, and love one another. They are often encouraged to give up material goods (kill their pigs, get rid of money or European goods, and so on), while new taboos are created on foods, sexual behavior, and clothing. As noted, another feature of the Melanesian cults, one found in the Taro Cult described above, is behavior that is highly emotional, "out-of-control," including convulsions and speaking in tongues (Worsley 1968: 61, 70, 76). One successful movement that began in 1919 in New Guinea, known as the Vailala Madness, was characterized by a peculiar form of possession, so much so that it was often referred to by names meaning "dizzy" or "crazy" (ibid.: 75). One observer reports: "[T]he natives ... were taking a few quick steps in front of them, and would then stand, jabber and gesticulate, at the same time swaying the head from side to side; also bending the body from side to side from the hips" (Williams, in ibid.: 75–76).

Worsley attempts to explain such phenomena as being an expression of the emotional reaction to frustrations resulting from contact with Europeans:

> The hysterical elements are only too plain, and can be interpreted in terms of the frustrations arising from changed social conditions, the inability to find correct ways of dealing with these new problems due to lack of material techniques and knowledge, and the powerful emotions engendered by conscious mobilization to overthrow the old, deeply established ways and to adopt new ones. (Ibid.: 89–90)

However, if these extraordinary performances were merely the expression of strong emotion, what accounts for the fact that "there were three categories of people whom Williams termed 'Automaniacs': those who were swept away involuntarily, those who simulated possession, and those who could voluntarily induce it" (ibid.: 76)? Why should anyone try to encourage or fake a trance if the trance is merely an expression of emotional frustration? The fact that possession "was usually a collective phenomenon" (ibid.: 61)—that many individuals went into trance together rather than privately—suggests also that such displays are more than simply the expression of emotional tension. If, as we have suggested, the significant effect of the behavior was to *communicate* commitment to the prophet, and thereby to members of the cult, the encouragement of the public performance of trances, and the fact that some people might try to fake them or learn how to induce them, is understandable. It also makes sense why intensive emotional behavior should be such a common feature in newly formed cults, wherever they occur. Emotional behavior that encourages an emotional response in others is often found where individuals who have had little or no previous contact with one another are urged to commit themselves quickly and intensely, and to demonstrate that commitment immediately.

Often members were encouraged to give up many of their material possessions in anticipation of the coming millennium, where all things would be provided supernaturally. In the Milne Bay Prophet movement, which took place in 1893, it was predicted that a storm would come and wipe out the coastal villages, so all the people "were to abandon their houses and retreat inland to seek refuge from the storm. Houses were burnt down and the people moved" (ibid.: 52). All goods obtained from the white man were banned. No work was done in the gardens, and three to four hundred pigs, the most important source of native wealth, were killed and consumed (ibid.: 53). Such sacrifice contradicts the argument, implied in the name "cargo cult" itself, that the aim of the people involved in cargo cults is to amass cargo.

Such sacrifice is not restricted to Melanesian religious movements. Worsley reports: "Southern Bantu died in their thousands in the nineteenth century through killing off their cattle and destroying their crops in response to a prophet's appeal; in this century, Eskimos in Greenland became so convinced of the imminence of the millennium that they stopped hunting and ate into their stores of food" (ibid.: 225).

By such activities—hysterical possession, sacrifice, and taboo—followers of the prophet communicate their acceptance of his or her influence, their willingness to suffer for the prophet, and for one another. They communicate thereby the acceptance of the message common to all Melanesian prophets: "the love of one's cult-brethren; new forms of sexual relationship, abandonment of stealing, lying, cheating, theft; devotion to the interests of the community and not merely of the self" (ibid.: 251). In a word, they demonstrate family-like kinship behavior toward one another. In addition, what they are giving up (money, pigs, and so forth) are all sources of competition. A very strict sexual morality was usually emphasized in the Melanesian cults—"no adultery" was a common tenet. Some Melanesian cults, however, encouraged unusual sexual freedom. For example, in one movement in the New Hebrides, people were encouraged to perform sex in public and to be open about their sexual liaisons (ibid.: 151). Worsley interprets both types of behavior—"sexual communism and sexual asceticism"—as attempts to reject old, outworn forms of morality no longer suitable to the new life. One function of the creation of new rules and breaking of the old, according to Worsley, is to unite people: "It welds the devotees together into a new fraternity of people who have deliberately flouted the most sacred rules of the old society. ... The ritual breaking of taboos is thus a most powerful mechanism of political integration and generates intense emotional energy" (ibid.: 249–50).

How the breaking of taboos should generate or liberate energy and weld people together is not clear from Worsley's discussion. The "new morality" and emphasis on sexual purity is explained by Worsley in quite another way, but is equally unconvincing: "Such doctrines are the spiritual concomitants of the new life if the political and economic changes are to be infused with any humanist content" (ibid.: 251).

We suggest that the prophet's emphasis on sexual behavior, as on all social behavior, is to achieve certain kinds of social relationships. By discouraging promiscuity, for example, sexual conflicts are reduced, both between the same sexes and between spouses. But what of the encouragement of sexual freedom? Worsley writes of the cult that advocated open sexual congress: "[H]usbands should show no jealousy, for this would disturb the state of harmony which the cult was trying to establish" (ibid.: 151).

Because of the importance of sexual behavior and its competitive consequences, sexual behavior must always be of great concern to prophets. Mother Ann Lee, the prophet of the Shakers, claimed to have received a supernatural vision that identified "the root of evil in the act of sexual intercourse." She encouraged her followers, who were originally English Quakers, to leave England and come to the United States in 1774. There they lived together in "families" of celibates, sharing all property in common. Her followers claimed to expect the millennium to occur at any moment, since Christ in the form of Ann Lee had already returned. In their years of greatest vigor, in the early 1800s, the Shakers numbered more than five thousand. Following Mother Lee's advice, they loved one another like brothers and sisters—not sexually—and consequently left no descendants. Only a few Shakers survive today (Albanese 1981: 155–56).

The Oneida Perfectionists, on the other hand, established by the prophet John Humphrey Noyes in Vermont in 1844, and later in New York, prohibited *exclusive* sexual relationships. Indeed, "complex marriage" was required:

> [E]very man was husband to every woman in the community, and every woman was wife to every man. Only mutual agreement was needed to engage in sexual relations. … Sex should become the great bond of a community that mirrored the heavenly unity: it should not bring with it the divisiveness that prevented the members of one body in Christ from genuinely loving each and all. (Ibid.: 158)

By 1878 the community had acquired more than three hundred members. Albanese writes: "The joy and ease of life in the community had been purchased by a near-monastic discipline embracing all aspects of daily existence" (ibid.). Further, "Oneidans saw their community as a living witness to the end of what Noyes called the 'sin-system.' Apostasy, unbelief, obedience to mammon, private property, and death … had been destroyed at Oneida" (ibid.: 159).

> [However] by the time the second generation … had grown to maturity, internal dissension became a factor. … They reacted against the ways of their elders, sometimes by outright agnosticism and sometimes by secret disapproval of what they regarded as the *immorality* of complex marriage. The misgivings of these Perfectionists, combined with the hostility of outsiders, … finally led Noyes to flee to Canada and to urge the dissolution of the community. (Ibid.: 158, our emphasis).

Neither extreme strategy—sexual abstinence nor sexual communism—would appear to be successful in leaving descendants. But clearly both attempts are *aimed* at promoting cooperation—brotherly love—by reducing sexual competition.

In the United States there are many new religious movements that have gained converts during recent decades. One such cult is Hare Krishna, which was founded in New York in 1966 with the teachings of A. C. Bhaktivedanta Prabhupada, by a guru trained in this Hindu sect in India (Judah 1974: 464). This guru quickly attracted followers in New York, mainly among young people, and the first temple was set up there. By 1974, the movement had spread to twenty-two cities in the United States, as well as to Germany, Canada, Australia, Hong Kong, Japan, England, France, Holland, and Trinidad (ibid.: 463). The devotees of the cult live together communally in groups of between twelve and twenty-four and hold services in the temple that may be attended by outsiders.

Members of this cult are urged to devote their lives to developing "Krishna consciousness"—a "deepening of one's love of God and man" (ibid.: 465). They shave their heads and wear distinctive orange robes. The four most important requirements of a cult member: he or she "must refrain from eating meat, fish, or eggs; must not gamble nor have illicit sex; must not take drugs or intoxicants; must chant sixteen rounds on his prayer beads daily" (ibid.: 470). Celibacy is the ideal, although sexual relations are permitted between married couples for the purpose of having children (ibid.: 471). Besides gambling, other "idle amusements" such as movies and television are also prohibited (ibid.). Only specially prepared food may be eaten (ibid.). The day of a Hare Krishna devotee begins at 3:45 A.M. and follows a rigid schedule of praying, chanting, reading, and selling in the streets.

It is obvious from this description that the life of a Hare Krishna member is one of discipline. What makes it appealing to so many young people? There is certainly no economic benefit; most of the members come from middle-class families (ibid.: 464), and the pursuit of material and other pleasures is discouraged. What a member of Hare Krishna acquires is a "family." Through encouraged selflessness, members of the cult establish close relationships with one another. They live together like a family; they spend many hours in prayer and study and give up many of the pleasures of their former life. They place themselves completely under the authority of their leader or guru, who encourages the suppression of self-interest. Thus, a "family" is established in which the members regularly demonstrate to one another their willingness to make sacrifices for "love of God and man." Through this behavior the adherents to the cult, in their words, "[find] more happiness than they had known before, and a greater pleasure than drugs had ever been able to supply" (ibid.: 476).

In recent decades, cults referred to as Satanism have become popular in the United States. These cults focus on the practice of magic and often perform rituals said to be aimed at Satan and that parody Christian rituals. An example is the black mass, in which the Lord's Prayer is said backward and a cross is hung upside down over the naked body of a woman, used as the altar (Moody 1974: 367). Their selection of the term "Satanism" appears to have more to do with a rejection of Christianity than any interest in being "supernaturally" evil. Although they declare themselves in league with Satan, just as the alleged witches persecuted in Europe were accused of being, they actually have far more in common with members of Christian churches than they do with the alleged European "witches." That is because they regularly cooperate within their identifiable congregation led by a religious leader.

Moody has studied one such satanic cult, the First Church of the Trapezoid, the Church of Satan, located in San Francisco. He writes that the Satanists teach that man is evil, and encourage and applaud members for expressing their "evil" thoughts. They "persuade their new members to revel in their own humanity, to give free reign to their natural impulses and indulge their appetites without fear of guilt" (ibid.: 365). "Evil" is itself not seen as bad but, on the contrary, as natural—"human, free, unafraid, and joyful," (ibid.) and without the guilt and fear of retribution for sins said to be taught by Christianity.

This cult seems to challenge the basic argument of this book. Rather than emphasizing selflessness, as found, for example, in cargo cults, Christianity, and the Hare Krishna movement, the Satanists seem to emphasize self-indulgence— behavior that should threaten cooperation and social relationships.

A look at the actual behavior encouraged and exhibited between members, however, quickly dispels this notion. According to Moody, the new member "comes into contact with others who are friendly and accepting and who, by example, encourage him to voice his fears. They persuade him that he is not different or detestable" (ibid.: 371). After an initial series of tests and interviews, the initiate is asked to join his "new friends" to view the rituals (ibid.: 365). This invitation is seen as a "symbol of acceptance and warmth, of belonging" (ibid.: 371).

As noted, a characteristic of the satanic cults is that many of the rites are "grotesque" parodies of Christian ceremonies, often involving behavior considered by outsiders as outrageous, even shameful. One ritual is a form of communion in which urine and a beet soaked in vaginal fluid are substituted for wine and bread (ibid.: 367). Some rituals involve aggressive actions against Christian symbols, such as the cross, breaking them or urinating on them (ibid.: 368). We suggest that these coordinated actions communicate not merely a rejection of Christianity but also a willingness to suffer disgust or humiliation for one another.

In addition to establishing important social relationships, Satanists learn skills that improve their social behavior toward outsiders. According to Moody, those attracted to the satanic church tend to be individuals who have difficulties with their social relationships, who are seen by others as somewhat "abnormal" and socially inept (ibid.: 360). In addition to instructing his followers in techniques of "Greater Magic"—such as charms, spells, chants, curses—the minister (and others) gives instruction in what is called "Lesser Magic" (ibid.: 371). Lesser Magic involves techniques to influence people in their everyday life, equivalent to what Moody calls the "social graces" (ibid.: 375). For example, part of the instruction in love magic (called the "invocation of lust") involves advice on good grooming, how to make oneself more attractive, how best to show one's interest in a member of the opposite sex, how to flatter, and so on (ibid.: 371–72). As a result of this training, the Satanist "grows more confident and socially adept, and the general quality of his relationship with others improves" (ibid.: 375). Often, "in the eyes of the larger society this former 'deviant' may be thought to have undergone a pleasing and unexpected personality modification" (ibid.: 380).

Behavior of individuals, not beliefs, can be identified and responded to by others, and it is particular behavior that is encouraged in all cults, including modern churches. Indeed, it is particular behavior (including speech) that identifies a cult. This can be observed in a typical Sunday's service of a Presbyterian Church:

1. People, carefully dressed, exhibiting quiet restraint, enter the church shortly before 10:00 A.M., sit quietly, and listen to quiet organ music.
2. The choir, distinctively but identically dressed, enters and sits quietly in a special place.
3. The minister, distinctively dressed, enters from the side and sits quietly, seeming to meditate.
4. The minister mounts to the pulpit, asks the congregation to bow their heads, and gives a prayer, often about general human problems in the world, emphasizing a concern for and interest in "humanity"; also for loved ones who are away—sons, daughters, spouses. He then says "Amen," ending the prayer.
5. The congregation stands in unison, recites the Apostles' Creed, and sings *Gloria Patria*.
6. The congregation then sits and participates in "Responsive Reading," readings by the minister (usually biblical) interspersed by readings by the congregation in unison (usually printed on the back page of the hymn-books).
7. The congregation stands and sings a hymn, usually chosen by the minister when writing his sermon and aimed at contributing to its message. A short, appropriate sermon is directed to the children, who then leave for "Sunday School" classrooms.
8. Announcements follow, usually by the minister but sometimes by heads of committees of non-Sunday church activities, such as fund-raising drives or changes in a weekly meeting; also, appreciative remarks about donations of flowers by individual members, often made "in memory of" recently deceased spouses or children.
9. Carefully rehearsed singing is performed by either the choir or a soloist. It is conducted by a paid, professional choir director. Generally, a song is chosen to fit the minister's sermon (requiring prior coordination).
10. Collection of the offering occurs by ushers passing plates, accompanied by organ music, which is usually soothing, pleasurable, and not rousing, which might divert attention from the collection. As the ushers bring

the collection to the front of the church and stand, the minister prays, pledging the use of the funds to God's purposes.

11. The sermon is given. It has been prepared by the minister during the week before the service and lasts about a half-hour. This message urges, encourages, and inspires good social—kinshiplike—behavior: to be fair, honest, trustworthy, trusting, responsible, caring, and so on. In addition, sermons almost invariably emphasize the New Testament: God's word as given by Jesus.

12. At the conclusion of the sermon, the congregation then rises and sings a hymn more or less appropriate to the sermon.

13. While the congregation remains standing, the minister gives a short benediction (a short blessing ending the religious service) to the congregation, leaves his pulpit, and strides briskly to the back of the church. Meanwhile, the choir sings another benediction to the congregation.

14. As the congregation then rises and begins slowly to leave, the minister shakes hands and warmly greets many of the individual members, who often praise or mention the message in the sermon. The members of the congregation also greet each other.

Thus, it is behavior that identifiably characterizes this church, and not only the behavior of the minister, the choir director, and the various helpers such as ushers. It is the behavior of the congregation itself that constitutes a religion. By displaying the characteristic behavior of their chosen church—being silent at certain times, singing or reciting at certain times, weekly offerings, attendance itself, acceptance of the influence of the religious leaders and communicating acceptance of their supernatural claims—members communicate their willingness to cooperate.

Every social ritual requires, and thereby encourages, cooperation, and this appears to be its most important feature. In regard to clothing, people are usually encouraged to be clean, neat, dressed in a manner that is more formal than casual; such attire communicates concern and respect for the other members of the congregation. The choir (in our example) is identified by distinctive and formal wear, and emphasizes their coordinated role as performers. The minister, too, is identified by formal and unique dress, which distinguishes him as the religious leader.

In respect to speaking, singing, and praying in church, such behavior not only demonstrates unity—it promotes it. To do things in unison, individuals must adjust their behavior to one another; they must cooperate. Singing together, for example, not only is cooperative but also demonstrates an interest in cooperating and also increases the pleasure of being together. The creed said in unison communicates one's commitment in front of the entire congregation to accept the Presbyterian tenets. The offering is voluntary and often pledged a year in advance. What can be said about all these activities is that through them individuals demonstrate a willingness to accept one another's influence.

In the sermon, people are urged to behave with honesty and integrity, even to outsiders. Social behavior influences others to respond in the same way. Through such behavior social relationships are created and renewed.

Fundamental to the whole enterprise is meeting regularly with fellow members and demonstrating concern for them, for without that there is no church. When a member misses several services, upon his or her return the absence is noted by other members, who greet the person with a statement that he or she has been missed. New members are sometimes urged to break former relationships, sometimes even close family ties. As previously mentioned, Jesus urged his followers to leave their families and follow him: "For I am come to set a man at variance against his father, and the daughter against her mother.... And a man's foes shall be they of his own household. He that loveth father or mother more than me is not worthy of me. ... And he that taketh not his cross, and followeth after me, is not worthy of me" (Matthew 10: 35–38, KJV). Family-like cooperation between nonfamily members is basic to all cults.

We turn now to specific claims of supernatural behavior found in a variety of cults created by prophets. We attempt to demonstrate what exhortation communicates and how it contributes to the formation of kinshiplike cooperative social relationships.

Glossolalia

Behavior said to be supernaturally caused is not uncommon in present-day Christian religions; such activities include prophecy, faith healing, and other miraculous occurrences. One such practice is "speaking in tongues," or glossolalia: speaking in an apparent, but unidentifiable, language.

Although speaking in tongues was practiced in the early Christian church, and has been occasionally practiced by various sects since, it did not become widespread until the twentieth century (Stagg, Henson, and Glenn-Oates 1967: 45–46). Since about 1900 it has been most strongly associated with the Pentecostal movement, which also emphasizes salvation, faith healing, and the Second Coming of Christ (ibid.: 68). However, from about 1960 this practice has spread to other Christian denominations with a speed that has been described as "little short of miraculous" (ibid.: 12). Members of many Protestant denominations—Episcopalians, Evangelicals, Presbyterians, and Baptists (ibid.: 70)—and Catholics have taken up glossolalia, often causing considerable controversy and concern among church leaders (ibid.: 12–13; Samarin 1972: 48). Some leaders have banned its practice, as did the Episcopal bishops of California and Missouri (Jaquith 1967: 2).

Goodman, an anthropologist, has made a detailed study of glossolalia in two Apostolic churches (an offshoot of Pentecostalism), one in Mexico City and the other in the Mayan village of Utzpac in the Yucatan. Her observations form the basis of the analysis here. In these two churches, speaking in tongues forms a part of almost every service. In Mexico City, glossolalia usually occurs during the altar call, when individuals come forward and pray aloud at the altar. During this part of the service, some people demonstrate "receiving the Holy Spirit" by speaking in tongues (1972: 19). In the Yucatan church, glossolalia was even more important: in addition to its performance during the regular services, praying in tongues was used to exorcise the Devil and was "interpreted" as specific advice from God on particular problems of the church (ibid.: 18–19).

Although some of those who speak in tongues state that they may be known human languages, such as Latin or Greek (Goodman 1972: 10; Stagg, Henson, and Glenn-Oates 1967: 15), most of the people in these congregations consider it an unknown language that can be understood only by God and those who have been inspired by him to interpret it (Goodman 1972: 10, 19). This phenomenon is generally explained in two ways by those who practice it. First, it is said to be an indication that the speaker is possessed by the Holy Spirit. This is supported by citing the biblical description of the day of the Pentecost, when Christ's apostles "were all filled with the Holy Spirit and began to speak in other tongues, as the Spirit gave them utterance" (Acts 2: 4, KJV). It is also recognized as a prayer to God, inspired by the Holy Spirit. As described by Paul, "one who speaks in a tongue speaks not to me but to God" (1 Cor. 14: 2, KJV; Goodman 1972: 18).

Church members are expected to speak in tongues and seek to do so after they have been baptized with water. Some do not achieve it immediately but are strongly encouraged to do so by the minister and members of the congregation. Goodman reports that "to drive yet another supplicant into the manifestation is a constantly reenacted communal effort" (1972: 88). The minister urges the importance of this behavior in his sermons, as when one preacher encouraged his followers to "just let it happen." Goodman observed two women guiding a third, saying, "Jesus wants you: open your mouth. ... Let him come to you" (ibid.: 91). She notes that those who spoke in tongues, especially for the first time, exhibited such signs of emotional intensity as profuse sweating, crying, rapid breathing, goose pimples, trembling and spasms, and unusual body movements: some fell to the floor, others became stiff and rigid (ibid.: 58–59). To a witness, these signs along with the seemingly miraculous acquisition of a strange language can be quite impressive. One man, writing in *Voice,* a periodical devoted to the subject of glossolalia, claimed that the miracle of others speaking in tongues was so overwhelming that he became instantly convinced of the value of their religion: "This is what I want, I told myself, I want to experience God!" (Samarin 1972: 77–78).

The experience of speaking in tongues is said to have "joyful" effects. A typical comment from one of Goodman's informants: "Afterward I felt strong, and well, and all my problems were forgotten" (1972: 29). More important, however, it is seen as the cause of a major change in behavior. All the individuals questioned by Goodman agreed that their accomplishment of this practice changed their lives for the better: "[N]ow I am saved, and my life is very different" (ibid.: 25). Indeed, Pentecostals everywhere credit glossolalia with curing alcoholism, mental problems, immorality, marital difficulties, and even physiological disease (Stagg, Henson, and Glenn-Oates 1967: 16). One of Goodman's informants, Felipe, reports that he was able to stop smoking (which cured his asthma), drinking, and throwing his money away (1972: 45–47). Emilio was a young man who often got drunk and ended up sleeping on the streets or lost all his money playing cards, but all of this changed (ibid.: 48–49). The minister of the church in Utzpac, after living "a bad life, with smoking and drinking, and drugs, and women, well, just everything that you can imagine," and after losing all of his property in an illegal business deal, changed his ways, eventually becoming a minister (ibid.: 41–42).

Linguists who have studied the utterances of glossolalia have universally concluded that they are not a human language, known or unknown. According to Samarin, who studied glossolalia in a number of countries:

> In every case, glossolalia turns out to be linguistic nonsense. A person filled by the Holy Spirit does not speak a foreign human tongue, although glossolalists believe that it is the language of angels. ... Glossolalia consists of strings of meaningless syllables made up of sounds taken from those familiar to the speaker and put together more or less haphazardly. (Ibid.: 49–50)

Thus, the phenomenon to be explained in regard to glossolalia is not the acquisition of a foreign tongue. Rather, we must ask what influences individuals to perform in this way, and why such behavior is accepted as being the consequence of supernatural influence. What are the identifiable effects of such a claim and behavior that influence individuals to encourage it in others and seek to exhibit it themselves?

Some psychologists have suggested that glossolalia occurs as the result of an abnormal psychological state in the speaker, either because of his or her peculiar personality, a particular psychological problem, or because the person is in an altered state of consciousness, such as trance, hypnosis, or hysteria (Samarin

1972). Although Goodman argues that glossolalia always occurs in a trance state (1972: 59), other researchers have found little evidence to support this; many of those who speak in tongues can do it in what appears to be a normal state (Jaquith 1967; Samarin 1972). Furthermore, there seems to be no support for the suggestion that glossolalists have any sort of distinctive psychological problems. Samarin claims that "there is, in fact, no evidence whatsoever to suggest—Zlet alone prove—that glossolalists are all of a single psychological type and that this personality of [theirs] predisposes ... them to speak in tongues" (1972: 79). In addition, even if glossolalia could be shown to be associated with some peculiar psychological condition, that fact could not explain why it is actively encouraged in some churches, why it is attributed to supernatural influence, and why it appears to be associated with profound changes in secular behavior.

Goodman has suggested that one reason glossolalia is encouraged is that it unites the members of the congregation: "[It] is the single most powerful cohesive factor of the group" (1972: 88). She says that the congregation unites in its efforts to encourage new members to speak in tongues, and that the practice distinguishes them from other members of the community. She claims that precisely because glossolalia makes the church members a subject of ridicule to outsiders, it serves the purpose of uniting them especially well. Yet it is difficult to see why the members should want to alienate outsiders, especially when they are trying to attract outsiders to their congregation. Further, this explanation does not account for glossolalia itself; anything distinctive could serve as well.

The behavior of speaking in tongues has two aspects. First, to a naive audience it does seem extraordinary. Anyone who has tried to learn a foreign language knows that speaking one is not an easily acquired skill; a person who does so after a year or two of study would be unusual. A person who would speak such a language spontaneously would be extraordinary indeed. He or she would appear to do something a person cannot accomplish by his or her own efforts. It would be miraculous.

A second feature of the glossolalist's performance is that it often exhibits an emotional intensity and apparent lack of conscious control. That is especially true of a convert's initial experience with it. As Goodman reports, the person may sweat, faint, even have convulsions, and appear as if hypnotized or in a trance. He or she is said to be under the influence of something outside of him or herself. The person is said to be possessed by the Holy Spirit.

Although it cannot be verified that a person speaking in tongues is under the influence of something supernatural, his or her behavior can be shown to influence, and be influenced by, living humans. Speaking in tongues occurs regularly in response to the encouragement by the preacher and members of the congregation. By his or her performance, the glossolalist demonstrates acceptance of this influence, while the intensity and sincerity of the behavior communicates the intensity of the person's acceptance. By standing before others and speaking in tongues, an individual publicly communicates a commitment to those encouraging the behavior.

When the audience acknowledges the performance as resulting from the Holy Ghost, they are not only recognizing the person's commitment to them but also accepting that person. A case where the influence of the Holy Ghost was denied illustrates this point: a young man walked into the church for the first time and began speaking in tongues, but he never returned. His behavior was interpreted by the congregation as not being truly inspired by the Holy Ghost, but perhaps even as the work of the Devil (ibid.: 10). Thus, when a person speaking in tongues is not seen as being sincerely committed, that person is not accepted, and the supernatural intervention denied.

Why would some churches, particularly the more stable or conservative, resist, sometimes vehemently, speaking in tongues? We suggest that the members of such churches are not interested in the emotional, intense promise of commitment that glossolalia communicates. They are interested in protecting and renewing their existing social relationships, not in establishing new ones at the expense of the old. Dramatic responsiveness such as speaking in tongues and falling down possessed should tend to be encouraged only between those who are strongly interested in creating immediate social relationships; an intense, sincere promise is better than nothing. Indeed, such promises may eventually lead to stable social relationships, a result that now characterizes many established cults or churches, such as the Methodists, which also originally were strongly "emotional."

Confession

Among the activities of the Inuit and Ndembu shamans described in the chapter on shamanism (Chapter Seven) was the encouragement of confession. Let us briefly examine this phenomenon, and the reason why Pope John Paul I, in a letter to his mother, cited the proverb "A sin confessed is half forgiven" (United Press International, September 2, 1978).

Confession is usually explained as being the result of a desire on the part of the confessor to express or vitiate his or her guilt, thereby enhancing the sense of well-being. But it is important to keep in mind that guilt, literally, is the fact of having committed a wrong, and confession, literally the acknowledgement of that wrong. Because a crime cannot be undone, therefore, actual guilt can be neither modified nor eliminated, and hence, confession cannot be explained by its reduction of actual guilt. Confession can, however, influence the consequences of a crime or sin.

The two important questions in regard to confession are, Why do people encourage it, and why do people confess? The most palpable effect of a sin, crime, or wrong is on social relationships. Although a sin may be defined as a crime against God, its identifiable effect is against the living. Both ancestors and communities depend on social relationships and hence discourage behavior that threatens them.

Confession has several important consequences. As noted earlier, Rasmussen (1972) recognized for the Inuit that "much comes to light that no one had ever dreamed of"; by exposing his or her crime, the confessor makes it difficult to continue it. Those who become aware of his or her past crime are likely to be suspicious of any future behavior that could be associated with that crime. In addition, confession invariably carries with it a promise to desist; if the crime were repeated, therefore, it would include a broken promise. Confession reduces crime and thereby benefits the community, and to the extent it consists of codescendants, it benefits their ancestors. However, as Pope John Paul I implied, the encouragement of confession carries with it the obligation to forgive, or more accurately, to reduce the punishment, for confession must be made appealing to the offender. If some forgiveness were not implied, an individual who confessed would be exposed to the same punishment that he or she would receive were that person caught. The reason why confession may reduce anxiety is not that it reduces guilt but that it reduces punishment, which can range from slight disapproval to death.

Thus, confession obligates: it obliges the encourager to forgive and the confessor to desist. And both parties gain: the likelihood of that offense being continued is reduced, and the confessor to some degree vitiates the reaction to the crime. However, both also lose: the confessor cannot so easily continue the crime, for others will remember it, and, because punishment must be reduced, the intimidation achieved by punishment is also reduced. The sources of confession lie in the interest of individuals: (1) to reduce the behavior of others that threatens them and their social relationships, and (2) to diminish the negative reaction against the guilty ones for their own crimes. The overall effect of confession is to promote social behavior and its consequent relationships.

Conclusion

The fundamental question in regard to religious phenomena is what the supernatural claim—the religious metaphor—adds to a message. In regard to cults, the question is, What does it add to the social relationships between leader and follower, and between cofollowers?

Because a supernatural claim is not verifiable by the senses, it is not subject to revision by the senses. It therefore forces the potential follower either to accept or to reject the prophet's message in total; it cannot be accepted as only partially true. When it is written down, it is even more resistant to modification. Fourteen hundred years after Muhammad, two thousand years after Jesus, and thirty-five hundred years after Moses, their extant messages remain more or less intact. There may be new interpretations, but so long as the original message remains accessible, every interpretation remains vulnerable to it. This prevents new or popular knowledge from being used casually to modify the prophet's message. When a new "supernatural" message is accepted, the enunciator is accepted as a new prophet: Jesus' modification of Moses and the other prophets, Muhammad's modification of Jesus and Moses, Joseph Smith's and John Wesley's modification of Jesus, and so on. For new religious claims to be accepted, their authority, apparently, must be accepted as divine.

The reason why religious groups tend to create deeper, more enduring social relationships than are found in other social groups is that the relationships created are like those between kin in a family: they are based on trust, commitment, and the unquestioning acceptance of their prophet's or ancestor's parental-like guidance.

Chapter 13

Conclusion

Social behavior, including cooperation, is the basis of all social relationships and the transmission of traditions. Such behavior is a product both of genes and the environment (including the behavior of others, especially ancestors and codescendants). Cooperative relationships, while precious, are fragile and must be continuously encouraged and protected. Because of the importance of extensive cooperation to the human descendant-leaving strategy, human ancestors regularly encourage cooperation among their descendants. Religion, as part of this strategy, is objectively characterized not by belief but by cooperation based on the communicated acceptance of supernatural claims. Religious behavior is *aimed* at encouraging future cooperation between the participants.

Our argument has been that the various kinds of religious behavior are aimed at encouraging social behavior. This includes cooperation, and the relationships resulting from it, among followers in certain specific ways. This is achieved by the nonskeptical acceptance of another person's influence, the encouragement of respect for ancestors, and the metaphorical extension of kinship. Additionally, it can be achieved by the communication through magic of care, anger, and desire; and by the reduction of acrimony in decision-making, the acceptance of "supernatural" claims of evilness, the communication of suffering, the vicarious influence on descendants through stories, and by claims of the existence of a Creator God and supernatural humans.

Apparently, all the activities discussed in this book associated with supernatural claims can also occur without such claims. Children regularly accept the influence of their parents without skepticism. Respect for dead ancestors can be encouraged without a supernatural claim. Modern sporting teams often identify themselves with an animal. Football coaches are hanged in effigy, and pictures of political leaders are burned without associated supernatural claims. People send "get well" cards, a coin flip can be used to make a decision, and political leaders usually are said to be only extraordinary. Individuals are often criticized unfairly, without "supernatural" allegations of evilness. Taboo, sacrifice, and pain can be urged and accepted without accompanying supernatural justifications, and traditional stories need not contain supernatural elements.

The essential question in regard to the study of religion is what accounts for the religious behavior—specifically, what accounts for the communicated acceptance of another person's supernatural claim? The argument of this book is that the distinctive feature of such acceptance is that it communicates a willingness to accept another person's influence nonskeptically. We have proposed that the important effect of this acceptance is that it helps to create enduring, family-like cooperation between family and nonfamily members alike. The communicated denial that a religious claim is metaphor is a fundamental aspect of this communication of nonskepticism.

The transmission of both traditions and social relationships depends on the acceptance of authority. Perhaps all authority depends to some degree on nonskeptical acceptance. Furthermore, all authority may be fundamentally parental; certainly, a "close" kinship idiom often seems to be used.

Parental guidance and its acceptance is not only widespread, it is crucial to human descendant-leaving success. To some extent, a parent-child relationship always includes nonskeptical acceptance. Religion, like no other behavior, through the explicit communication of nonskeptical acceptance, communicates the acceptance of authority, for religious behavior communicates commitment. Furthermore, when a common authority is accepted—a parent, leader, or prophet—enduring, important cooperation between the coacceptors is always encouraged. In addition, a parent who communicates his or her own acceptance of ancestors also encourages such acceptance in his or her descendants—filial piety can be traditional. Likewise, a prophet often encourages such acceptance among followers by claiming that he or she is merely obeying God, their "father" (or "mother"), who would be their ultimate ancestor.

To study anything requires the critical and independent use of the senses, and hence skepticism, but religion is distinguished by activities that discourage skepticism. The word skepticism comes from a Greek word meaning "to look" or "to look out," and implies a doubting or questioning attitude. A skeptic is one who independently doubts the validity of what is claimed to be knowledge, and hence, includes seekers of truth. Doubting, however, threatens cooperation. Martin Luther accordingly wrote: *Quia est auditu fides, non ex visu* ("Faith comes from listening, not from looking") (Erikson 1962: 207).

Yet both knowledge, which is based on the senses (and hence on skepticism), and cooperation are of fundamental importance in the acquisition of traditions. Social learning involves both sensory discrimination and the acceptance of the influence of others. For mammals, close kinship cooperation is influenced by the actual memory of particular experiences of the behavior of others: how one was mothered, for example, influences how one mothers. The cooperation between parent and child is the basis not only of traditions in general but, most important, of those traditions that help to create such cooperation.

Because of the fundamental importance of cooperation, statements made by others are virtually always evaluated in regard to their likely effect on social behavior and, hence, social relationships. Such evaluation can lead to apparently true statements being rejected (like those of Galileo, as well as those of modern evolutionary theory), and patently false statements being accepted (like those made by racists). Given the importance of cooperation, this continuous evaluation of the social consequences of statements, regardless of their truth, is understandable, but also a major impediment in the study of humans. Indeed, paradoxically, science itself is characterized by enduring cooperation between scientists, whose cooperation is aimed explicitly at increasing knowledge based on their skepticism of one another's claims.

Religious statements distinguished by claims whose truth must not be assessed by the senses cannot be shown to be literally true. The meaning of such statements therefore does not depend on their literal truth or their verifiability. If such statements are meaningful, and not seen simply as incorrect or lies, they must refer to something other than their literal referents. Recall that a metaphor is identified as a statement (1) that is not true according to the senses, and (2) that is responded to as if it were a simile.

By that standard, religious statements can be shown to be metaphorical. Religious claims, on the basis of the senses, are not literally true. At the same time, they are not responded to as if they were a lie. They are accepted *as if* they were true, and thus as a simile. That they are accepted as a simile is identified by the response to them. When people claim to be actual kangaroos, for example, and yet continue to behave like humans, we identify such a claim as metaphor. The difference between religious and ordinary metaphor lies in the response: religious metaphor is said to be literally true—that it is not metaphor. Based on the skeptical use of our senses, however, religion remains identifiably metaphorical.

Whether or not religious statements are in some unidentifiable way "true," those who accept them identifiably respond to the behavior of others and, hence, to the social consequences of those statements. Although religious statements cannot demonstrably be shown to reflect beliefs, they can be shown to influence behavior.

The crucial problem in the study of religion is the significance of communicating acceptance of religious metaphor. Most anthropologists have concluded that religious statements are consequences of beliefs, that they literally reflect beliefs—that religious statements, in a word, are not metaphorical: Australian Aboriginal peoples are said to speak of being kangaroos, wombats, koalas, and so on, because they *believe* they are. Magicians, diviners, and their audiences really *believe* their techniques work; prophets and their followers really *believe* the prophet is divine and immortal; Catholics really *believe* they are consuming the body and blood of Jesus weekly at communion. The identifiable evidence offered for such conclusions, however, is virtually always limited to claims made by the people themselves. Indeed, what other basis could there be for such a conclusion? But a moment's reflection leads to the opposite conclusion, for their identifiable behavior and appearance belie such claims. If people failed to distinguish kangaroos from humans, communication from techniques that physically/mechanically work, bread and wine from flesh and blood, they would not long survive. On the basis of the senses, the objects consumed at communion, identifiable both to the participant and the outside observer, remain food and drink—it is religious statements alone that distinguish bread and wine as the blood and body of Jesus. The sense organs of Catholics and Australian Aboriginal peoples do not differ from those of "nonbelievers."

What we have tried to do in this book is to identify explicitly what individuals are implicitly discriminating and responding to in regard to religious behavior. What people discriminate and respond to can be identified, despite their unwillingness or lack of ability to state explicitly their own true motivations. Indeed, it is the failure of humans to explain their behavior that justifies the very existence of social science. Statements are messages aimed at influencing other people; we cannot logically assume that any statement necessarily reflects or expresses a particular motivation or belief. Motivations must not be assumed. The task of social scientists is to account for human behavior, including communicative behavior, by identifying the influences that cause it, not by merely asserting them. One important influence involved in human communication is the identified and remembered effects on receivers. Another is selection continuously working through time on the inheritable elements involved in the communication.

Common Religious Similes

Let us conclude by discussing some of the similes implied by the metaphors frequently found in religious behavior. The fundamental simile underlying religion itself (defined as the communicated acceptance of another person's "supernatural" claim) seems to be the acceptance of the influence of the shaman/prophet/priest voicing the claim as if he or she were the ancestor's true representative. Deceased ancestors and ancestral gods, as just discussed, are treated like living ancestors, to some extent.

A creator God is the first ancestor and often the source of everything important to his descendants, including geographical features, domestic and wild animals, and so on. But most important, he created one's kinsmen and traditions. When he is said to be directly involved in human conception, all humans become his "offspring"—they become one "blood"—and hence are "siblings." Defying kin or traditions, therefore, defies the ancestral God, and defying God is to defy traditions and kinsmen. A creator God is a metaphor for a dead ancestor, itself a metaphor for a living ancestor, the identifiable source of both traditions and kin. Thus, the alleged messages of a creator God should be accepted *like* those of a dead ancestor, whose influence should be accepted *like* that of a living ancestor.

A closely related phenomenon is the soul. Apparently, in every society individuals speak of human souls. The soul is that part of life said to continue to live after death. It is, therefore, that part of an obviously dead ancestor that is lifelike in being both influential and influenceable. Everyone at birth is a potential ancestor and, hence, allegedly influential after death; everyone therefore has a soul. The metaphor "soul" communicates a simile for life—it is as if that individual were still alive (even though he or she is dead), and is therefore influenceable and can influence.

Ancestor worship, as a religious activity, is distinguished by the claim that, although dead, ancestors retain their interest in their living descendants. The minimal difference between this metaphor and a statement that can be literally true is the use of the present rather than the past tense. In other words, the ancestors "are" still interested rather than "were" or "would have been." That part of the dead ancestor said to be influenceable and influential is his or her soul, since, obviously, it is not his or her bones that remain, or his or her flesh and blood, which would have decomposed. Ancestor worship implies the soul.

The importance to all humans of cooperation with ancestors is basic to their acquisition of traditions and the establishment of their most important social relationships—that between kinsmen. Respect for dead ancestors itself depends on respect for living ancestors. A ritual elaboration communicating respect for remote ancestors (who thereby link individuals to many codescendants), combined with a metaphor asserting the continued interest of those dead ancestors in their descendants, is all that is necessary for the existence of ancestor worship. Ancestor worship, in view of its ubiquity and its concern with souls (as Tylor and Spencer have argued), may be as good a candidate as any for the original religion. Spirits (or spiritual beings), either good or evil, are anthropomorphic. Hence, metaphors referring to them represent good and evil human beings—particularly their cooperative and socially destructive actions. In other words, spirits represent—are like—living humans in certain respects.

The totem metaphor simply embellishes social (meaning kinship, in the strict sense) relationships by evoking an association between individuals and their totem animal or plant. By adding another dimension to social relationships, such embellishment makes the social relationships themselves more attractive, interesting, and salient. It also emphasizes the uniqueness or distinctiveness of a set of codescendants, as if they were a separate species.

The similes underlying the various techniques and metaphors of magic are that the communications are like killing, loving, curing, hating, or supporting an individual. They communicate a willingness to do those things. The simile of the divination metaphor is that the future or secret divined by the various techniques is like knowledge and can therefore be used to make successful decisions. For example, the Hewa sometimes use divination to determine whether someone who lies dying has been "eaten" by a *pisai* (witch). They first ask the suffering person who the *pisai* was, suggesting names, until the person responds affirmatively. If the person does not, they put a bundle of leaves on his or her chest that is then used to divine the alleged cannibal. In either case, the means of decision-making require collusion, thus promoting cooperation in their decision to kill the alleged *pisai*.

The witch is only like evil; he or she only symbolizes it. The accusation requires widespread acceptance before it is acted upon. The identifiable "evilness" is an actual threat to the accusers' social relationships and hierarchy.

The "supernatural" metaphors involved in suffering (taboo, pain, or sacrifice) are usually described as requirements coming from God, or the ancestors, who are said to want their descendants to suffer in particular ways. The Hewa avoid eating mushrooms and sexual intercourse for six days after eating wild pig, abstain from drinking water from sunrise to sunset during certain rituals, and refrain from sitting down the entire night when dancing for others as a sacrifice to their ancestors. Because gods/ancestors metaphorically represent living ancestors, the effect of such acceptance is to encourage their "descendants" to suffer for living ancestors and their codescendants.

The claim that prophets and shamans are themselves supernatural is a metaphor whose simile encourages the acceptance of their influence as if they themselves were living ancestors. The Hewa are an example of a society with only informal shamans, individuals who informally claim to speak for the ancestors more often than others. These are the individuals who tend to have the most influence when applying traditional supernatural claims (such as stories about *pisai* causing death) to a specific current situation (such as the death of an elderly man). Hence, their role as interpreters of tradition can have serious and far-reaching consequences. When a claim is that the first ancestor created all peoples, and not just a tribe, it follows that all peoples are codescendants—that they are "brothers"—and should accept the prophet and act accordingly. This is the basis for conversion. Claims of death and rebirth—of shamans, prophets, initiates, and followers (including reborn Christians)—encourage these new kinshiplike relationships.

The fundamental simile of myth is that it is like actual experiences. Through these vicarious experiences the audience acquires social knowledge. The Hewa tell traditional stories about *pisai,* and as we have seen, such stories profoundly influence the behavior of Hewa in ways that have life-and-death consequences, for many generations.

The meanings of the words "truth," "knowledge," and "reality" in religious contexts are also usually metaphorical, for religious statements are distinguished by their inability to be shown to be true. The purpose of using claims of truth, knowledge, and reality, in association with supernatural claims, must be to encourage the listeners to accept the religious claims *as if* they were objectively true statements or actual knowledge and, then, to act as if they were true (to some extent).

The acceptance of any metaphor depends on (and hence, encourages) collusion, for it is a statement that is not discernibly true. Explicitly stating that a metaphor is a metaphor destroys it, and hence, its communicative power, for it then becomes merely a simile. To "believers" (followers, acceptors), therefore, it is crucial that the identification of religious statements as metaphor be denied, for the basis of their cooperation with one another is the explicit acceptance of such claims as literally true—as nonmetaphorical.

Conclusion

In these pages we have attempted to demonstrate that our knowledge of religion—indeed of any human activity—can be increased significantly if analysis is restricted to what is identifiable, particularly behavior and its consequences. The most important consequences are, first, those likely to be identified and remembered by the people themselves, and, second, those that influence descendant-leaving success. This book represents only an initial attempt to discover the relationship between traditions, cooperation, and descendant-leaving success. The subject matter of social science is already traditions and social relationships. A significant increase in the understanding of humans can be expected if social scientists were to restrict their study severely to what is identifiable by the senses, analyze the complex relationship between traditions and cooperation, and discover their descendant-leaving consequences. We must seek to identify those environments that favor or disfavor the descendant-leaving success of particular activities. The study of humans will then begin to reveal our distinctive natures.

If the argument presented in this book is accepted in principle, an important consequence follows. The wellspring of human behavior is not what social scientists in the past have led us to assume. Humans are not fundamentally selfish, egotistical beings with hedonistic appetites. Nor are they group-preserving saints. The distinctive nature of humans, the way in which humans have successfully left descendants for millennia, includes complex and specific cooperation with personally identified and remembered individuals. Social relationships are consequences of that cooperation.

This finally brings us to the question of whether religious behavior is good or bad. Such value judgments are not implied by explanations about how the world is, but legitimately rest on our evaluation of the consequences of a behavior (see Wright 1994: 386). Our interest was initially drawn to religion because of the "bad" consequences of an innocent woman being killed. However, our attempts to explain that behavior drew our attention to the "good" consequences of religious behavior: increased cooperation among coacceptors of supernatural claims. Similarly, in modern religions, sacrificing for the defense of one's own religious group or hierarchy may be at the expense of other religions, other people and their hierarchies. Not surprisingly, recent authors who focus on only one of these two consequences of religious behavior have come to quite different conclusions about whether religion is good or bad. David Sloan Wilson (2002), for example, focusing on the cooperative social relationships *among* individuals resulting from religious behavior, sees religion as good. Richard Dawkins (1998; 2006), on the other hand, focusing on the consequences of the sacrifices encouraged by religion for individuals who *don't communicate acceptance of the same supernatural claims* (for example, the victims of suicide bombers), condemns religion as something that needs to be eradicated. Each of these claims has a point, because what is seen as moral from the "inside" may be seen as immoral from the "outside." A similar difference would be found in the opinions of members of the two Hewa households in regard to the killing of the "witch."

Religion has been used to encourage all kinds of behavior that is not itself religious, including war, charity, feasts, and countless ceremonies and holidays. What we have attempted to do in this book is to identify the effect of religious behavior per se that has led to its being selected for: sacrifice that creates and maintains a religious hierarchy and its consequent social behavior, including cooperation among cofollowers. Such sacrifice is an extension of the behavior found regularly among close kinsmen. We leave it to others to decide whether the consequences of religious behavior are desirable.

References

Albanese, C. L. 1981. *American Religions and Religion.* Belmont, CA: Wadsworth.

Alexander, R. D. 1979. *Darwinism and Human Affairs.* Seattle: University of Washington Press.

———. 1987. *The Biology of Moral Systems.* New York: Aldine de Gruyter.

Arensberg, C. 1968. *The Irish Countryman.* Garden City, NY: Natural History Press.

Aristotle. 1954. *The Rhetoric and the Poetics,* trans. W. Rhys Roberts and I. Bywater. New York: Random House.

Armstrong, K. 2001. *Buddha.* New York: Penguin.

Asad, T. 1983. "Anthropological Conceptions of Religion: Reflections on Geertz." *Man* 18(2): 237–59.

Ashbrook, J. B., and C. R. Albright. 1997. *The Humanizing Brain: Where Religion and Neuroscience Meet.* Cleveland, OH: Pilgrim Press.

Atran, S. 2002. *In Gods We Trust: The Evolutionary Landscape of Religion.* New York: Oxford University Press.

Avital, E., and E. Jablonka. 2001. *Animal Traditions: Behavioural Inheritance and Evolution.* Cambridge, UK: Cambridge University Press.

Balicki, A. 1967. "Shamanistic Behavior among the Netsilik Eskimo." In J. Middleton, ed., *Magic, Witchcraft, and Curing.* New York: Natural History Press.

Baron, R. A., and D. Byrne. 1977. *Social Psychology.* Boston: Allyn and Bacon.

Barrett, J. L. 2000. "Exploring the Natural Foundations of Religion." *Trends in Cognitive Sciences* 4(1): 29–34.

———. 2004. *Why Would Anyone Believe in God?* Walnut Creek, CA: AltaMira Press.

Barth, F. 1987. *Cosmologies in the Making.* Cambridge, UK: Cambridge University Press.

Bellah, R. N. 1964. "Religious Evolution." *American Sociological Review* 29: 258–374.

Benson, S. 1977. "Supernatural as a Western Category." *Ethos* 5: 31–53.

Berger, P. L. 1974. "Some Second Thoughts on Substantive versus Functional Definitions of Religion." *Journal for the Scientific Study of Religion* 13(2): 125–34.

Bichmann, W. 1979. "Primary Health Care and Traditional Medicine: Considering the Background of Changing Health Care Concepts in Africa." *Social Science and Medicine* 13: 175–82.

Blackmore, S. 1999. *The Meme Machine.* Oxford, UK: Oxford University Press.

Bloch, M. 2002. "Are Religious Beliefs Counterintuitive?" In N. K. Frankenberry, ed., *Radical Interpretation in Religion,* 129–46. Cambridge, UK: Cambridge University Press.

Blume, M. 2007. "The Reproductive Benefits of Religiosity: Empirical Findings of Religion, Reproduction, and Female Choice Towards a Sociobiology of Religion." Paper presented at International Conference on the Biological Evolution of Religiosity, Hanse-Wissenschaftskolleg Delmenhorst, Germany, September 28–October 1, 2007.

Boas, F. 1930. *The Religion of the Kwakiutl Indians,* Part II, *Translations.* New York: Columbia University Press.

———. 1964. *The Central Eskimo.* Lincoln: University of Nebraska Press. (First published in 1888).

Bouchard, T. 2007. "Religiousness, Authoritarianism, and Conservatism: A Psychometric/Quantitative Genetic Approach to the Explanation for Their Universality and Their Evolution." Paper presented at International Conference on the Biological Evolution of Religiosity, Hanse-Wissenschaftskolleg Delmenhorst, Germany, September 28–October 1, 2007.

Bourguignon, E. 1976. *Possession.* San Francisco: Chandler and Sharp.

Bowra, M. 1944. *Sophoclean Tragedy.* Oxford, UK: Clarendon Press.

Boyd, R., and P. Richerson. 1985. *Culture and Evolutionary Process.* Chicago: University of Chicago Press.

Boyer, P. 1996. "What Makes Anthropomorphism Natural: Intuitive Ontology and Cultural Representations." *Journal of the Royal Anthropological Institute* 2: 283–97.

———. 2001. *Religion Explained: The Evolutionary Origins of Religious Thought.* New York: Basic Books.

Boyer, P., and S. Nissenbaum. 1974. *Salem Possessed.* Cambridge, MA: Harvard University Press.

Briggs, R. 1996. *Witches and Neighbours: The Social and Cultural Context of European Witchcraft.* London: HarperCollins.

Brown, D. 1991. *Human Universals.* New York: McGraw-Hill.

Brown, M. F. 1993. "Dark Side of the Shaman." In A. C. Lehmann and J. E. Myers, eds., *Magic, Witchcraft, and Religion,* 3d ed. Mountain View, CA: Mayfield.

Bulbulia, J. 2004. "Religious Costs as Adaptations That Signal Altruistic Intention." *Evolution and Cognition* 10: 19–42.

Burkert, W. 1996. *Creation of the Sacred: Tracks of Biology in Early Religions.* Cambridge, MA: Harvard University Press.

Burridge, K. O. L. 1967. "Levi-Strauss and Myth." In E. Leach, ed., *The Structural Study of Myth and Totemism*. London: Tavistock.

Campbell, D. T. 1975. "On the Conflicts between Biological and Social Evolution and between Psychology and Moral Tradition." *American Psychologist* 30: 1103–26.

———. 1991. "A Naturalistic Theory of Archaic Moral Orders." *Zygon* 26: 91–114.

Cannon, W. B. 1942. "'Voodoo' Death." *American Anthropologist* 44: 169–81.

Caporael, L. R. 1976. "Ergotism: The Satan Loosed in Salem?" *Science* 192: 21–26.

Castro, L., and M. A. Toro. 2004. "The Evolution of Culture: From Primate Social Learning to Human Culture." *Proceedings of the National Academy of Sciences* 101(27): 10235–40.

Chagnon, N. 1983. *Yąnomamö: The Fierce People,* 3d ed. New York: Holt, Rinehart, and Winston.

Cicero, M. T. 1950. *De Divinatione: Brutus on the Nature of Gods, on Divination, on Duties,* trans. H. M. Poteat. Chicago: University of Chicago Press. (First published in 44 B.C.).

Coe, K. 2003. *The Ancestress Hypothesis: Visual Art as Adaptation*. New Brunswick, NJ: Rutgers University Press.

Coe, K., N. Aiken, and C. T. Palmer. 2006. "Once upon a Time: Ancestors and the Evolutionary Significance of Stories." *Anthropological Forum* 16(1): 21–40.

Coe, K., and C. T. Palmer. 2007. "The Words of Our Ancestors: Kinship, Tradition, and Moral Codes." *World Cultures* 16(1): 2–32.

Cohn, N. 1970. "The Myth of Satan and His Human Servants." In M. Douglas, ed., *Witchcraft, Confessions, and Accusations*. London: Tavistock.

Cohn, W. 1962. "Is Religion Universal? Problems of Definition." *Journal for the Scientific Study of Religion* 2(1): 25–32.

Cotterell, A. 1980. *A Dictionary of World Mythology*. New York: G. P. Putnam's Sons.

Crapanzano, V., and V. Garrison. 1977. *Case Studies in Spirit Possession*. New York: John Wiley and Sons.

Darwin, C. 1871. *The Descent of Man, and Selection in Relation to Sex*. Princeton, NJ: Princeton University Press. (Reprinted in 1981).

———. 1994. *The Origin of Species by Means of Natural Selection*. London: Senate. (First published in 1859).

Davies, R. E. 1963. *Methodism*. Harmondsworth, UK: Penguin.

Dawkins, R. 1976. *The Selfish Gene*. Oxford, UK: Oxford University Press.

———. 1998. "The Emptiness of Theology." *Free Inquiry* 18(2): 6.

———. 2006. *The God Delusion*. New York: Houghton Mifflin.

Dennett, D. 1995. *Darwin's Dangerous Idea*. New York: Simon and Schuster.

———. 2006. *Breaking the Spell: Religion as a Natural Phenomenon*. New York: Viking.

De Rios, M. D. 1984. *Hallucinogens in Cross-Cultural Perspective.* Albuquerque: University of New Mexico Press.

Diamond, J. 1978. "The Tasmanian." *Nature* 273: 185–86.

Dodds, E. R. 1968. "On Misunderstanding the *Oedipus Rex.*" In M. O'Brien, ed., *Twentieth-Century Interpretations of* Oedipus Rex. Englewood Cliffs, NJ: Prentice-Hall.

Douglas, M. 1966. *Purity and Danger.* London: Routledge and Kegan Paul.

———. 1967. "The Meaning of Myth." In E. Leach, ed., *The Structural Study of Myth and Totemism.* London: Tavistock.

———. 1968. "Pollution." In D. L. Sills, ed., *The International Encyclopedia of the Social Sciences,* 12: 336–41. New York: Crowell, Collier, and Macmillan.

———. 1970. "Introduction." In M. Douglas, ed., *Witchcraft, Confessions, and Accusations.* London: Tavistock.

———. 1975. "Heathen Darkness." In M. Douglas, ed., *Implicit Meanings.* London: Routledge and Kegan Paul.

Douglas, S. 1978. *Wizard of the Four Winds.* New York: Free Press.

Dove, M. R. 1993. "Uncertainty, Humility, and Adaptation in the Tropical Forest: The Agricultural Augury of the Kantu." *Ethnology* 40(2): 145–67.

———. 1996. "Process versus Product in Bornean Augury: A Traditional Knowledge System's Solution to the Problem of Knowing." In R. Ellen and K. Fukui, eds., *Redefining Nature: Ecology, Culture and Domestication.* Oxford: Berg.

Dundes, A. 1962. "Creation of the 'Mythopoeic Male.'" *American Anthropologist* 64(5): Part 1.

Durkheim, E. 1961. *The Elementary Forms of the Religious Life.* New York: Collier. (First published in 1912).

Edgerton, R. B. 1993. "A Traditional African Psychiatrist." In A. C. Lehmann and J. E. Myers, eds., *Magic, Witchcraft, and Religion,* 3d ed. Mountain View, CA: Mayfield.

Ehrenberg, V. 1968. "Sophoclean Rulers." In M. O'Brien, ed., *Twentieth-Century Interpretations of* Oedipus Rex. Englewood Cliffs, NJ: Prentice-Hall.

Eickelman, D. F. 1981. *The Middle East: An Anthropological Approach.* Englewood Cliffs, NJ: Prentice-Hall.

Eliade, M. 1964. *Shamanism: Archaic Techniques of Ecstasy,* trans. W. R. Trask. New York: Pantheon Books/Random House.

———. 1987. *The Encyclopedia of Religion.* New York: Macmillan.

Elkin, A. P. 1964. *The Australian Aborigines.* Garden City, NY: Doubleday.

Erasmus, C. J. 1977. *In Search of the Common Good: Utopian Experiments Past and Future.* New York: Free Press/Macmillan.

Erikson, E. H. 1962. *Young Man Luther: A Study in Psychoanalysis and History.* New York: W. W. Norton.

Erikson, K. 1966. *Wayward Puritans: A Study in the Sociology of Deviance.* New York: Wiley.

Evans-Pritchard, E. E. 1937. *Witchcraft, Oracles, and Magic among the Azande.* Oxford, UK: Clarendon Press.

———. 1940. *The Nuer.* Oxford, UK: Clarendon Press.

———. 1965. *Theories of Primitive Religion.* Oxford, UK: Clarendon Press.

Feierman, J. 2006. "The Ethology of Psychiatric Populations II: Darwinian Neuropsychiatry." *Clinical Neuropsychiatry* 3(2): 87–109.

Fernandez, J. W. 1972. "Tabernanthe Iboga." In P. T. Furst, ed., *Flesh of the Gods.* New York: Praeger.

Feuerlicht, R. 1972. *Joe McCarthy and McCarthyism.* New York: McGraw-Hill.

Firth, R. 1964. "Shaman." In J. Gould and W. L. Kolb, eds., *A Dictionary of the Social Sciences.* New York: Free Press.

———. 1972. "Offering and Sacrifice: Problems of Organization." In W. Lessa and E. Z. Vogt, eds., *Reader in Comparative Religion: An Anthropological Approach,* 3d ed. New York: Harper and Row.

Fortes, M. 1945. *The Dynamics of Clanship among the Tallensi.* New York: Oxford University Press.

———. 1949. *The Web of Kinship among the Tallensi.* New York: Oxford University Press.

———. 1976. "An Introductory Comment." In W. H. Newell, ed., *Ancestors.* The Hague: Mouton.

Frazer, J. G. 1951. *The Golden Bough: A Study in Magic and Religion.* New York: Macmillan. (First published in 1922).

———. 1979. "Sympathetic Magic." In W. Lessa and E. Z. Vogt, eds., *Reader in Comparative Religion: An Anthropological Approach,* 4th ed. New York: Harper and Row.

Freeman, D. 1983. *Margaret Mead and Samoa.* Cambridge, MA: Harvard University Press.

Freud, S. 1935. *A General Introduction to Psychoanalysis,* trans. J. Riviere. New York: Liverright.

———. 1950. *Totem and Taboo: Some Points of Agreement between the Mental Lives of Savages and Neurotics.* New York: W. W. Norton. (First published in 1913).

Furst, P. T. 1972. *Flesh of the Gods.* New York: Praeger.

Garrett, W. R. 1974. "Troublesome Transcendence: The Supernatural in the Scientific Study of Religion." *Sociological Analysis* 35(3): 167–80.

Geertz, C. 1960. *The Religion of Java.* New York: Free Press.

———. 1966. "Religion as a Cultural System." In M. Banton, ed., *Anthropological Approaches to Religion.* London: Tavistock.

———. 1973. *The Interpretation of Cultures.* New York: Basic Books.

Geertz, H., and C. Geertz. 1975. *Kinship in Bali.* Chicago: University of Chicago Press.

Gergen, K. J. 1969. *The Psychology of Behavior Exchange.* Reading, MA: Addison-Wesley.

Gibson, A. J. 1961. "Chresmology: A Comparative Study of Oracles." *Kroeber Anthropological Society Papers* 24: 19–37.

Giovannoli, J. 1999. *The Biology of Belief: How Our Biology Biases Our Beliefs and Perceptions.* Rosetta Press.com.

Goodman, F. D. 1972. *Speaking in Tongues.* Chicago: University of Chicago Press.

———. 1988. *Ecstasy, Ritual, and Alternative Reality: Religion in a Pluralistic World.* Bloomington: Indiana University Press.

Goody, J. 1961. "Religion and Ritual: The Definitional Problem." *British Journal of Sociology* 12(2): 142–64.

Gould, T. 1970. *Oedipus the King by Sophocles.* Englewood Cliffs, NJ: Prentice-Hall.

Graves, R. 1978. *The Greek Myths: Volume Two.* Harmondsworth, UK: Penguin.

Grim, J. A. 1983. *The Shaman.* Norman: University of Oklahoma Press.

Guillaume, A. 1955. *The Life of Muhammad: A Translation of Ibn Ishaq's Sirat Rasul Allah.* Oxford, UK: Oxford University Press.

Guthrie, S. 2001. "Rethinking Animism." *Journal of the Royal Anthropological Institute* 7(1): 156–57.

Hahn, R. A. 1973. "Understanding Beliefs: An Essay on the Methodology of the Statement and Analysis of Belief Systems." *Current Anthropology* 14(3): 207–29.

Hall, D., ed. 1991. *Witch-Hunting in Seventeenth-Century New England: A Documentary History, 1638–1692.* Chicago: Northwestern University Press.

Hamilton, W. D. 1964. "The Genetical Evolution of Social Behavior, Parts 1 and 2." *Journal of Theoretical Biology* 7: 1–52.

Harner, M. 1973. *Hallucinogens and Shamanism.* New York: Oxford University Press.

Harris, M. 1974. *Cows, Pigs, Wars, and Witches: The Riddles of Culture.* New York: Random House.

———. 1989. *Our Kind.* New York: HarperCollins.

Hart, C. W. M., A. R. Pilling, and J. Goodale. 1988. *The Tiwi of North Australia.* New York: Holt, Rinehart, and Winston.

Haviland, W. A. 1978. *Anthropology.* New York: Holt, Rinehart, and Winston.

———. 1983. *Cultural Anthropology.* New York: CBS College Publishing.

Haviland, W., H. Prins, D. Walrath, and B. McBride. 2005. *Cultural Anthropology: The Human Challenge,* 11th ed. Belmont, CA: Wadsworth.

Hilty, D. M. 1988. "Religious Belief, Participation, and Consequences: An Exploratory and Confirmatory Analysis." *Journal for the Scientific Study of Religion* 27(2): 243–59.

Hinde, R. A. 1999. *Why Gods Persist: A Scientific Approach to Religion.* London: Routledge.

Hippler, A. 1978. "Culture and Personality Perspective of the Yolngu of

Northeastern Arnhem Land." Part 1, "Early Socialization." *Journal of Psychological Anthropology* 1: 221–44.

Hogbin, I. 1964. *A Guadalcanal Society.* New York: Holt, Rinehart, and Winston.

Horton, R. 1960. "A Definition of Religion and Its Uses." *Journal of the Royal Anthropological Institute* 90(2): 201–26.

Hostetler, J., and G. E. Huntington. 1996. *The Hutterites in North America,* 3d ed. New York: Holt, Rinehart, and Winston.

Howells, W. 1962. *The Heathens: Primitive Man and His Religion.* Garden City, NY: Doubleday. (Reprinted in 1986).

———. 1993. "The Shaman." In A. C. Lehmann and J. E. Myers, eds., *Magic, Witchcraft, and Religion,* 3d ed. Mountain View, CA: Mayfield.

Hulkrantz, A. 1983. "The Concept of the Supernatural in Primal Religion." *History of Religions* 22(3): 231–53.

Hunter, D. E., and P. Whitten. 1976. *Encyclopedia of Anthropology.* New York: Harper and Row.

Irons, W. 2001. "Religion as a Hard-to-Fake Sign of Commitment." In R. M. Neese, ed., *Evolution and the Capacity for Commitment,* 292–309. New York: Russell Sage Foundation.

James, W. 1902. *Varieties of Religious Experience.* London: Fontana Press.

Jaquith, J. R. 1967. "Toward a Typology of Formal Communicative Behaviors: Glossolalia." *Anthropological Linguistics* 9(8): 1-8.

Jebb, R. C. 1904. *The Tragedies of Sophocles.* Freeport, NY: Books for Libraries Press. (Reprinted in 1972).

———. 1966. *The Oedipus Tyrannus of Sophocles.* Cambridge, UK: Cambridge University Press. (First published in 1885).

Judah, J. S. 1974. "The Hare Krishna Movement." In I. Zaretsky and M. Leone, eds., *Religious Movements in Contemporary America.* Princeton, NJ: Princeton University Press.

Keesing, R. M. 1970. "Shrines, Ancestors, and Cognatic Descent: The Kwaio and Tallensi." *American Anthropologist* 72: 755–75.

Kirkpatrick, L. A. 1999. "Towards an Evolutionary Psychology of Religion and Personality." *Journal of Personality* 67: 921–49.

Kirsch, T. G. 2004. "Restaging the Will to Believe: Religious Pluralism, Anti-Syncretism, and the Problem of Belief." *American Anthropologist* 106(4): 699–709.

Kluckhohn, C. 1972. "Myths and Rituals: A General Theory." In W. Lessa and E. Vogt, eds., *Reader in Comparative Religion: An Anthropological Approach,* 3d ed. New York: Harper and Row.

Kluckhohn, C., and D. Leighton. 1962. *The Navajo.* Garden City, NY: Anchor Books/Doubleday.

Knauft, B. M. 1985. *Good Company and Violence.* Berkeley: University of California Press.

230 ✳ References

Kohn, W. 1967. "'Religion' in Nonwestern Cultures." *American Anthropologist* 69(1): 73–76.

Kors, A. C., and E. Peters, eds. 2001. *Witchcraft in Europe, 400–1700: A Documentary History*, 2d ed. Philadelphia: University of Pennsylvania Press.

Kottak, C. P. 1974. *Cultural Anthropology*. New York: Random House.

Kroeber, A. 1952. *The Nature of Culture*. Chicago: University of Chicago Press.

Kuper, H. 1977. "The Swazi: A South African Kingdom." In G. Spindler and L. Spindler, eds., *Cultures around the World: Five Cases*. New York: Holt, Rinehart, and Winston.

La Barre, W. 1972. "Hallucinogens and the Shamanic Origins of Religion." In P. T. Furst, ed., *The Flesh of the Gods*. New York: Praeger.

Leach, E. R. 1966. "Ritualization in Man in Relation to Conceptual and Social Development." *Philosophical Transactions of the Royal Society of London,* Series B, 772(251): 403–8.

———. 1967. "Introduction." In E. Leach, ed., *The Structural Study of Myth and Totemism*. London: Tavistock.

Lee, R. 1984. *The Dobu !Kung*. New York: Holt, Rinehart, and Winston.

Lehmann, A. C., and J. E. Myers. 1993. "Introduction." In A. C. Lehmann and J. E. Myers, eds., *Magic, Witchcraft, and Religion*, 3d ed. Mountain View, CA: Mayfield.

Lessa, W. A., and E. Z. Vogt, eds. 1979. *Reader in Comparative Religion: An Anthropological Approach*, 4th ed. New York: Harper and Row.

Levi-Strauss, C. 1963a. *Structural Anthropology*. New York: Basic Books.

———. 1963b. *Totemism*. Boston: Beacon Press.

———. 1966. *The Savage Mind*. London: Weidenfeld and Nicolson.

Levine, R. 1973. *Culture, Behavior, and Personality*. Chicago: Aldine.

Levinson, D. 1996. *Religion: A Cross-cultural Dictionary*. New York: Oxford University Press.

Levy-Bruhl, L. 1966. *Primitive Mentality*, trans. L. Clare. Boston: Beacon Press. (First published in 1922).

Lewis, I. M. 1971. *Ecstatic Religion*. Harmondsworth, UK: Penguin.

Lowie, R. H. 1935. *The Crow Indians*. New York: Holt, Rinehart, and Winston.

———. 1952. *Primitive Religion*. New York: Crossett and Dunlap.

Luckmann, T. 1967. *The Invisible Religion*. New York: Macmillan.

Luthin, R. 1973. "McCarthy as Demagogue." In Earl Latham, ed., *The Meaning of McCarthyism*. Boston: D. C. Heath.

Machalek, R. 1977. "Definitional Strategies in the Study of Religion." *Journal for the Scientific Study of Religion* 16(4): 395–401.

Maddox, J. L. 1923. *The Medicine Man*. New York: Macmillan.

Mair, L. 1969. *Witchcraft*. New York: McGraw-Hill.

Malinowski, B. 1929. *The Sexual Life of Savages*. New York: Harcourt, Brace.

———. 1931. "Culture." In E. R. Seligman and A. Johnson, eds., *Encyclopedia of the Social Sciences* 4: 634–42.

————. 1954. *Magic, Science, and Religion.* Garden City, NY: Doubleday. (First published in 1948).

————. 1961. *Argonauts of the Western Pacific.* New York: Dutton. (First published in 1922).

Mandelbaum, D. G. 1966. "Transcendental and Pragmatic Aspects of Religion." *American Anthropologist* 68(5): 1174–91.

McClenon, J. 1994. *Wondrous Events: Foundations of Religious Belief.* Philadelphia: University of Pennsylvania Press.

————. 2002. *Wondrous Healing: Shamanism, Human Evolution, and the Origin of Religion.* De Kalb: Northern Illinois University Press.

Middleton, J. 1960. *Lugbara Religion.* Oxford, UK: Oxford University Press.

————. 1966. "The Resolution of Conflict among the Lugbara of Uganda." In M. J. Schwartz, V. Turner, and A. Tuden, eds., *Political Anthropology.* Chicago: Aldine.

Midelfort, H. C. E. 1972. *Witch Hunting in Southwestern Germany, 1562–1684: The Social and Intellectual Foundations.* Palo Alto, CA: Stanford University Press.

Molloy, M. 1999. *Experiencing the World's Religions: Traditions, Challenge, and Change.* Mountain View, CA: Mayfield.

Moody, E. J. 1974. "Magical Therapy: An Anthropological Investigation of Contemporary Satanism." In I. Zaretsky and M. Leone, eds., *Religious Movements in Contemporary America.* Princeton, NJ: Princeton University Press.

Mooney, J. 1965. *The Ghost Dance Religion and the Sioux Outbreak of 1890.* Chicago: University of Chicago Press. (First published in 1896).

Moore, O. K. 1957. "Divination: A New Perspective." *American Anthropologist* 59: 69–74.

Moore, T. 2000. "Placebos, Faith, and Morals: Or Why Religion?" Paper presented at Human Behavior and Evolution Society meeting, Amherst College.

Mullen, P. 1969. "The Function of Magic Folk Beliefs among Texas Coastal Fishermen." *Journal of American Folklore* 82: 214–25.

Murdock, G. 1971. "Anthropology's Mythology." *Journal of the Royal Anthropological Society* (Huxley Memorial Lecture, 1971): 17–21.

Nadel, S. F. 1946. "A Study of Shamanism in the Nuba Mountains." *Journal of the Royal Anthropological Institute* 76(1): 25–37.

————. 1954. *Nupe Religion.* London: Routledge.

————. 1977. "Magic Thinking." *Canberra Anthropology* 1(1): 1–14.

Needham, R. 1972. *Belief, Language, and Experience.* Chicago: University of Chicago Press.

Nelson, L. D. 1986. "Comment on Segal's 'Have the Social Sciences Been Converted?'" *Journal for the Scientific Study of Religion* 25(3): 367–68.

Nesse, R., and A. Lloyd. 1992. "The Evolution of Psychodynamic Mechanisms." In J. Barkow, L. Cosmides, and J. Tooby, eds., *The Adapted Mind.* New York: Oxford University Press.

Newberg, A., E. D'Aquili, and V. Ruse. 2001. *Why God Won't Go Away: Brain Science and the Biology of Belief.* New York: Ballantine.

Nuttin, J. 1975. *The Illusion of Attitude Change.* New York: Academic.

O'Brien, M. J., ed. 1968. *Twentieth Century Interpretations of* Oedipus Rex. Englewood Cliffs, NJ: Prentice-Hall.

Opler, M. E. 1972. "An Interpretation of Ambivalence of Two American Indian Tribes." In W. Lessa and E. Z. Vogt, eds., *Reader in Comparative Religion: An Anthropological Approach,* 3d ed. New York: Harper and Row.

Palmer, C. T. 1989. "The Ritual Taboos of Fishermen: An Alternative Explanation." *Maritime Anthropological Studies* 2(1): 59–68.

Palmer, C. T., B. Fredrickson, and C. Tilley. 1997. "Categories and Gatherings: Group Selection and the Mythology of Cultural Anthropology." *Evolution and Human Behavior* 18: 291–308.

Palmer, C. T., and L. Steadman. 1997. "Human Kinship as a Descendant-Leaving Strategy: A Solution to an Evolutionary Puzzle." *Journal of Social and Evolutionary Systems* 20(1): 39–51.

———. 2004. "With or Without Belief: A New Approach to the Definition and Explanation of Religion." *Evolution and Cognition* 10(1): 138–47.

Palmer, C. T., L. B. Steadman, and C. Cassidy. 2006a. "Traditional Religious Ritual Sacrifice: Cultural Materialism, Costly Signaling, or Descendant-Leaving Strategy?" *Journal of Ritual Studies* 20(2): 33–42.

Palmer, C. T., J. Wright, S. A. Wright, C. Cassidy, T. VanPool, and K. Coe. 2006b. "The Many Manipulations of Morty Mouse: Children's Stories and the Parental Encouragement of Altruism." *Journal of Anthropological Research* 62(2): 235–57.

Park, G. 1967. "Divination and Its Social Contexts." In J. Middleton, ed., *Magic, Witchcraft, and Curing.* Austin: University of Texas Press.

———. 1974. *The Idea of Social Structure.* Garden City, NY: Anchor Books/Doubleday.

Patterson, M. 1974. "Sorcery and Witchcraft in Melanesia." *Oceania* 45(2): 132–60, 212–34.

———. 2000. "Sorcery and Witchcraft." In Raymond Sculpin, ed., *Religion and Culture: An Anthropological Perspective.* Englewood Cliffs, NJ: Prentice-Hall.

Pinker, S. 1997. *How the Mind Works.* New York: W. W. Norton.

Poggie, J. J., Jr., and R. Pollnac. 1988. "Danger and Rituals of Avoidance among New England Fishermen." *Maritime Anthropological Studies* 1(1): 66–78.

Poggie, J. J., Jr., R. Pollnac, and C. Gersuny. 1976. "Risk as a Basis for Taboos among Fishermen in Southern New England." *Journal for the Scientific Study of Religion* 15: 257–62.

Pulliam, H., and C. Dunford. 1980. *Programmed to Learn.* New York: Columbia University Press.

Pyysiainen, I. 2004. *Magic, Miracles, and Religion: A Scientist's Perspective* (Cognitive Science of Religion Series). Walnut Creek, CA: AltaMira Press.

Radcliffe-Brown, A. R. 1931. "The Social Organization of Australian Tribes." *Oceania Monograph* 1. Sydney.

————. 1979. "Taboo" (Frazer Lecture). In W. A. Lessa and E. Z. Vogt, eds., *Reader in Comparative Religion: An Anthropological Approach,* 4th ed. New York: HarperCollins. (First published in 1939).

Radin, P. 1957. *Primitive Religion: Its Nature and Origin.* New York: Dover.

Rappaport, R. 1979. "Ritual, Sanctity, and Cybernetics." In W. A. Lessa and E. Z. Vogt, eds., *Reader in Comparative Religion: An Anthropological Approach,* 4th ed. New York: HarperCollins. (First published in 1971).

Rasmussen, K. 1971. "A Shaman's Journey to the Sea Spirit." In W. Lessa and E. Z. Vogt, eds., *Reader in Comparative Religion: An Anthropological Approach,* 3d ed. New York: Harper and Row.

Read, K. E. 1965. *The High Valley.* New York: Charles Scribner's Sons.

Richerson, P., and R. Boyd. 1989. "The Role of Evolved Predispositions in Cultural Evolution; or, Human Sociobiology Meets Pascal's Wager." *Ethology and Sociobiology* 10: 195–219.

Rogers, E. M. 1983. *Diffusion of Innovations.* New York: Free Press.

Rovere, R. 1973. "McCarthy: An Unfavorable Summary." In E. Latham, ed., *The Meaning of McCarthyism.* Boston: D. C. Heath.

Saler, B. 1973. "Comment." *Current Anthropology* 14(3): 227.

Samarin, W. J. 1972. "Glossolalia." *Psychology Today* 6 (August): 48–50, 77–79.

Sander, E. P. 1993. *The Historical Figure of Jesus.* London: Allen Lane.

Scalise Sugiyama, M. S. 2001. "Food, Foragers, and Folklore: The Role of Narrative in Human Subsistence." *Evolution and Human Behavior* 22(4): 221–40.

Schneider, H. K. 1981. *The Africans: An Ethnological Account.* Englewood Cliffs, NJ: Prentice-Hall.

Schneider, L. 1970. "The Sociology of Religion: Some Areas of Theoretical Potential." *Sociological Analysis* 31(3): 131–45.

Segal, R. A. 1985. "Have the Social Sciences Been Converted?" *Journal for the Scientific Study of Religion* 24(3): 321–24.

Shermer, M. 2002. *Why People Believe Weird Things: Pseudoscience, Superstition, and Other Confusions of Our Time.* New York: Henry Holt.

Shore, B. 1996. *Culture in Mind: Cognition, Culture, and the Problem of Meaning.* New York: Oxford University Press.

Shultes, R. E., and A. Hofmann. 1992. *Plants of the Gods.* Rochester, VT: Healing Arts Press.

Siskind, J. 1973. "Visions and Cures among the Sharanahua." In M. J. Harner, ed., *Hallucinogens and Shamanism.* Oxford: Oxford University Press.

Slotkin, J. S. 1955. "The Peyote Way." *Tomorrow* 4: 64–70.

Smith, E., and R. Bliege Bird. 2000. "Turtle Hunting and Tombstone Opening: Public Generosity as Costly Signalling." *Evolution and Human Behavior* 21(4): 245–62.

Sosis, R. 2000. "Costly Signaling and Torch Fishing on Ifaluk Atoll." *Evolution and Human Behavior* 21(4): 223–44.

Sosis, R., and C. Alcorta. 2003. "Signaling, Solidarity, and the Sacred: The Evolution of Religious Behavior." *Evolutionary Anthropology* 12: 264–74.

Sosis, R., and B. Ruffle. 2003. "Religious Ritual and Cooperation: Testing for a Relationship on Israeli Religious and Secular Kibbutzim." *Current Anthropology* 44: 713–22.

Speck, F. G. 1935. *Naskapi*. Norman: University of Oklahoma Press.

Spencer, H. 1972. "An Ecclesiastical System as a Social Bond." In J. D. Y. Peel, ed., *On Social Evolution*, 217–24. Chicago: University of Chicago Press. (First published in 1876 as *The Principles of Sociology*, vol. 3, part 6).

Sperber, D. 1996. *Explaining Culture: A Naturalistic Approach*. Oxford, UK: Blackwell.

Spiro, M. E. 1966. "Religion: Problems of Definition and Explanation." In M. Banton, ed., *Anthropological Approaches to the Study of Religion*. London: Tavistock.

———. 1967. *Burmese Supernaturalism*. Philadelphia: Institute for the Study of Human Issues.

Stagg, F., E. Henson, and W. E. Glenn-Oates. 1967. *Glossolalia: Tongue Speaking in Biblical, Historical, and Psychological Perspective*. Nashville, TN: Abingdon.

Stanner, W. E. H. 1956. "The Dreaming." In T. A. G. Hungerford, ed., *Australian Signpost*, 51–65. Melbourne: F. W. Cheshire.

Starkey, M. L. 1969. *The Devil in Massachusetts*. New York: Anchor Books/ Doubleday.

Steadman, L. B. 1971. "Neighbours and Killers: Residence and Dominance among the Hewa of New Guinea." Ph.D. diss., Canberra, Australian National University.

———. 1975. "Cannibal Witches among the Hewa." *Oceania* 12: 114–21.

———. 1985. "The Killing of Witches." *Oceania* 56: 106–23.

Steadman, L. B., and C. Merbs. 1982. "Kuru and Cannibalism?" *American Anthropologist* 84: 611–27.

Steadman, L. B., and C. T. Palmer. 1994. "Visiting Dead Ancestors: Shamans as Interpreters of Religious Traditions." *Zygon* 29: 173–89.

———. 1995. "Religion as an Identifiable Traditional Behavior Subject to Natural Selection." *Journal of Social and Evolutionary Systems* 18(2): 149–64.

———. 1997. "Myths as Instructions from Ancestors: The Example of Oedipus." *Zygon* 32: 341–50.

Steadman, L. B., C. T. Palmer, and C. Tilley. 1996. "The Universality of Ancestor Worship." *Ethnology* 35(1): 63–76.

Strenski, I. 1974. "Falsifying Deep Structures." *Man* 9: 571–84.

Swanson, G. 1960. *Birth of the Gods*. Ann Arbor: University of Michigan Press.

Thompson, J. A. 2001. "Does God Help Me or Do I Help God or Neither?" In S. Akhtar and H. Parens, eds., *Does God Help?* Northvale, NJ: Jason Aronson.

Thornhill, R., and C. T. Palmer. 2000. *A Natural History of Rape.* Cambridge: Massachusetts Institute of Technology Press.

Tonkinson, R. 1978. *The Mardujara of Australia.* New York: Holt, Rinehart, and Winston.

———. 1991. *The Mardu of Australia.* New York: Holt, Rinehart, and Winston.

Torrey, E. F. 1972. *The Mind Game: Witchdoctors and Psychiatrists.* New York: Emerson Hall.

Trevor-Roper, H. R. 1968. *The Crisis of the Seventeenth Century: Religion, the Reformation, and Social Change.* New York: Harper and Row.

Tunstall, J. 1962. *The Fishermen.* London: Macgibbon and Kee.

Turner, V. 1964. "A Ndembu Doctor in Practice." In A. Kiev, ed., *Magic, Faith, and Healing: Studies in Primitive Psychology Today.* New York: Free Press/Macmillan.

———. 1972. *Drums of Affliction.* Oxford, UK: Oxford University Press.

———. 1979. "Divination as a Phase in a Social Process." In W. A. Lessa and E. Z. Vogt, eds., *Reader in Comparative Religion: An Anthropological Approach,* 4th ed. New York: HarperCollins.

———. 1993. "Religious Specialists." In A. C. Lehmann and J. E. Myers, eds., *Magic, Witchcraft, and Religion,* 3d ed. Mountain View, CA: Mayfield.

Tylor, E. B. 1958. *Religion in Primitive Culture.* New York: HarperCollins. (First published in 1873 as vol. 2 of *Primitive Culture,* 2d edition).

United Press International. 1978. "Letter Admits Lie to Mom." *Arizona Republic,* September 2, sec. C.

van Baal, J. 1981. *Man's Quest for Partnership.* Assen, The Netherlands: Van Gorcum.

van den Berghe, P. L. 1979. *Human Family Systems: An Evolutionary View.* New York: Elsevier North Holland.

van Ginkel, R. 1987. "Pigs, Priests and Other Puzzles: Fishermen's Taboos in Anthropological Perspective." *Ethnologia Europea* 17: 57–68.

Varney, H. 1973. "McCarthy: A Favorable Summary." In Earl Latham, ed., *The Meaning of McCarthyism.* Boston: D. C. Heath.

Verkamp, B. J. 1995. *The Evolution of Religion: A Re-Examination.* Scranton, PA: University of Scranton Press.

Vogt, E. Z., and R. Hyman. 1959. *Water Witching U.S.A.* Chicago: University of Chicago Press.

Von Furer-Haimendorf, C. 1993. "Priests." In A. C. Lehmann and J. E. Myers, eds., *Magic, Witchcraft, and Religion,* 3d ed. Mountain View, CA: Mayfield.

Wadley, R., A. Pashia, and C. T. Palmer. 2006. "Religious Scepticism and Its Social Context: An Analysis of Iban Shamanism." *Anthropological Forum* 16(1): 41–54.

Waines, D. 2003. *An Introduction to Islam,* 2d ed. Cambridge, UK: Cambridge University Press.

Wallace, A. 1958. "Dreams and the Wishes of the Soul: A Type of Psychoanalytic

Theory among the Seventeenth Century Iroquois." *American Anthropologist* 60(2): 234–48.

Warner, W. L. 1937. *A Black Civilization: A Social Study of an Australian Tribe.* New York: Harper and Row.

Watling, E. F. 1947. *Sophocles: The Theban Plays.* Harmondsworth, UK: Penguin.

Weigert, A. J. 1974. "Functional, Substantive, or Political? A Comment on Berger's Second Thoughts on Defining Religion." *Journal for the Scientific Study of Religion* 13(4): 483–86.

Wells, W. R. 1921. "Is Supernaturalistic Belief Essential in a Definition of Religion?" *Journal of Philosophy* 18(10): 269–74.

Whitehouse, H. 1996. "Rites of Terror: Emotion, Metaphor, and Memory in Melanesian Initiation Cults." *Journal of the Royal Anthropological Institute* 2: 703–15.

Williams, F. E. 1928. *Orokaiva Magic.* Oxford, UK: Oxford University Press.

Williams, G. C. 1966. *Adaptation and Natural Selection.* Princeton, NJ: Princeton University Press.

Wilson, D. S. 2002. *Darwin's Cathedral: Evolution, Religion, and the Nature of Society.* Chicago: University of Chicago Press.

Wilson, E. 1972. "The Zuni Shalako Ceremony." In W. Lessa and E. Z. Vogt, eds., *Reader in Comparative Religion: An Anthropological Approach,* 3d ed. New York: Harper and Row.

Wilson, E. O. 1978. *On Human Nature.* Cambridge, MA: Harvard University Press.

Winkelman, M. 2002. "Shamanism and Cognitive Evolution." *Cambridge Archaeological Journal* 12: 71–101.

———. 2004. "Shamanism as the Original Neurotheology." *Zygon* 39: 193–217.

Wolf, E. 1958. "The Virgin of Guadalupe: A Mexican National Symbol." *Journal of American Folklore* 71: 34–39.

Worsley, P. 1968. *The Trumpet Shall Sound: A Study of "Cargo" Cults in Melanesia.* New York: Schocken.

Wright, R. 1994. *The Moral Animal.* New York: Vintage.

Yalman, N. 1967. "The Raw: The Cooked: Nature: Culture—Observations on le Cru et le Cuit." In E. Leach, ed., *The Structural Study of Myth and Totemism.* London: Tavistock.

Yinger, M. J. 1970. *The Scientific Study of Religion.* New York: Macmillan.

———. 1977. "A Comparative Study of the Substructures of Religion." *Journal for the Scientific Study of Religion* 16(1): 67–86.

Zulaika, J. 1981. *Terranova: The Ethos and Luck of Deep Sea Fishermen.* Philadelphia: Institute for the Study of Human Issues.

Index

acrimony, 13, 42, 137, 213
adaptations, 28–29, 34–35, 41, 48. *See also* by-products
adultery: as cause of conflict among Hewa, 174; criticized by shamans, 112, 117; divination of, 144–146; in Melanesian cults, 199; as sin, 189
Africa, 56, 59, 67, 115–116, 124, 139
afterlife, 24, 101. *See also* death; funerals; mourning; rebirth
Aguaruna, 115
aim, 3, 20–21, 39, 46–47, 53, 216; of cargo cults, 198; of magic, 128, 131, 133, 135; of myth, 89, 90, 99; of religious behavior, 22, 24, 48, 52, 213; of rituals, 61, 76, 78, 160, 201, 204; of science, 201; of shamans, 113; of taboos, 151, 200; of witch-hunts, 184; of witch-killing, 173–174, 177, 183–184. *See also* goal
alcheringa, 27, 82
Alcoholics Anonymous, 14, 109
Alcorta, C., 4–5, 28–30, 32, 153
Allah, 52, 190. *See also* Islam; Muhammad; Muslims
allies, 84–85, 116, 153, 161, 176
All Saints Day, 69
altered states of consciousness. *See under* consciousness
altruism, 28, 32–35, 50, 83–84, 184
Amaterasu, 58
amen, 203
ancestors, x, 12, 17, 21, 25, 27–28, 31–34, 38, 40–73, 76, 78–79, 81–84, 96, 103–104, 108–118, 122, 126, 128, 131, 134, 136, 144, 146–147, 152–154, 156–158, 160, 175, 185, 187, 189–192, 195–196, 210–211, 213–214, 217–219; ancestress, 58, 105. *See also* dead, the
ancestor worship, 17, 27–28, 41–42, 52, 54–71, 78, 96, 187, 217–218; defined, 42
ancestral names, 56, 62–63, 67–68, 72. *See also* descent names
angels, 190, 207
anger. *See under* emotion
Anglicanism, 193–194
animals, 20, 42, 44, 49, 51–54, 56, 61, 71–76, 78, 81, 87, 105–106, 129, 138, 143, 150, 152–153, 157, 214, 217–218; bears, 71; birds, 52–53, 74, 76; buffalo, 158–159; caribou, 142–143; cattle, 59, 150–152, 198; chickens, 137–138, 144, 157; chicks, 71; chimpanzees, 53; clams, 151; cows, 60, 149–151, 174; coyotes, 53; crocodiles, 196; crows, 40, 76; dogs, 76; eels, 196; fish, 196; fowl, 145, 159; foxes, 71, 129; frogs, 196; goats, 59–60, 150–152, 157, 172; hawks, 71, 151; kangaroos, 39–40, 71–72, 74–76, 122, 130, 215–216; koalas, 216; lions, 71, 126; lizards, 129; mammals, 21, 25, 49, 52–53, 215; monkeys, 53; mules, 71; owls, 39–40, 75–76; oxen, 150, 157; pigs, 1, 71–72, 126, 149–152, 171, 174–175, 197–199, 218; primates, 52; rams, 71–72, 75–77; rats, 21, 39, 71; reptiles, 52; sheep, 59, 75, 150–152; snakes, 157; spiders, 129; termites, 146; tigers, 71; vultures, 151; water buffalo, 150; witchety grubs, 39,

Burkert, W., 5, 28, 129, 137
by-products, 29, 32, 35. *See also* adaptations

Cadmus, 88, 100
California, 206
Calvin, John, 165
Campbell, D., 21, 28
Canada, 142, 200
cannibalism, 1–2, 35, 100, 135, 161, 163, 171, 218
Cannon, W., 132–133
cargo cults, 191–192, 195–198, 202
caribou. *See under* animals
Catholicism, 6, 39–40, 165, 173, 190–191; blood and body of Christ, 39–40, 216; conflict with Protestants and witch-killing, 165, 167, 173; glossolalia, 205; priests, 24, 191. *See also* communion
celibacy, 153, 199, 201
Central Eskimo, The, 105
ceremonies, 4, 7, 57, 60, 68, 76, 101, 105, 112, 133, 157–160, 172, 191, 195–196, 202, 220; ceremonial words, 74; curing ceremonies, 115–117, 134–135. *See also* rituals
Chagnon, N., 57, 110–111, 115
chance: in divination, 138, 142–143; in magic, 123, 129; Oedipus and, 90, 100. *See also* probability; randomization
channeling, 14
charisma, 116
charlatans, 109–110, 114
charms, 133, 164, 202
Cheyenne. *See under* Native Americans
chickens. *See under* animals
children. *See under* kin terms; offspring
chimpanzees. *See under* animals
China, 142
choir, 203–204
Christ, 10, 39–40, 199–200, 206; second coming of, 205. *See also* Jesus
Christianity, 4, 42, 69, 186, 201–202; anti-Christian, 184; Christians, 10, 73, 76, 166, 178, 184, 192, 197, 201–202, 205, 219
Chrysippus, 93, 97
churches, 4, 10, 69, 104, 166, 180, 191–192, 194, 197, 201–209; First Church of the Trapezoid, 201; of Satan, 201–202
Cicero, 68, 99, 137–138

clans, 25, 27, 39–40, 62–63, 67–68, 72–74, 76–79, 105, 109, 111, 158, 169. *See also* totemism
clergy, 179
Clodius, 137, 147
close kin. *See under* kinship
codescendants, 27, 42, 46, 48, 51–52, 54, 57–59, 61–68, 72–79, 81, 84, 118, 122, 136, 169, 185, 192, 210, 213, 217–219. *See also* clans; descendants; kinship; kin terms
cofollowers, 39, 41, 43, 51, 211, 221
cognitive psychology, 10, 19, 28, 128; cognitive fluidity, 81. *See also* evolutionary psychology
collusion, 39–40, 122, 137, 144, 147, 178, 218–219
Colonus, 84
commandments, 189
commitment, 16, 29, 32, 35, 43, 73, 153–154, 160, 177, 183, 188–191, 194, 198, 205, 209, 211, 214. *See also* costly signaling theory
communicated acceptance of supernatural claims, ix, 16–17, 19, 30, 36–43, 54–57, 70, 73–73, 83–84, 100, 108, 113, 115, 118, 121, 130, 133, 136–141, 144, 147, 177–178, 183–184, 186–188, 190–191, 196, 204, 207, 211, 213–214, 216, 219, 220. *See also* religion; religious behavior; skepticism; supernatural, the; supernatural claims; talk
communication: defined, 37–38. *See also* behavior; communicated acceptance of supernatural claims; magic; talk
communion, 4, 8, 39–40, 191, 202, 216
communism, 6, 181–184; sexual, 199–200
competition, 49, 51–52, 54, 67, 174–175, 181, 184, 199–200
confession, 106, 117, 166, 177, 209–210
confidence, 6, 21, 24, 37, 79–81, 127–128, 139–141, 186, 202
congregations, 66, 106, 108, 117, 191, 201, 203–206, 208–209
consciousness, 9, 20, 38, 143, 197, 201, 207–208; altered states of, 207; Krishna, 201; semi-, 107; un-, 85–86, 99, 141, 158, 193
consequences, 3, 9, 17, 24, 26, 31, 36, 38,

Wilson, D. S., 28–29, 220
Wilson, E., 157–158
Wilson, E. O., 28, 38
Witchcraft, Oracles, and Magic Among the Azande, 144
Witch-doctors, 138. *See also* shamans
witches, 17, 38, 42; Azande, 7, 139, 144–146, 168; defined, 43, 163–164, 183; Europe, 165–168, 171–173, 176–178, 181, 184, 201; explanations of, 172–184; Hewa, 2, 34, 70, 168–178, 181, 184, 218, 220; McCarthy period, 178, 181–182, 184; Melanesia, 164; Salem, 178–181, 184; stereotype of, 168. *See also Cows, Pigs, Wars, and Witches*; innocence; water witching; *Witchcraft, Oracles and Magic Among the Azande*
wizards, 125
women, 1–3, 27, 34–35, 67, 70, 78, 88, 93, 106, 117, 135, 159, 164, 167, 169–172, 174–175, 179, 181, 184, 193, 200–201, 206–207, 216, 220

world religions, x, 41, 43, 185–187, 192. *See also* modern religions
Worsely, P., 191–192, 195–199
worship. *See* ancestor worship
Wounded Knee, 196
Wovoka, 197
Wright, R., 28, 33, 50, 54, 220

Yakut, 105
Yąnomamö, 56–57, 108, 111, 115
Yathrib. *See* Medina
Yinger, M., 5–6
yoga, 8
Yolngu, 74
yoyoya, 164
Yucatan, 206

Zande. *See under* Azande
Zeus, 88, 95–96
zombies, 158
Zuni. *See under* Native Americans
Zwingli, Ulrich, 165

About the Authors

Lyle B. Steadman is a graduate of Occidental College (BA), UCLA (MA), and the Australian National University, where he earned a Ph.D. in sociocultural anthropology. He spent a total of two-and-a-half years doing fieldwork with the Hewa, a Stone Age group of agriculturalists in Papua New Guinea. For more than three decades he taught courses at Arizona State University in comparative religion, kinship, the evolution of human sexuality, the peoples of the Pacific, and the sociocultural evolution of humans.

Craig T. Palmer earned his Ph.D. in cultural anthropology at Arizona State University in 1988. He performs fieldwork in Newfoundland, and has published on religion, evolution, kinship, traditions, ecology, sexual aggression, ritual, storytelling, and fishing villages. He is associate professor of anthropology at the University of Missouri–Columbia.

Made in the USA
Monee, IL
14 January 2020

20336975R00146